Build Your Own Framework with Visual FoxPro

Ken Chazotte

Hentzenwerke Publishing

Published by:
Hentzenwerke Publishing
980 East Circle Drive
Whitefish Bay WI 53217 USA

Hentzenwerke Publishing books are available through booksellers and directly from the publisher. Contact Hentzenwerke Publishing at:
414.332.9876
414.332.9463 (fax)
www.hentzenwerke.com
books@hentzenwerke.com

Build Your Own Framework with Visual FoxPro
    By Ken Chazotte
    Technical Editor: Joe A. Johnston
    Copy Editor: Jeana Frazier
    Cover Art: "Structural" by Todd Gnacinski, Milwaukee, WI

ISBN: 1-930919-53-0

Manufactured in the United States of America.

Dedication

To my wife, who had confidence in me, even when I did not.

To my son: Achievements result from ideas, effort, persistence, and faith.

Our Contract with You, The Reader

In which we, the folks who make up Hentzenwerke Publishing, describe what you, the reader, can expect from this book and from us.

Hi there!

I've been writing professionally (in other words, eventually getting a paycheck for my scribbles) since 1974, and writing about software development since 1992. As an author, I've worked with a half-dozen different publishers and corresponded with thousands of readers over the years. As a software developer and all-around geek, I've also acquired a library of more than 100 computer and software-related books.

Thus, when I donned the publisher's cap seven years ago to produce the *1997 Developer's Guide,* I had some pretty good ideas of what I liked (and didn't like) from publishers, what readers liked and didn't like, and what I, as a reader, liked and didn't like.

Now, with our new titles for 2004, we're entering our seventh season. (For those who are keeping track, the '97 DevGuide was our first, albeit abbreviated, season, the batch of six "Essentials" for Visual FoxPro 6.0 in 1999 was our second, and, in keeping with the sports analogy, the books we published in 2000 through 2003 comprised our third and subsequent seasons.)

John Wooden, the famed UCLA basketball coach, posited that teams aren't consistent; they're always getting better—or worse. We'd like to get better…

One of my goals for this season is to build a closer relationship with you, the reader. In order for us to do this, you've got to know what you should expect from us.

- You have the right to expect that your order will be processed quickly and correctly, and that your book will be delivered to you in new condition.

- You have the right to expect that the content of your book is technically accurate and up-to-date, that the explanations are clear, and that the layout is easy to read and follow without a lot of fluff or nonsense.

- You have the right to expect access to source code, errata, FAQs, and other information that's relevant to the book via our Web site.

- You have the right to expect an electronic version of your printed book to be available via our Web site.

- You have the right to expect that, if you report errors to us, your report will be responded to promptly, and that the appropriate notice will be included in the errata and/or FAQs for the book.

Naturally, there are some limits that we bump up against. There are humans involved, and they make mistakes. A book of 500 pages contains, on average, 150,000 words and several megabytes of source code. It's not possible to edit and re-edit multiple times to catch every last misspelling and typo, nor is it possible to test the source code on every permutation of development environment and operating system—and still price the book affordably.

Once printed, bindings break, ink gets smeared, signatures get missed during binding. On the delivery side, Web sites go down, packages get lost in the mail.

Nonetheless, we'll make our best effort to correct these problems—once you let us know about them.

In return, when you have a question or run into a problem, we ask that you first consult the errata and/or FAQs for your book on our Web site. If you don't find the answer there, please e-mail us at **books@hentzenwerke.com** with as much information and detail as possible, including 1) the steps to reproduce the problem, 2) what happened, and 3) what you expected to happen, together with 4) any other relevant information.

I'd like to stress that we need you to communicate questions and problems clearly. For example…

- Bad reports:

  "Your downloads don't work."

  "Your Web site is down."

  "The code in Chapter 10 caused an error."

  These types of complaints don't contain enough information for us to help you.

- Good reports:

  "I get a 404 error when I click on the **Download Source Code** link on www.hentzenwerke.com/book/downloads.html."

  "I performed the following steps to run the source code program DisplayTest.PRG in Chapter 10, and I received an error that said 'Variable m.liCounter not found.'"

  Now this is something we can help you with.

We'll do our best to get back to you within a couple of days, either with an answer or at least an acknowledgment that we've received your inquiry and that we're working on it.

On behalf of the authors, technical editors, copy editors, layout artists, graphical artists, indexers, and all the other folks who have worked to put this book in your hands, I'd like to thank you for purchasing this book, and I hope that it will prove to be a valuable addition to your technical library. Please let us know what you think about this book—we're looking forward to hearing from you.

As Groucho Marx once observed, "Outside of a dog, a book is a man's best friend. Inside of a dog, it's too dark to read."

Whil Hentzen
Hentzenwerke Publishing
February 2004

List of Chapters

Table of Contents

Acknowledgements

As an accountant and business manager, I was responsible for analyzing large amounts of data from a mainframe accounting system. At the time, FoxPro 2.5 for Windows was the natural choice for processing what often amounted to hundreds of thousands of records.

It turns out the mainframe system wasn't capturing all the information we needed. So my first thank-you goes to Gary Meyer, whose faith in me led to the development of a new job-costing system and the beginning of my journey into programming.

It was the early '90s and many people believed that the raw power of FoxPro was its best feature. Others, like me, learned that the true power of FoxPro was in the community of developers who were always willing to help, educate, and share. To everyone who has contributed to this community—authors, editors, and online responders—thank you.

It was my desire to belong and contribute to the FoxPro community that led me to my second DevCon in San Diego, 2001. In the wake of 9/11, I was stranded, like so many others, far from home. I met Leslie Koorhan next to a sign posted in the lobby asking for people willing to share a ride to New Jersey. We drove 42 hours straight on our return home. For those of you who know Leslie, I managed to get a few words in … I believe it was somewhere in Ohio. Thank you, Leslie, for encouraging me to send a proposal to Whil Hentzen.

Of course, a big thank-you goes to Whil. Whil and I went back and forth on the proposal for months before he agreed to publish the book. Almost two years have passed since we reached an agreement. Without his continued support and guidance, I would not have been able to complete this book.

Last, but not least, my technical editor Joe Johnston and his wife, Rhonda, deserve enormous thanks. One challenging aspect of writing a framework book is that changes in one chapter could (and usually did) require changes in another chapter. To complicate matters, this book was originally written for Visual FoxPro 7.0 and much of the book had to be rewritten to accommodate version 8.0. In addition to the normal technical editing responsibilities, Joe and Rhonda were exceptional in maintaining consistency across chapters.

—*Ken Chazotte*

About the Authors

Ken Chazotte

Ken Chazotte is an independent consultant based in Marlboro, New Jersey. Ken started his professional life as an accountant and business manager. In 1998, he officially entered the Information Technologies field as a project manager responsible for the implementation of a JD Edwards enterprise resource planning (ERP) system. Since then, Ken has been designing and developing custom solutions using Visual FoxPro, Microsoft .NET, Transact SQL, SQL Server, and JavaScript.

Ken is a co-chair of the Central New Jersey Microsoft Developers Group (CNJMSDev) and has also been a contributor to *FoxPro Advisor* and *Component Developer (CoDe) Magazine*. You can reach him at **ken@chazotte.com** or find out more about CNJMSDev at **http://www.cnjmsdev.org**.

Joe A. Johnston

Joe Johnston is a Microsoft Certified Professional in VB Desktop and VB Distributed, and also is a Microsoft Certified Partner. Based in Chesapeake, Virginia, he has pursued several lines of industry, driven by the heroes in his life: his father, Donald, who is one of the most intelligent human beings he knows; his mother, Sharyn, who is now and has always been his best friend; his grandmother, Elvira, who taught him to passionately pursue his goals and never do anything halfway; and his completer, his wife, Rhonda, who is the greatest gift he ever received. Joe went from Certified Automobile Mechanic to United States Military (Desert Shield/Desert Storm as a micro-miniature electronics technician) to his true calling, software development.

Joe is currently Chief Technical Officer of CyberJetX Corporation, where he works with VS.NET, VFP, SQL Server, MTS/COM+, and Flash MX 2004 to create solutions or utilities for acute issues regarding data and software systems. You can reach him at **cto@cyberjetx.com**.

xx

How to Download the Files

Hentzenwerke Publishing generally provides two sets of files to accompany its books. The first is the source code referenced throughout the text. Note that some books do not have source code; in those cases, a placeholder file is provided in lieu of the source code in order to alert you of the fact. The second is the e-book version (or versions) of the book. Depending on the book, we provide e-books in either the compiled HTML Help (.CHM) format, Adobe Acrobat (.PDF) format, or both. Here's how to get them.

Both the source code and e-book file(s) are available for download from the Hentzenwerke Web site. In order to obtain them, follow these instructions:

1. Point your Web browser to **www.hentzenwerke.com**.

2. Look for the link that says "Download."

3. A page describing the download process will appear. This page has two sections:

   - **Section 1:** If you were issued a user name/password directly from Hentzenwerke Publishing, you can enter them into this page.

   - **Section 2:** If you did not receive a user name/password from Hentzenwerke Publishing, don't worry! Just enter your e-mail alias and look for the question about your book. Note that you'll need your physical book when you answer the question.

4. A page that lists the hyperlinks for the appropriate downloads will appear.

Note that the e-book file(s) are covered by the same copyright laws as the printed book. Reproduction and/or distribution of these files is against the law.

If you have questions or problems, the fastest way to get a response is to e-mail us at **books@hentzenwerke.com**.

Chapter 1
Introduction

Building an application framework is a challenging and rewarding experience. This book will teach you how to build your own framework by using examples while offering guidance.

Who should read this book?

This book provides some perspective on how to build a polished and robust application. It is intended for intermediate and experienced programmers who want to learn to create their own framework or who are interested in learning techniques to enhance their own work. If you are comfortable with programming, regardless of the language, you should be able to follow along.

If you are new to programming, the Visual FoxPro Help file is an excellent reference while you are learning the syntax and mechanics of programming. Additionally, there are many excellent books in the Hentzenwerke collection to guide you in the early stages of learning application development. Take your time. Refer to these resources as you read about the concepts presented in this book. Fully understanding these concepts will make you a much stronger programmer, as opposed to "going it alone."

What is an application framework?

A framework is a reusable integration of components engineered to facilitate development of a particular type of application.

 This definition of a framework is based on the definition provided in Design Patterns (Gamma, Helm, Johnson, Vlissides; Addison-Wesley, 1995). The definition supplied in the book: "A framework is a set of cooperating classes that make up a reusable design for a specific class of software."

The representation of a framework varies with the type of application being built. The following example illustrates what constitutes a component, an application, and a framework.

Consider an automated teller machine (ATM). The software you interact with is an example of a client/server application. Each part of the application—the bankcard reader, the screen display, the buttons on the keypad—is a component of the application. Next, consider how the user interacts with an ATM while withdrawing money from his or her account. The sequence may be summarized as follows:

1. Swipe your card.

2. Type in your password.

3. Select an account (Checking, Savings…).

4. Enter the amount you want to withdraw.

5. Confirm that you want to withdraw the money.

6. Retrieve the money from the machine.

7. Indicate that you do not want to conduct another transaction.

Consider step 5: "Confirm that you want to withdraw the money." The event sequence that occurs when the user confirms the withdrawal might be as follows:

1. Make a connection to the back-end database server.

   - Did the connection succeed?

     - Continue

   - Did the connection fail?

     - Inform the user that the system is unavailable at this time.

2. Does the ATM have enough cash to complete the transaction?

   - Yes

     - Continue

   - No

     - Inform the user that the machine does not have sufficient funds to complete the transaction.

3. Verify the transaction.

   - Does the user have enough money in his/her account to cover the transaction?

     - Yes

       - Continue

     - No

       - Inform the user that he/she does not have sufficient funds to complete the transaction.

4. Post the transaction.

   - Reduce the user's account by the amount of the withdrawal.

   - Reduce the machine's cash balance by the amount of the withdrawal.

An alternative to having the application developer program all facets of the transaction is to use a framework. In this example, the framework developer would be responsible for coordinating the major elements of the transaction. Additionally, the framework developer would most likely take a holistic perspective and define the problem differently.

1. Data connection:

   - At any time, if a connection fails, show a "System Not Available" message.

- Periodically check to see if a connection can be re-established.

- If a connection can be re-established, show the "Welcome" screen.

2. For all transactions:

- Assume the connection to the database is valid.

- Provide a place for the developer to validate the information.

- Run the validation code.

   If the validation code fails:

   - Show the message generated by the application developer indicating the information supplied is not valid.

   If the validation code succeeds:

   - Proceed with the posting process.

   - Provide a place for the developer to post the transaction.

   - Run the post code.

   If the transaction fails:

   - Show the message generated by the application developer indicating the transaction failed.

   If the transaction succeeds:

   - Show the "Transaction Succeeded" message.

So what's left for the application developer? Developing the validation and transaction code (business rules) and appropriate message screens (interface design).

This example illustrates the roles of component, framework, and application developers. As you can see, the component developer is associated with the functionality of a single task—for example, connecting to a database. The framework developer focuses on coordinating existing components and adding general functionality, while the application developer provides application-specific functionality.

Why use a framework?

Developing polished, robust applications is a complex and time-consuming task. A framework handles many of the repetitive tasks associated with application development, allowing the application developer to focus on the specific features unique to a specific application.

Frameworks offer major enhancements to productivity. As demonstrated in the illustration, much of the integration code is written and tested prior to starting the application. True, there is a learning curve associated with using a framework. However, when you are familiar with the framework and the methodologies it employs, you will find that your focus shifts more toward the tasks of the application rather than the details of the implementation.

Varying skill sets are required to develop an application; a few of these are user interface development, database design, and writing business logic. Frameworks can be used to segregate these tasks, allowing you to focus on one area of development at a time. This is particularly helpful in a team environment where certain developers may be more adept in one area of development.

Frameworks tend to solve problems by using a standardized approach. Approaching each development effort in a consistent manner makes transitioning between applications, between developers, or even between different parts of your own code more efficient and less prone to error. Reusable designs that follow a standardized approach can be automated. Frameworks generally provide wizards and builders that reinforce the framework methodology. Wizards and builders further improve productivity by reducing the effort to implement an application.

How is a framework different from a class library?

A class library is a collection of programming tools or components a developer may use when building an application. Components in a class library accomplish specific, often complex, tasks. To use a component, you do not need to know the details of how the task is completed. For example, a hammer is a carpenter's tool. It can drive a nail or remove a nail. To use the hammer, the carpenter does not need to know about metallurgy, physics, or ergonomic design.

Components offer discrete functionality useful in a variety of applications. The data connection discussed at the beginning of the chapter is an example of functionality that could be made into a component. The developer of this component would be knowledgeable about database connection protocols and the types of issues that cause connections to fail. Framework and application developers benefit from using the connection, but do not need to know "how" it works. Components are useful to both application and framework developers.

The framework developer defines the relationship between components and provides much of the code that integrates them. The framework developer leaves "empty spaces" for the application developer to fill in later, defining only the specifications for the desired functionality. When deciding how and when to integrate components, a framework developer follows a plan called the "framework architecture," which is often formalized in an architecture document.

A framework developer typically organizes basic framework functionality into a class library, but this is not required.

The type of application the framework supports dictates the components that a framework contains and how they are integrated. For example, the requirements and structure of an Internet application are entirely different from a traditional FoxPro (fat client) application. Internet applications are stateless, requiring a host of services to manage information between requests. State-full applications "remember" information and require none of the state-management functionality.

Elements of a framework

A framework is comprised of a variety of tools, services and modules. The tools and services provided by each framework will vary depending upon the goals of the framework and type of application to be developed. Here is a listing of the key framework elements:

- Procedures

- Classes

- Tools and components

- Application services

  - Messaging

  - Event logging

- Forms management

- Data management

- Business objects

- Interface controls

- System navigation

  - Menus

  - Toolbars

  - Buttons

- Security

- Error handling

Reasons to create your own framework

Building your own framework offers several advantages that a purchased framework simply cannot. Most important is the thorough understanding of exactly what is happening at each moment in your code.

Learning to use someone else's framework takes time. A lot of time. Developing your own framework takes even more time, but you can be certain that the resulting product will meet your requirements.

At some point your framework, regardless of who developed it, will not meet your needs. Commercial frameworks are intended for a wide audience and may contain features or a certain level of complexity that are of no benefit to you. There is no feeling more frustrating, and no task less productive, than trying to modify someone else's framework to accomplish something for which it was not designed.

A custom framework is lean, supporting only your personal methodology and preferences. When you've properly designed a framework, reworking it to meet a new set of requirements takes less time than reworking someone else's framework.

I started building my first class library as a learning opportunity. Each time I learned something new, it went into the library. I then started to focus on how I was building my applications. Sure, they all worked, but was I building them in the best way possible? Unlike building a class library, where I was cataloging what I learned, building a framework actually made me a stronger, more well rounded, and more productive programmer.

Reasons to avoid developing your own framework

The biggest drawback to building a quality framework is the time required. You may feel as though much of the work required to produce a framework would have been incurred by writing the application. This is partially true. An extra level of effort is required to ensure that the components you create will work beyond the situation for which they were created. For example, it is not enough to know how to save data in a buffered table; you have to know how to save data in *all* tables, without knowing beforehand the names of the tables or their buffering status.

This leads to a second drawback. It's difficult to develop a framework while you are developing a single application. The requirements used to define the needs of the application are generally not reflective of applications in general. Viewed from the narrow perspective of one project, the following requirement might be missed.

```
Requirement: A developer must have the ability to limit the number of instances
of a form available to the end user.
```

The final reason to avoid developing your own framework is that your experience, imagination, or talents are limiting factors. The other side of the learning curve is that you didn't include all the things you didn't know, or didn't think of.

Framework mindset

When you are developing a framework, you are creating a product that other developers will use to help them build applications. Your job as the framework developer is to make the application developer as productive as possible. Even if you are developing the framework for your own use, it is helpful to separate your roles as framework developer and application developer. When you have your framework hat on, you are thinking, "How can I make my next project (application) better?" When you have your application hat on, you are thinking, "How can I best meet the specific needs of my client?"

Throughout the book, the terms "you" and "framework developer" are synonymous. These terms are used when discussing tasks you should be completing or your objectives when designing and implementing your framework. The terms "application developer" or "developer" refer to the developers that will use your framework. The term "client" is used to represent the project stakeholder—the person or group for which the application is written. If you are a corporate developer, your clients may be members of your company in other departments. If you are a consultant, clients are the ones writing the checks. The term "end user" or "user" represents people that use an application built with your framework. An end user may or may not be a client.

These terms are used throughout the book to clearly distinguish between developing a framework and developing an application from the framework you've created.

Overview

Building a framework can be broken into four phases: planning, component development, integration, and productivity enhancement.

During the planning phase you define requirements, select an architecture, and create a project plan. These activities and the concepts required to complete these steps successfully are covered in the first three chapters of the book.

The component-development phase represents the start of the coding phase. In this phase you develop classes that are responsible for one thing. This one thing could be simple, such as a class that knows how to format and display ZIP code information, to a complex task such as starting an application. Another aspect of developing components is creating the base components that integrate the architectural elements of your framework. Chapters 3 through 9 focus on base components, while chapters 10 through 13 focus on major architectural components.

The integration phase involves linking functionalities that exist in two or more classes. In some cases, you will link classes together directly to create framework components. In other cases, you will create subcomponents that are in turn coordinated to create framework components or that are shared among many components. Chapters 14 through 16 illustrate several ways to link the elements of your framework together.

Finally, with the integration complete, you will want to create tools that reinforce your design decisions and that can help to relieve the mundane aspects of development. Chapters 17 through 19 look at some critical tools you will need to support your framework and make your development efforts more productive.

How should I read this book?

Sequentially. Then, once you have read it cover to cover, refer back to specific sections as needed.

Each chapter builds on the chapter that precedes it. Constantly repeating material from previous chapters is redundant and unpleasant to read. Each chapter assumes that you have read the chapters before it.

The purpose of developing a framework is to make developing an application simpler or more efficient. Take the time to review the samples provided. At times, the framework code is complex. The examples illustrate how the framework can simplify development, even though the framework code may be complex.

A word about the approach presented in this book

In this book, I'll lead you through the process of building a framework called "MyFrame." Each step of the development process is explained in detail, citing general, as well as FoxPro-specific, design considerations you will encounter as you build your framework.

There is no "one way" to create a framework. If there were, it would have been created already and we would all be using it. Creating a framework has more to do with coordinating the many components involved in the framework rather than how a particular feature is implemented. Your framework will be as much a reflection of your personal preferences as the types of applications you build.

The entire book is one big example of how to create a framework. In several chapters, I've prepared examples that illustrate how the framework may be used. The final chapter includes a comprehensive example illustrating how to use the framework. If you don't like the way a particular item is implemented, feel free to change it; after all, it is your framework.

In addition, FoxPro is a wonderfully rich programming environment. As a rule, any task that can be implemented with FoxPro can be implemented in more than one way. This book is about coordination and planning, not exploring the many ways FoxPro avails itself to solving a particular problem.

Your framework will not be developed in one big blast of development nirvana. Developing a framework is an iterative process. Most likely, your first pass will be to implement the features you require. After using the framework for a while, you might want to implement additional features, and possibly change some things established in the prior pass. After a while, the cycle is repeated again … and again … and, well, you get the idea.

As each requirement is fulfilled and each layer added, you will understand the dependencies that exist between components, how to avoid creating dependencies, and the types of considerations you'll face when requirements change.

Unfortunately, this type of development is difficult to capture in a book. As the reader, you expect, and rightly so, to be able to find the chapter titled "Forms." Scattering functionality throughout the book would make this book difficult to use as a reference when developing your own framework. Instead, consider this book as the first iteration, or "Version 1.0" of your framework.

Icons used in this book

Throughout this book, you'll see the following icons used to point out special notes, tips, and download information.

 Information of special interest, related topics, or important notes are indicated by this icon.

 Tips—marked by this icon—include ideas for shortcuts, alternate ways of accomplishing tasks that can make your life easier or save time, or techniques that aren't immediately obvious.

 Paragraphs marked with this icon indicate that you can download the referenced code or tool from ***www.hentzenwerke.com***.

Summary

This book is about defining framework objectives and choosing implementation strategies that maximize the potential for reuse. Framework design encompasses all aspects of application development: general programming principles, object-oriented programming techniques, requirements analysis, refactoring, user interface development, class interface development, documentation, and a thorough understanding of the problem domain.

Developing a framework requires you to *put it all together*. Upon completing your framework, you will be a better, more productive developer who is able to produce full-featured applications efficiently.

Updates and corrections to this chapter can be found on Hentzenwerke's Web site, **www.hentzenwerke.com**. Click "Catalog" and navigate to the page for this book.

Chapter 2
Project Planning

Framework development is a complex activity requiring thousands of decisions. Taking the time to formulate your expectations and plan your development efforts is essential to successfully completing a framework. In this chapter, I'll highlight the key documents that will help you organize and plan your framework.

A good project manager uses several tools during the analysis and development stages of any software development project. A framework is probably the most complicated category of software to develop; developing a solid implementation plan is critical to successfully completing your framework.

A good implementation plan is actually a compilation of several documents. These documents include, but are not limited to, a steering document, requirements list, design plan, implementation plan, and a test plan.

Thoroughly analyzing your requirements and developing a detailed implementation plan will highlight areas where flexibility is needed or potential conflicts exist. You may find requirements that seem to be at odds, yet each seems equally important. Developing a requirements list takes time. However, identifying these "trouble spots" in the analysis or design phase is much more productive than after you have spent hours writing code.

In this chapter, you will learn what items go into a implementation plan and how to prepare one. You will see an explanation of the items contained in the implementation plan. In addition, you will see a sample of the requirements list, design plan, task list, and test plan used to develop the MyFrame framework. The sample illustrates the level of detail that you should strive for when preparing for your own development effort. As you read through the chapters, you will see that the presentation resembles the Requirement, Design, Plan, and Test paradigm presented in this chapter.

Steering document

The steering document is the starting point for designing your framework. It consists of a goal statement, as well as guidelines and objectives, and is the basis for preparing the remainder of your implementation plan. It should be "high level," defining the purpose for developing the framework and some overall attributes about the completed project as a whole.

In this section, I'll review the steering document used to develop MyFrame. The steering document contains a goal statement, guidelines for development, and objectives for developing the framework. The contents of the document are shown in **bold text**, while comments about the document are shown in regular text.

The goal statement

The goal statement should capture the reason you are developing your own framework. It should be singular in purpose and easily understood. Avoid putting too much detail or specific requirements into the goal statement. Many things will change as you progress through the development process, but the goal of the framework should not change.

Developing a framework is different than developing an application. When you build an application, you know that you are building an "accounting application" or a "content management system." When you build a framework you don't know what types of systems will be built with it.

The goal for the framework should reflect something about the types of applications that can be built with your framework. Optionally you could describe the level of support your framework provides for building those types of applications. An example of a goal statement might be: "To provide the basic templates and tools necessary for creating air traffic control software."

Here is the goal statement for MyFrame:

The goal of MyFrame is to provide the necessary components for producing fully functional client/server or LAN-based applications.

This statement is clear and unlikely to change during the course of development. It conveys to the developer the types of applications that can be built with this framework and that the necessary tools to build an application are included as part of the framework.

Guidelines

Guidelines are evaluative statements about the framework as a whole. They reflect how the framework is constructed, or how it is to be used. Ultimately, the success of a framework depends on how it is perceived. When preparing your guidelines, think of the characteristics you would want in a framework if you were going to purchase one.

The following guidelines for MyFrame are presented in **bold text**. Additional explanations included as part of the book are in plain text.

Developer Friendly

Information should be conveyed to the developer about the how the MyFrame framework works and where to place application code.

A framework is effectively useless without documentation or guidelines for how to use it. Introduce the developer to your framework with an overview of the framework's structure and some examples of how to use the framework. If you are building a framework for your own use, sketching out these documents or examples will help to further clarify many of your design decisions and development tasks.

Once a developer begins working with the framework, builders or wizards can be used to help with the learning process. Builders and wizards help in a number of ways. First, they inform the developer about the types of information required to make a class or group of classes functional. Additionally, they can validate the developer's selections (or prevent them from making incorrect entries), which can reduce the overall "frustration factor" associated with learning a new framework.

ASSERTS can be used to inform the developer when the expected conditions for a program are not satisfied. In addition to suspending execution (when SET ASSERTS is ON), the message in an ASSERT can be used to explain why a particular piece of information is required.

One of the key roles fulfilled by a framework is that the complexity or redundancy of application development is hidden from the end developer. As a framework developer, you provide the application infrastructure. You should provide developers with ways to customize and utilize your infrastructure. Make sure the areas where the developers are to place code are clearly identifiable. Strive for a "fill-in-the-blanks" or "connect-the-dots" approach.

These are just some of the ways to make your framework developer friendly. Remember that this is a guideline. As you develop your framework you'll be in a better position to assess how a piece of code or a feature can be made developer friendly.

Consistent
MyFrame should be constructed in an orderly and organized fashion.

Developers should expect to find similar problems handled in similar ways, even if that developer is you. Identify when you choose not to follow standards, and why. Developers should not have to remember the exceptions to your rules. For example, if you decide to provide a SetCaption() method for all your forms, adhere to that. Don't set the caption directly with code in some places and use SetCaption() in others.

Maintaining consistency throughout the framework is essential to ensure that the developer does not get frustrated with it.

Reusable (Single Point Accountability)
The framework functionality in MyFrame should be implemented once. Once implemented, the implementation should be used wherever that functionality is required.

This guideline is similar to the consistency principle.

One of the biggest benefits attributed to object orientation is that it facilitates code reuse. The promotion generally goes something like, "Once you program that pesky function, you'll never have to code it again." True. The bigger benefit, in my opinion, occurs when requests are made for changes. Knowing where to make the change, and having the change automatically ripple through the entire application, is a powerful feature for users of your framework.

Flexible and Configurable
The developer must be able to extend the classes and functionality provided in MyFrame.

You cannot create a framework that will handle every need of every developer. Instead, you should consider where flexibility may be required and give the developer a way to extend the framework to meet his or her own needs.

There are several means to provide flexibility. The most obvious may be to provide a property that can be set to alter the behavior of a class. For example, you can instruct a form to act as a modal form by changing the WindowType property. However, as you'll see later, many other alternatives exist.

With flexibility comes complexity, which can be a major deterrence to reuse. When simple tasks seem to take an inordinate amount of effort or require the configuration of many different components, the tendency is to avoid using those components. If the framework is considered overly complex, developers will feel frustrated.

Always consider flexibility from two perspectives: yours as the developer of the framework, and the developers who will use your framework. It is entirely appropriate, and likely, that you will write complex code in order to make the job of subsequent developers simpler.

In no case, however, does flexibility mean that you explain how a developer can modify your framework by altering framework code. Instead, you want to provide alternatives and hooks to extend the classes you provide.

Reduce Application Development Time
MyFrame should reduce the effort required to produce a quality application.

Be careful not to micromanage this guideline. Sure, if a form takes 100 percent longer to produce, you may want to rework its structure. Conversely, if using special tags for varying types of comments requires 5 percent more time, but returns 500 percent during the project documentation phase, developers will most likely see this as a positive use of their time.

Objectives
Objectives are high-level requirements for the framework. The term "high level" implies that you cannot map an objective to one element in the framework. Instead, objectives permeate the entire framework.

Be careful not to confuse objectives with requirements. Having the ability to work with arrays is not an objective of the framework. It may be a requirement of the framework, but it is certainly not an objective. You are not building an entire application framework so that you can work with arrays.

State the objectives in a way that does not define how the objective is achieved. For example, the first objective is that the framework must work with multiple sources of data. It does *not* state:

> "The framework should contain one class that is mapped to a particular type of data. This class will serve as the interface between each type of data. A new class will be created for each new source of data."

This explanation is actually a design decision (and the way that multiple data sources are handled in MyFrame). Working with multiple data types affects much more than one individual class; it affects how you navigate between records, how you write data validation code, and a host of other issues, as you will see throughout the remainder of the book.

The following objectives for MyFrame are presented in **bold text**. Additional explanations included as part of the book are in plain text.

Multiple Data Sources
The system must have the ability to work with multiple sources of data.

Data is not limited to DBF files only. Application data can exist in remote databases accessible via ODBC, Web Services, Microsoft Outlook, or a variety of other sources.

What does it mean to be able to work with multiple sources of data? Does it mean that a single form can write to data in a SQL Server database as well as a FoxPro table? Can contact information stored in a FoxPro table be connected to Outlook appointments? Can a form originally written using a FoxPro table be switched to SQL Server without having to redevelop the form?

To me, working with multiple data types means all these things. This is not to say that the framework will accomplish all these things "automatically." It means that the tools are provided to accomplish these things. If the application developer is willing to change the way he or she thinks about designing an application, these questions can be answered affirmatively.

Multiple projects

I am always working on several projects at the same time, and each project is at various stages of completion. Although my framework doesn't change much anymore, when I do make a change it is usually something that would be beneficial to all projects in development.

There is nothing more frustrating than working on several projects at once and having to add new features to each project individually. One key principle of inheritance is that that you should only have to make code changes in one place. Having multiple copies of the same files on disk just violates this basic concept.

The term "project" here refers to each application being developed. Do not confuse the term "project" with the term "project manager." A project manager is (in FoxPro) a tool that organizes the files in your project and facilitates the compilation and distribution process.

Modular Construction

Whenever possible, MyFrame should be constructed in modular fashion.

Modular construction means that your framework and resulting systems are structured in logical pieces. Much of framework construction is the integration of components. However, once they're integrated, modifying one or more framework modules can change the behavior of the entire application.

FoxPro Designers

The MyFrame framework should work within the FoxPro Design Tools.

The objectives stated to this point are ones that you will most likely use as the basis for your own framework. Working within the FoxPro designers is a stated objective of the MyFrame framework for the following reasons:

- Developers are familiar with the FoxPro interface.

- The FoxPro interface has been user tested.

- The FoxPro interface is supported by the FoxPro documentation.

This is not to say that your framework must work exclusively with the FoxPro designers. In fact, many frameworks come with tools that either overcome the limitations of the FoxPro designers, or that support their specific design philosophy, or both.

Portable

The MyFrame framework and framework files should start in any directory.

I use the phrase "start in any directory" to indicate that whether the framework is loaded on your D:\ drive, or C:\drive, or any other directory, it should work without fail.

Implementation plan

There are no hard and fast rules as to what belongs in an implementation plan. In my experience, the most helpful project implementation plans include a detailed listing of framework requirements, design guidelines to direct the development process, a task list detailing specific development activities, and a test plan to assess the success of the project.

Each element of the implementation plan may be developed independently. In practice, however, the development of a comprehensive implementation plan is an iterative process. In this section, I will explain the type of things that go into each section and provide samples of the implementation plan for MyFrame.

Requirements list

The requirements section contains a detailed listing of features and capabilities the framework must have. Requirements are quantifiable. They can be measured. At the end of the day, either a requirement is satisfied, or it isn't.

State requirements clearly and in a quantifiable manner. Precisely defining your requirements reduces the chance for misinterpretations. Stating requirements in a manner that can be measured further reinforces the requirement and assists when developing a test plan.

Design (implementation)

The requirements list will probably resemble a "laundry list" of items to be included in the framework. Taken in isolation, each requirement could (possibly) be implemented in a variety of ways. For example, one requirement may be that users must be able to sort a particular result set. In isolation, that could mean that the result set could be sorted in memory using an array or persisted by storing the result set in a table.

In the design section of the implementation plan, you categorize one or more requirements and define a cohesive development strategy to satisfy those requirements.

Once you've completed your design, check the solution against the guidelines and objectives for the project. Ask yourself, "Does my design violate any of the objectives or requirements of the framework?"

Consider the following guideline and requirement:

- Guideline: The framework should be user friendly.

- Requirement: Each action taken in the system must be reversible or confirmed prior to taking the action.

A system that asks a user, "Are you sure you want to log on to the system?" after he enters his user name and password and clicks a Logon button, satisfies the requirement but probably fails the "user friendly" test. The user took the time to provide a user name and password, and click the Logon button, so it's safe to assume the user wanted to log on to the system. The additional confirmation is an extra step that the user may consider "unfriendly."

Task list

This is a list of the specific development actions to be taken to construct the framework. Your requirements list and design guidelines are the basis for the items appearing in your task list.

Test plan

The test plan is a list of tests that, when run successfully, ensure that your framework is satisfying its design specifications.

Sample (excerpt)

This section contains an excerpt taken from the MyFrame implementation plan. The level of detail in your implementation plan will vary. A rule of thumb might be that the more people working on the project, the greater level of detail is required—especially if you are working on a large project where several different classes and modules have to integrate with each other.

The familiarity of your developers with the project at hand is also a factor in how detailed each item might be. The more familiar, the less detail and more "bullet-like" your implementation plan will be.

Finally, development standards will also limit the level of detail required in your implementation plan. For example, if a development step is labeled "Develop customer maintenance screen" and your development standards dictate that all maintenance screens must have Save and Cancel buttons, it is unnecessary to repeat these items for every maintenance screen in your system.

The following excerpt is related to creating the startup routine. It assumes you are familiar with application development and is presented in a terse bullet format. If you are unfamiliar with any of the items presented in the example, relax ... a full explanation of each item is presented in Chapter 5, "Beginning Development."

REQUIREMENTS

- One file starts all applications.

- Starting the application also "starts" the framework.

- Use relative paths only.

- Start of application configures environment.

- Close of application restores environment.

DESIGN

One of the overall objectives for the project is to support multiple project development. One class serves as the "control" for starting and shutting down an application. This class is then subclassed as each new project is started.

A single file is required as the "main" file for each project. One program will be created to start each project. The stub program will contain the code for setting the default directory and search paths.

As a matter of preference, I like keeping the code for starting the application (Main.prg) close to the code responsible for handling all the activities as the program is started and closed. Therefore, the application class is created as a PRG class.

One program file is required to store the framework application object definition (Main_frame.prg) and another is required to store the application object and starting code for each application (Main.prg).

Task Plan

- Create a file for the framework class definition (.\MyFrame\FrameSource\Main_Frame.prg).

- Create the application class.

- Define the startup sequence for the application class.

- Define the shutdown sequence for the application.

- Create a file for the Application Class Definition.

- Add startup code responsible for setting default and search paths.

- Create the application-specific application class definition.

Test Plan

Test of startup and shutdown sequence
    Non-compiled
        Check path
            Load framework
                (Path should now be set to the project's root directory)
                (Environment settings: Set to application-specific settings)
            Release framework
                (Old path is restored)
                (Original environment settings are restored)

Conventions

The first thing I do when I get a new piece of software is look through the menu and start poking. I expect the menu to be organized and indicative of the types of things the software can do. Assuming the software is reasonably organized, I know it won't take long to figure out how to use it, even before reading the documentation. I expect that you don't need to be persuaded about the importance of presenting an orderly and consistent user interface to the end user.

When building a framework, the application developer is your end user, and he or she expects the same degree of consistency in the interface: your code. Adhering to the following conventions is one way to ensure consistency.

Write clear, readable code. Application developers will read your code to gain understanding and insight into how they can better use your framework. Provide meaningful comments that explain what is happening and why. Avoid commenting on syntax; instead, focus on the objectives and why an action was taken, not just what the action was. Read through your code a few days after completing it. Are the variables named appropriately? Is the intent of the code clear from the comments provided or from the code itself?

This section focuses on the conventions you should consider for your framework, followed by a systematic approach to organizing the framework files.

Conventions are a set of rules describing how to format your code. For example:

- Indent case statements three spaces.

- Use CamelCase notation.

Follow the conventions recommended by Microsoft in the Visual FoxPro Help file. Most developers are familiar with or are already using these conventions. The conventions you choose to follow when developing the framework can be as loose, or as stringent, as you feel comfortable with. Establish a set of conventions for your code and follow it. You may add to or take away from the conventions as you see fit. Remember, one of your objectives is to make the development process smoother. Try not to make the conventions too restrictive or complicated. And finally, conventions are optional. Never impose conventions on the application developer.

Comments

Every piece of code should clearly state its intention. I have read somewhere that each piece of code should be documented in such a way that, if the code were removed, the reader would still understand its purpose. Taken in moderation, this is a good principle to follow. However, the best-case scenario is when the code is self-documenting. For an example of self-documenting code, see the LoadApp() method in Chapter 5, "Beginning Development," under the section titled "aApplication."

Place the comments in appropriate places. Consider a method named PrintSalaryHistory(). How PrintSalaryHistory() retrieves and calculates information is irrelevant to the calling program. Comments for PrintSalaryHistory() are better placed directly in the PrintSalaryHistory() method. On the other hand, if a precondition exists it would be better to state as much in both the calling method and the called method. An example of a precondition might be "Prior to calling PrintSalaryHistory(), the employee table must be open, selected, and on the record of the employee you wish to print."

 Preconditions that must be explained in more than one place may be an indication that coupling between classes or methods exists.

Be careful not to over-comment. It is difficult enough to trace through code without having to read every thought a developer had while he or she assembled the code. The following is an example of over-commenting:

```
*-- The customers table is not opened when the form loads.
*-- It is only opened if the user tries to search for a customer.
*-- Since this form is one of the few forms where a private data session is
*-- not used and the customers table was not opened from the data environment,
*-- it is sometimes left open.
*-- Even though the table is opened in shared mode, and causes no problems if
*-- it remains open, it's cleaner to make sure it is closed.
*-- By the way, this next line of code I found in the FoxPro Advisor's tips
*-- section. Boy, it sure seems easier. I used to close tables like this:
*--   IF USED("TableName")
*--       USE IN "TableName"
*--   ENDIF
*--   Now I close them like this:
USE IN SELECT ("Customers")
```

Instead try:

```
*-- Cleanup
USE IN SELECT ("Customers")
```

The same is true of code that has been extensively modified over time. Obtaining a clear understanding of what code achieves is often muddied by comments about what the code used to achieve. Keep the comments in your code related to the code in effect. Place modification histories at the beginning or end of each code block; then, if the modification is of interest, the information is still readily available.

Comment blocks of code rather than individual lines. I use the term "block of code" to indicate functions, programs, or, in the case of classes, the class itself. A class may contain several methods that, in effect, function to achieve a single goal. Commenting each method is tedious and is often not as helpful as a single explanation defining the purpose of the class and role of the more important methods. A technique first introduced by Drew Speedie (a framework developer) is to include a method in each class named "zReadMe()". zReadMe() will always sort toward the bottom of an alphabetically sorted list and is therefore easily found in the FoxPro designers.

Here's an example of a comment block in a header:

```
*=============================================
*| Purpose......A sentence or two describing what the
*|              code does.
*@ Author.......The name of the developer
*| Created......The date the program was created
*| About........This is a free-form area provided to expand
*)              on the purpose of the code, explain how
*)              the code is structured, or any other
*)              relevant information.
*| Dependencies: Another free-form area describing
*)               conditions expected to be true for the code
*)               to work properly. If possible, try stating
*)               dependencies as ASSERTions.
*//Mod.List.....A listing of the dates, developer(s) and
*)              reasons for the modifications
*=============================================
```

You may have noticed that various parts of the header are marked with different comment strings. FoxPro 8.0 introduces a new tool called Code References, which searches source code files for a particular string. Using the Code References tool, it would be possible to obtain a list of all developers that worked on a project by conducting a project-wide search for "*@". Other comment tags used in MyFrame are:

```
*--Comment tags
*// Modification
*ToDo:
*-? Question:
 *) Continuation of any comment
 *--
 NOTE:
 &&
```

Names (general)

When naming something, try to make the name meaningful in the context for which the name will be used. UpdateTableBuffer() is an appropriate name for a method on a data class. However, Save() might be a better name for a similar method on a form. Using descriptive names for variables and methods helps to keep the code readable. IntelliSense, first introduced in FoxPro 7.0, dramatically reduces the "pain in the butt" factor associated with using long names.

Names (formatting)

Most FoxPro developers expect to see names in CamelCase, where the first letter of each word in a name is capitalized. Using CamelCase makes it easier to read names comprised of more than one word. Several examples have been used already in this chapter, including PrintSalaryHistory() and UpdateTableBuffer().

In some circumstances, a prefix is added to the name to convey additional information about the item. For instance, variables are often prefixed with two letters, the first indicating the scope of the variable and the second indicating the data type of the variable. Therefore, lcDescription would indicate that the variable "Description" was local in scope and of type character.

Most FoxPro developers are familiar with or are already using the prefixes listed in the Visual FoxPro Help file. These prefixes are listed in the following tables.

Table 1. Prefixes indicating scope.

Scope	Description	Example
l	Local	lnCounter
p	Private (default)	pnStatus
g	Public (global)	gnOldRecno
t	Parameter	tnRecNo

Table 2. Prefixes indicating variable types.

Type	Description	Example
a	Array	aMonths
c	Character	cLastName
y	Currency	yCurrentValue
d	Date	dBirthDay
t	Datetime	tLastModified
b	Double	bValue
f	Float	fInterest
l	Logical	lFlag
n	Numeric	nCounter
o	Object	oEmployee
u	Unknown	uReturnValue

Table 3. Prefixes indicating class.

Prefix	Object	Example
chk	CheckBox	chkReadOnly
col	Collection	colFormObjects
cbo	ComboBox	cboEnglish
cmd	CommandButton	cmdCancel
cmg	CommandGroup	cmgChoices
cnt	Container	cntMoverList
ctl	Control	ctlFileList
cad	CursorAdapter	cadInventory
<user-defined>	Custom	user-defined
dte	DataEnvironment	dteSalesForm
edt	EditBox	edtTextArea
frm	Form	frmFileOpen
frs	FormSet	frsDataEntry
grd	Grid	grdPrices
grc	Column	grcCurrentPrice
grh	Header	grhTotalInventory
hpl	HyperLink	hplHomeURL
img	Image	imgIcon
lbl	Label	lblHelpMessage
lin	Line	linVertical
lst	ListBox	lstPolicyCodes
olb	OLEBoundControl	olbObject1
ole	OLE	oleObject1
opt	OptionButton	optFrench
opg	OptionGroup	opgType
pag	Page	pagDataUpdate
pgf	PageFrame	pgfLeft
prj	ProjectHook	prjBuildAll
sep	Separator	sepToolSection1
shp	Shape	shpCircle
spn	Spinner	spnValues
txt	TextBox	txtGetText
tmr	Timer	tmrAlarm
tbr	ToolBar	tbrEditReport
xad	XMLAdapter	xadRemoteXMLData
xfd	XMLField	xfdPrices
xtb	XMLTable	xtbInventory

Variables

Variables begin with a two-letter prefix. The first letter indicates the scope of the variable. The second variable indicates the type. The name is in CamelCase.

Properties

Property names are prefixed with the "type" of information intended to be stored in the property. The name follows the CamelCase convention; for example: oApp.cAppName.

Functions

Function names are in CamelCase.

Tables

Avoid using long names for tables or including spaces in the name. Yes, FoxPro supports long table names and spaces, but some other databases do not. Some of the functionality you provide in the framework will rely on persisted data stored in tables. Don't set yourself up for disaster. Using short names will prevent problems when porting to another database.

Another convention followed in MyFrame is to name the tables in the plural form and to provide one surrogate primary key for each table. An example of table names would be "Contacts" or "Invoices." The primary key is stated in the singular form such as ContactID or InvoiceID.

Fields

Avoid using long field names for the same reasons outlined when naming tables. Additionally, many FoxPro programmers prefix the name of each field in their tables with the field's type. Avoid that convention when naming fields. Many FoxPro data types are not comparable to data types in other database products. Using a prefix to indicate the field's type offers little benefit because the type is easily determined and probably won't convert well to another database product.

Methods

As a framework developer you'll use methods for two reasons. The first reason is to accomplish work. The second is to provide a place for the application developers to do work. I'll discuss this topic in much more depth throughout the book. Here's the important point while discussing conventions: There is a difference in how methods are used, and they each have their own conventions.

- Use CamelCase when naming methods where you do the work.

- When providing methods for application developers, do not expect them to be clairvoyant. Consistently inform them, "This is where the code goes." Prefix all methods that are specifically provided for future developers with "On" or "Is." Prefix methods provided to return information with "Get." Use CamelCase for the remainder of the method name.

  For example, "IsValid()" would indicate where a developer could place some validation code. "OnSave()" would indicate a place where a developer could take action during a save. "GetEmployeeListing()" would indicate a method where information was being returned. Developer hooks beginning with "Is" or "On" must return logical values (Boolean for purists). The "Get" methods return data.

I'll discuss data formats in Chapter 8, "Data Access."

Class definitions

Each class serves a purpose in the framework. For example, the "Cursor" class provides services that are useful for working with FoxPro cursors. The class name reflects what the class does.

In some cases, the class will be an abstract class serving only to define the interface for subclasses. Abstract classes are prefixed with an "a." Alternately, fully defined classes that are ready for use are prefixed with "my."

Each application created with the MyFrame framework does not use the MyFrame classes directly. Instead, each class is subclassed at the start of a new application. These classes are application-specific and are (optionally) prefixed with one to three letters specified by the application developer. To remain consistent throughout the book, all application classes will begin with "smp," which is short for "sample application."

 I'll cover much more about the roles classes play in Chapter 6, "Creating a Class Library." A full discussion of how classes are created at the start of each application is discussed in Chapter 18, "Starting New Projects."

Classes as form properties

When classes are used on forms, the class name is prefixed by three letters indicating the class type. For example, all text boxes are prefixed with "txt," labels with "lbl," and so on.

Summary

This chapter illustrated how to create a goal statement that defines the purpose for building your framework, as well as development guidelines and objectives to help guide you during the development cycle.

This chapter also illustrated several documents that will help you during the implementation of your framework. These documents include, but are not limited to, a requirements list, design plan, task list, and a test plan.

Finally, this chapter explained the need for adhering to conventions when developing your framework.

Updates and corrections to this chapter can be found on Hentzenwerke's Web site, **www.hentzenwerke.com**. Click "Catalog" and navigate to the page for this book.

Chapter 3
Framework Architecture

The architecture of a framework is a conceptual model of the major framework components. In this chapter you will learn what comprises a system's architecture as well as take a first "high-level" look at the architecture of the sample framework developed throughout this book.

Architecting your framework—that is, deciding when and how to arrange the many pieces of your framework—appears to be a daunting task. Deciding on a system's architecture early in the development process will save you countless headaches as you develop the framework. When you have taken the time to define your requirements, as we did in Chapter 2, building your framework can be a (relatively) painless process.

You can model the architecture by using drawings, diagrams, sequence diagrams, or any other document that conveys the structure of the framework. Collectively, the architecture documents should convey the high-level design of your framework. The architecture documents provide others with a way to quickly grasp your framework as well as to quickly remind you of the "big picture," which is easy to forget when you get down in the coding trenches.

The architecture for your framework is a reflection of the machines your system will run on and your choice for segregating responsibilities within the framework. Thoroughly defining your requirements will help you identify the physical and logical constraints to which your framework must adhere. For example, the fact that the MyFrame framework must be able to work with FoxPro data as well as client/server data indicates that the way in which data is accessed may vary. Knowing the need for flexibility in this area exists, we can structure the physical and logical structure of our framework to accommodate this need.

Physical constraints on your framework will affect the way that you organize and delegate responsibilities within your framework. In the previous example, knowing that data can be accessed in different ways means that all data access should be directed through a limited number of classes.

Another way to view your framework is in terms of the functions it will provide. A functional breakdown of the framework is necessary to avoid duplicating responsibilities in various points throughout the framework. The second part of this chapter identifies the major responsibilities of the framework.

The third and final section of this chapter shows the data schema for the framework. As you develop your own framework, you may feel it's too early in the process to define table relationships. However, I've included the data schema in this chapter to help you further understand the framework developed throughout the book.

Architectures and tiers

For years Microsoft has been pushing the three-tier or N-tier model for developing applications. A "tiered" application is one in which the components of an application are logically or physically separated. Most often, an application's architecture is divided into three tiers: Presentation, Business Logic, and Data Storage. The N-tier model is an expansion of the three-tier model. Typically, the N-tier model is based upon the three-tier model. The responsibility of one or more tiers is split into smaller tiers. The result is two (or more) smaller, specialized tiers.

The concept of tiered development is one that many FoxPro developers may not be familiar with because FoxPro is capable of producing components that "fit" into any tier. However, separating your application into tiers does have benefits. Among them is the ability to divide development tasks among developers and the flexibility to change one tier without affecting code in another tier.

Presentation layer

The presentation layer contains the elements of an application that end users can see on their forms. A developer responsible for creating the presentation layer is concerned with a user's visual experience with an application.

The primary concern is that the forms are formatted clearly and consistently throughout the application. When users are trained in the use of one form, they should feel comfortable with the mechanics of most forms throughout the system.

Selecting the appropriate controls for the form is also a concern for the presentation developer. For example, using a drop-down combo box to select one of a limited number of selections is appropriate. If the list of selections grows to more than a dozen or so elements, another control should be selected.

Logic layer

The rules of an application, commonly referred to as "business logic," may be separated into their own layer. The types of decisions included in the logic layer are varied.

In a simple case, the logic layer may include rules to enforce that a field is not left empty, or that a numeric entry falls within a range of values.

A more complicated case may be that a client cannot place an order if their outstanding credit exceeds their credit limit. In this example, information from several tables may be required to determine a client's credit limit and whether they have exceeded that level.

A developer responsible for the logic layer should be knowledgeable about the business for which the application is developed.

Data layer

The data layer is the portion of an application that is responsible for reading and writing information to a permanent data store. The developer responsible for the data layer is concerned with enforcing referential integrity and making sure that each entry into the database has transactional integrity—that is, each transaction is atomic, consistent, isolated, and durable.

Separation of power

Each tier has a role. As indicated in the previous descriptions, the development efforts required of developers vary with each tier. Choosing to partition an application into these layers is a logical separation of development tasks.

The separation may be physical as well. For example, when you choose to include a logic layer, a strong case can be made for including rules in either of the other layers. In a client/server application, sending a request to the database server, only to find the request cannot be processed because of an empty field, may consume unnecessary resources on the server for something that could easily have been handled in the presentation layer. Likewise, a process that affects many tables may be best handled on the server, rather than repeatedly requesting information from and sending information to the server during the same transaction.

Therefore, the distinction between tiers may be logical or physical, and the lines between the two are often blurred.

Physical

One physical characteristic of your application is whether it runs on more than one machine. By more than one machine, I'm not referring to a multiuser application. Rather, I mean that components of the application run on different machines. For example, in a client/server application, the presentation layer runs on the end-user's machine while the database layer runs on the server machine.

An application that runs on several machines can only communicate to the user from the client machine. Partitioning the application so that business logic or data services run on separate machines means that you are physically constrained from displaying messages to the user from within these partitions. For example, **Figure 1** shows one possible hardware configuration for a client/server application. Popping a MessageBox() from code executing on the logic or data servers would not be visible to the end user and would only serve to lock up the application.

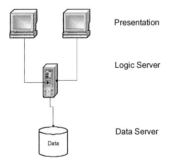

Presentation

Logic Server

Data Server

Figure 1. *Architecture for a three-tier model.*

Another aspect of physical design is the nature of the components themselves. Applications compiled into DLLs cannot present an interface to the user, even if they reside on the user's machine.

Knowing the physical limitations of your system architecture will affect the organization of your framework.

Logical

The organization of responsibilities in an application defines the framework's logical structure. As you develop your framework you will encounter many situations where you need functionality in one class that has already been implemented in another class. Logically organizing your framework reduces the likelihood that you will implement the same functionality more than once.

The approach in My Frame

The MyFrame architecture is an N-tier architecture. The conceptual mode is shown in **Figure 2**. The presentation layer consists of forms and form controls. The logic layer is divided into two sections: One section is for applying logic to data and the other for accessing the data. The data layer represents the database in which the data is stored.

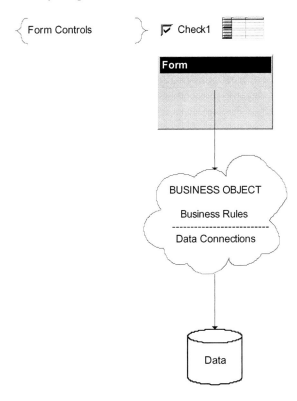

Figure 2. *The logical architecture for MyFrame.*

One of the requirements for MyFrame is to have the ability to work against multiple sources of data. So, for example, the framework may be asked to use FoxPro data in DBF format in one application and SQL Server in another application.

Separating the framework into layers minimizes the chances that changes to one layer will affect other layers in your framework and increases the flexibility of your framework. For example, changing databases may require you to change the classes used in the data connection layer. You are not required to change code in the logic or presentation layers.

The choice to develop MyFrame with an N-tier architecture is a self-imposed constraint. This constraint enables me to show you how to develop N-tier applications as well as how to make the framework useful in as many circumstances as possible.

However, as you will see, separating an application into tiers introduces additional complexity into the framework. The more tiers, the more complex the framework (and resulting application) becomes.

Responsibilities

The responsibilities for each tier can be summarized as follows:

Presentation layer

As mentioned, the presentation layer consists of forms and form controls. The form controls are responsible for collecting information from and presenting information to the user. To do this, each control must "know" how to read and write to information in the cursor.

The form is required to display the form controls. However, the form is also the coordinator of the controls it contains. Therefore, any action that requires interaction between one or more controls is coordinated via the form. For example, when resizing a form, the form contains the code for resizing and repositioning the controls.

 The code to resize controls can be placed elsewhere—for example, in an application object. However, it is more logical (to me at least) to keep code pertaining to form controls with the form.

Another responsibility of the presentation layer is to communicate with the user. This includes messages that may be generated in the data or logic layers. When a message is generated in the data or logic layers, it is communicated to the form. Information is never communicated directly to the user from either the logic or data layers.

Logic layer

The logic layer is responsible for validating information in the cursor. It is also responsible for coordinating the data access components during updates and retrieval of information. Additionally, the logic layer is where the developer will place the application-specific logic commonly referred to as the application's "business rules."

The business objects are based on the DataEnvironment class. Similar to the Form class, the data environment is the outermost container and is responsible for validating data and coordinating the controls it contains.

The Cursor, CursorAdapter, and Relation classes make up the data access layer. The data access layer is responsible for reading information from the underlying data source and placing it into a FoxPro cursor. The form controls are responsible for reading the underlying cursors and displaying their contents to users.

Data layer

The data layer is synonymous with the back-end database, which is the permanent data store for your application.

 Performance may be improved by including business logic in the back-end database. However, doing so requires that you rewrite much of the logic in order to change the back-end database. Business logic in the sample framework is included in the logic layer.

Functional view

A functional or modular view identifies major features of the framework. A class library is a very granular view of specific tasks that a class or classes perform. A functional view is a high-level view that illustrates the collaboration between the classes of your framework.

Additionally, this modular approach to framework construction makes it easier to change the behavior of the framework. If you want to change the capabilities of the Security module, for instance, you need only make changes in one place. Designing your framework in a modular fashion takes a little extra effort. But as your needs change from project to project, it will be easier to make the required changes.

Collectively, the modules provide kinds of functionality found in most frameworks. I use the term "module" to indicate that one or more classes are working together to accomplish a single objective. For example, the Location module "knows" how to set an object's location (top, left, width, and height). Controls call the GetLocation() and SetLocation() methods of the Location module, passing a reference to itself. The Location module is a single service that "knows" how to persist information and can set the location of forms, toolbars, and form controls.

The remainder of this section includes a brief explanation of the major services presented throughout the book.

Application Variable Server (myAppVars)

Every application has a number of "constants." For example, the name of the client for which you've developed your application could be hard coded into the application. But what if the name of the client changes? The Application Variables module stores application variables in one place and retrieves the appropriate value as needed.

Forms collection (myFormsCollection)

The forms collection is the framework equivalent of the forms collection provided by FoxPro.

Location manager (myLocations)

Often, you will want objects to be located where they were last positioned. The location manager in MyFrame remembers the locations of forms, toolbars, and in some cases, the controls on a form.

Messaging service (myMessages)

Messages displayed to the user should have a similar look and feel across an application. Additionally, some messages may change over time. The messaging service in MyFrame is a central module used to provide messaging services throughout the application.

Preferences manager (myPreferences)

Every user has preferences about how an application appears or behaves. The preferences manager is a central service that "remembers" the choices a user has made for his or her application.

Security module (mySecurity)

The security module manages the security settings and administration for users and groups of users.

System codes

Every system has various codes. In a purchasing application, a purchase order may have a code of Active, Closed, Canceled, and so on. Creating a separate table for the many codes is time consuming and adds little value to the end application. The system codes module provides one central place for managing all codes.

Toolbars collection

Similar to the forms collection, the toolbars collection contains a reference to each toolbar.

Reports manager (myReports)

Reporting is a huge development task required in most applications. The reports manager provides a consistent way to include and access reports in your application.

Error handler

This module provides error handling and system shutdown activities for all errors.

Framework data model

It is still early in the development cycle to lay out the data model for your framework. However, I'll present the data model for MyFrame (as shown in **Figure 3**) at this time to further illustrate the framework developed throughout the book.

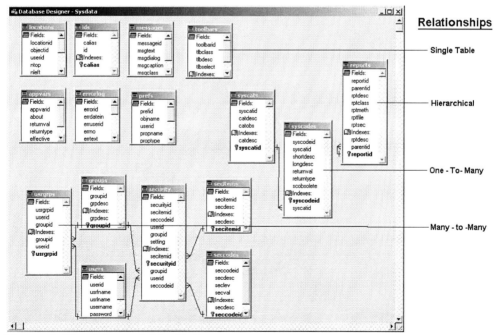

Figure 3. The data model for MyFrame.

Summary

This chapter introduced the major elements of a three-tier architecture and the responsibilities of each tier. Additionally, you learned that each tier can be viewed in terms of the physical constraints in which the framework must perform or the logical separation of responsibilities within the framework itself.

This chapter also introduced some aspects of the MyFrame framework developed throughout the book. I illustrated an approach to functionally segregating your framework by reviewing the functional view of the framework. Finally, I introduced the data model to further illustrate the framework construction.

> Updates and corrections to this chapter can be found on Hentzenwerke's Web site, **www.hentzenwerke.com**. Click "Catalog" and navigate to the page for this book.

Chapter 4
Techniques for Flexibility

Flexibility can mean a number of things to a developer. To a framework developer, flexibility boils down to this: "Will a developer using my framework be able to accomplish what he or she needs to accomplish without having to hack the code?" This chapter covers some of the primary techniques and patterns you can use to add flexibility to your framework.

Flexibility introduces a certain level of complexity to your framework. Understanding the mechanisms for providing flexibility will make it easier for you—and ultimately the application developer—to capitalize on the flexibility you have provided.

Flexibility does not just happen. It is a feature purposefully designed into your framework. Understanding the techniques for flexibility makes it easier (not easy) to map requirements to class designs. Once you become comfortable with the techniques, it will become second nature to ask yourself a question like "Is this feature likely to change in subclasses?" In other cases, flexibility is provided through collaboration between two or more classes. You will also find yourself thinking, "I've done something like this before. Can I reuse some or all of the classes I've already developed?"

The concepts and patterns presented in this chapter are only some of the many ways you can design flexibility into your framework. You can use them as illustrated or in combination. You may prefer to vary the approach depending on your particular style and circumstances. This chapter focuses on techniques used throughout the book.

Classes

A suggested benefit of object-oriented programming is that the resulting applications will be more flexible and the code more reusable. Unfortunately, the act of using classes does not magically result in more flexible and reusable code. To get the most out of object-oriented programming, you should be familiar with two techniques: avoiding hard coding and changing object composition.

Avoiding hard coding

The largest factor for promoting flexibility is to avoid hard coding anything. The term "hard coded" probably conjures an image of a fixed value in a piece of code. Here's an example of a hard coded value:

```
MESSAGEBOX("An Error Occurred")
```

The string "An Error Occurred" is hard coded into this one line of code. For the developer to change the message, he or she would have to find this one line of code and amend it.

Look closer. This is more than an example of a hard-coded string. This one line of code also hard codes the decision to use the MessageBox function. The application developer may wish to use a form other than the one displayed by the MessageBox function—possibly one that contains a Help button or a graphic or some other feature. Hard-coded design decisions, like using the MessageBox function, often occur in more than one line of code.

    Here I'll present three approaches to help you avoid hard coding values into your framework. Each approach is useful in different circumstances.

Properties

Rather than hard coding the error message, you could store the message text in a property of the class. Using a property to store a value carries the full benefit of object orientation. That is, subclasses inherit the property, and therefore the value of the property. The application developer may then choose to subclass the class you've provided and change the property value in the subclass without changing framework code.

    Note, however, that storing the message text in a property does not relieve the hard-coded design decision to use the MessageBox function. The examples presented in the upcoming section, "Patterns—Overview," illustrate ways to overcome hard-coded design decisions.

Predefined constants

Include files and predefined constants allow developers to define values in one central location, which exists outside of the source code. In the previous example, storing the message text in a property of the class works well when the value in question is limited to a single class and its subclasses. Predefined constants have the added benefit of being available to more than one class and can be used in programs as well.

    You probably wouldn't have a reason to hard code a particular error message in several parts of your application, but you might be likely to hard code the name of the application.

    Include files also have the added benefit of keeping all the "variables" for the application in a central location.

Data-driven (dynamic) solutions

The use of properties and predefined constants are examples of design-time flexibility. Once you've compiled the application, their values cannot be changed.

    Storing values in a permanent data store, such as a DBF file, is an example of a data-driven solution. Data-driven solutions are dynamic and can be changed after the application is compiled.

Changing object composition

Composite classes consist of more than one class. Changing the behavior or appearance of the classes that make up the composite class, by definition, changes the behavior or appearance of the composite class itself.

    Changing object composition means that you are changing the entire class and not simply changing a method or property of one of the classes. Swapping one object for another implies that the classes subject to changing object composition are interchangeable. In order for classes to be interchangeable they must have the same interface.

About the interface

Technically, an object's interface is the sum of its public properties and methods. However, objects that work together typically do not call every exposed property or method of another class. Instead, they work with a subset of an object's interface. The term "interface" in this book generally refers to the subset of exposed properties and methods that objects use to communicate with each other. An interface, then, is a communication agreement, or communication contract, between classes.

For example, assume you have a Textbox class, TextBoxWithErrorMessage, that has many public methods, one of which is SetErrorState(). Assume further that SetErrorState() accepts no parameters and returns a logical value. Any other Textbox class also having a SetErrorState() method that returns a logical value and accepts no parameters lives up to the communication contract of TextBoxWithErrorMessage and can therefore be considered interchangeable with TextBoxWithErrorMessage.

Abstract classes and interfaces

Abstract classes are often used to "implement an interface." In many cases, an abstract class contains no code—only properties, methods, and the parameters for the methods—leaving the "real" code to be implemented in subclasses.

Patterns—Overview

Design patterns are conceptual solutions to defined problems that can be useful in a variety of circumstances. Design patterns themselves are useful for communicating complex ideas with a single phrase.

Design patterns also promote consistency in your code. Once you have defined a problem, you are likely to identify a design pattern that satisfies the problem. You will also be likely to implement a design pattern in the same way in different parts of your code.

Design patterns have been created to identify many different types of problems. One of those problems is how to avoid hard coding design decisions into applications. With that in mind, this overview is intended to provide you with enough of an understanding about patterns so that when you see the term "proxy" you think "placeholder" and are aware of the impact a proxy will have on the design of your classes.

Some of the examples in this section illustrate how changing a class can change the behavior of the class that created it. The examples hard code the classes to implement. In practice you would use one of the techniques presented earlier to further extend the flexibility provided by these patterns.

Following is the sample form class used as the basis for many of the examples. Again, the simple MessageBox function is used to illustrate how to avoid hard coding this design decision into your framework. Additionally, the form has a hard-coded BackColor property. Here's the class definition:

```
DEFINE CLASS SampleForm AS FORM

  BACKCOLOR = RGB(255,255,0) && Yellow

    Function ShowMessage( tcMessage )
        =MessageBox( tcMessage )
    Endfunc

ENDDEFINE
```

Template method

A template method coordinates and directs activities. Typically, a template method does not perform the task or tasks at hand. Instead, other methods contain the code that does the actual work, and the template method specifies which methods or objects are called.

For example, the form class (presented in Chapter 12, "Forms") knows how to communicate with toolbars, add and remove itself from a forms collection, and grab a reference to the previously active form. The DoClose() method is a custom method that coordinates the release of a framework form. By controlling the form's close operation with a template method, you can change the sequence of the close method without affecting the individual steps. The DoClose() method is shown here:

```
*--An example of a template method
WITH THIS
    .VISIBLE=.F.
    .SaveLoc()
    .ReleaseToolbars()
    .RefreshToolbars()
    .RemoveFromFormsCollection()
    .oPreviousActiveForm = .NULL.

    IF .lReleaseOnClose
        .RELEASE()
    ENDIF
ENDWITH
```

Notice that the work (or code) of closing a form is not performed in the DoClose() method.

The template method is an important tool for you as a framework developer because it allows you to control a sequence of actions. Separating the control of an event sequence from the actual events makes it easier to change the sequence of events without affecting the individual methods.

This style of coding methods is advantageous whether you are coding an application or a framework. It is particularly important to a framework developer because you can design the template to call "hook" methods. A hook method is an empty method that exists for developers to insert code. The template method then can be used to structure your framework code and provide a safe way for other developers to extend the framework.

Templates also make it easier to reuse code within your class. In the previous example, a call is made to the RefreshToolbars() method. Although it is not shown here, the RefreshToolbars() method is called from several different methods of the form.

Template methods are common tools used in framework development—ones that you should use often.

Styles

A Style object knows how to configure an object. Two examples of how to implement a style class are presented; each is useful in different circumstances.

A Style object is not one of the patterns presented in the book Design Patterns *(Gamma, Helm, Johnson, Vlissides; Addison-Wesley, 1995). However, it is a conceptual approach to a defined problem useful in a variety of circumstances.*

In the first example, the Style class has one method that accepts an object for which the style is applied. In this case, the style changes the background color of an object to red.

```
DEFINE CLASS SampleStyle AS Custom

    FUNCTION ApplyStyle( toObject )

        IF PEMSTATUS (toObject, "BackColor", 5)
            toObject.BackColor = 255 &&Red
        ENDIF

    ENDFUNC
ENDDEFINE
```

The second example shows a style that knows how to configure its parent. A class like this might be useful when added to a form at run time or design time.

```
DEFINE CLASS AutoStyler AS Custom

  FUNCTION INIT()
            THIS.ApplyStyle()
  ENDFUNC

    FUNCTION ApplyStyle()
        IF TYPE( 'this.Parent' ) = 'O' and ;
        PEMSTATUS( this.parent, 'BackColor',5 )

            THIS.Parent.backcolor = 255
        ENDIF
    ENDFUNC
ENDDEFINE
```

It is easy to think of styles as setting properties associated with visual appearance, such as ForeColor and BackColor. However, a style can set any type of property or properties. Examples might be security settings, whether a form is read-only, and so on.

Mediator and event binding

A mediator links one action with one or more resulting actions. The most common use for a mediator is when the resulting actions vary. For example, a business application may have one or more business objects that must respond to some event. You hard code the calls to each business object as follows:

```
*--Simulate a system event
ObjectOne.DoEvent()
ObjectTwo.DoEvent()
ObjectThree.DoEvent()
```

However, this approach requires that you change the method each time the number of objects participating in the event increases.

A mediator is a separate object that decouples (separates) the caller of an event from the receivers of the event. When you use a mediator, the object initiating the event calls the mediator and "raises" the event. The mediator then forwards the request to any objects registered for the event.

An enhanced feature in FoxPro 8.0 is event binding. Event binding is similar to a mediator in that events or method calls in one object result in a method call in one or more objects. Event binding uses the BINDEVENT command to link objects, rather than using a separate object. BINDEVENT in previous versions of FoxPro was limited to working with COM objects. The version 8.0 enhancements allow BINDEVENT to link native FoxPro objects. Here is the syntax for event binding:

```
BINDEVENT(oEventSource, cEvent, oEventHandler, cDelegate [, nFlags])
```

The oEventSource parameter is the object reference to the initiator of the event. The cEvent parameter is the name of the method that causes the event to occur. The oEventHandler and cDelegate parameters are the object and method called. Specifying a value of 3 for the nFlags parameter tells the BINDEVENT command that you are linking two FoxPro objects.

The list box navigation controls illustrated in Chapter 13, "Data Entry Forms," use the BINDEVENT command to REQUERY themselves after the user deletes a record. The following line of code binds the list box to the custom form method OnDelete().

```
BINDEVENT(THISFORM,'OnDelete',THIS,'Requery',3)
```

Once this command is issued each time the OnDelete() method is invoked, the ListBox.Requery() method will fire as well.

Factory method

A factory method knows how to create an object. In the following example, the factory method instantiates the AutoStyle class from the previous example. Factory methods provide flexibility by allowing subclasses to instantiate different objects than are defined in the parent class (assuming one is defined in the parent class at all). The sample code for a factory method is shown here:

```
The AutoStyle definition is taken from the Styles example.
*--AutoStyle created with a factory
DEFINE CLASS SampleForm AS FORM

   FUNCTION INIT()
      THIS.MakeStyle()
   ENDFUNC

   FUNCTION MakeStyle()
      THIS.ADDOBJECT("oStyle","AutoStyle")
   ENDFUNC

ENDDEFINE
```

In this example, the AutoStyle class is added to the form. When the AutoStyle class is created, it changes the form's BackColor property to red.

 Factory methods in MyFrame begin with the prefix "Make."

Abstract factory

The book *Design Patterns* states that an abstract factory is used to "Provide an interface for creating families of related or dependent objects without specifying their concrete classes." An abstract factory is similar to a factory method in that it also knows how to create an object. However, the abstract factory returns a reference to the object rather than manipulating it directly.

In the following example, the abstract factory returns the AutoStyle class defined earlier. One point to mention is that the AutoStyle class is not contained within an object when it is created. In practice, the calling class would have to know to call the AutoStyle.ApplyStyle() method. Stated differently, the class returned by the factory method must support the ApplyStyle() interface.

The sample abstract factory is shown here:

```
DEFINE CLASS SampleFactory as Custom

    FUNCTION GetObject()
        RETURN CREATEOBJECT("AutoStyle")
    ENDFUNC

ENDDEFINE
```

Delegation (bridge)

Delegation is a way of extending the functionality of one class by implementing functionality in a second class. By changing the delegate, you change the behavior of the calling class. For example, the SampleForm class could have been written to delegate the messaging responsibility to a second class as follows:

```
*--Delegation Example
DEFINE CLASS SampleForm AS form
  ADD OBJECT oMessageBox AS SampleMessageBox

    FUNCTION ShowMessage( tcMessage)
        THIS.oMessageBox.ShowMessage( tcMessage )
  ENDFUNC

ENDDEFINE

DEFINE CLASS SampleMessageBox AS custom
    FUNCTION ShowMessage( tcMessage )
        Wait window tcMessage
  ENDFUNC
ENDDEFINE
```

This example illustrates how the design decision to use the MessageBox function can be changed. You can create additional classes to incorporate different messaging formats. For example, the ShowMessage() method of another class could change the status bar message or the _screen.Caption, or a form.

Proxy—Overview

A proxy serves as a placeholder for another object. Proxies are generally used to delay instantiation of memory-intensive objects until they are actually needed. For example, consider a page frame with seven pages and 30 items on a page. Loading all 210 objects could be a resource drain while the form is loading. A proxy, or in this case a series of proxies, would help by delaying the instantiation of items on pages 2 through 7.

The proxy class in MyFrame

A proxy is a placeholder for another object. The class MyProxy has a LoadProxy() method that is responsible for carrying out the tasks associated with a proxy. They are:

- Add a new object to the parent container.

- Resize the object to occupy the same space as the proxy.

- Make the object visible.

Two properties have been added to MyProxy: cClassToLoad and cNewClassName. To use this class, enter the class name you want to create in the cClassToLoad property and the name you want to assign to the class in the cNewClassName property.

The code for LoadProxy() is shown here:

```
*--MyProxy.LoadProxy()
LOCAL lcNewClass, loParent AS FORM, lcNewObjectName

lcNewClass = ALLTRIM(THIS.cClassToLoad)
lcNewObjectName = ALLTRIM(THIS.cNewClassName)

IF  ! EMPTY(lcNewClass)            AND;
        ! EMPTY(lcNewObjectName) AND;
        ! THIS.lLoaded           AND;
        TYPE("THIS.PARENT") = 'O'

    WITH THIS.PARENT

        *--Add The Object
        .ADDOBJECT(lcNewObjectName,lcNewClass)

        *--Set the position

        .&lcNewObjectName..TOP = THIS.TOP
        .&lcNewObjectName..HEIGHT = THIS.HEIGHT
        .&lcNewObjectName..WIDTH = THIS.WIDTH
        .&lcNewObjectName..LEFT = THIS.LEFT

        *--View it
        .&lcNewObjectName..VISIBLE = .T.
```

```
     *--Prevent it from loading again
     THIS.lLoaded = .T.

  ENDWITH

ENDIF
```

Label vs. custom classes

End users never see proxies. Their very purpose is to load some other class that users *do* want to see. Classes that are purely functional and that require no visual representation seem perfect candidates for the custom class. However, MyProxy is a subclass of aUtilityLbl, which is a label.

At various points in the MyFrame framework, I choose to use labels rather than the custom class. Labels allow me to convey extra information about the class at design time. In **Figure 1**, the label is the proxy. The custom class is added to show what the proxy would look like if it were based on the custom class.

When I wear my framework developer hat, I use the caption to convey information about how to use the class. As you can see in Figure 1, the caption for MyProxy explains how to use the class. When I'm wearing my application developer hat, I might place comments in the caption about why I chose to use a proxy.

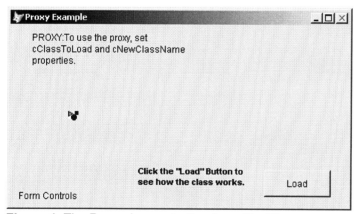

Figure 1. The Proxy demonstration form, TestProxy.scx.

To use the proxy, drop the class on a container object (form, page, and so on) and resize it as desired. Enter the name of the class you want to load in cClassToLoad and the resulting name of the class in cNewClassName. TestProxy.scx is included in the samples for this chapter.

Wrappers

The intent of a wrapper class is to change the interface of a class. Typically this is done to provide uniformity when working with various classes. Consider the delegate example presented earlier. In the example, each delegate is required to have a ShowMessage() method accepting one parameter. A wrapper class could be used to morph existing classes so they meet the interface requirements of SampleForm.

Summary

In this chapter, you have learned several techniques to incorporate flexibility into your framework. These techniques are used in various places throughout MyFrame, giving plenty of examples of how these concepts can be applied in practice.

Armed with the examples provided in the chapter and the examples of how they are applied in practice, you should be in a better position to understand how flexibility is incorporated into commercial frameworks and how to use these techniques in your work.

Updates and corrections to this chapter can be found on Hentzenwerke's Web site, **www.hentzenwerke.com**. Click "Catalog" and navigate to the page for this book.

Chapter 5
Beginning Development

The success of your framework depends upon the ability of the application developer to create fully functioning applications. Focus on quality and productivity. Ultimately those are the criteria on which your framework will be judged.

The first time I began developing a framework, it was exciting thinking of all the features I was going to include: a splash screen, business logic, resizable forms, and so on. I made coffee, sat in front of my computer, and then it really hit me: This is a huge project. Where do I start?

Like any computer project, a FoxPro project is a collection of files. The development of the MyFrame framework begins with an explanation of the framework folder structure and how to organize files to accommodate multiple projects. The next step is to create some of the framework files. In this chapter, I introduce procedure files: a header file, a configuration file, the framework class library, and the framework database. Throughout the book, the contents of these files are extended, much as you would do as you develop your own framework. If you have pre-existing procedure or class libraries, this is a good time to incorporate them into your new framework as well.

The last section in this chapter introduces an application object and the main program responsible for loading and unloading the framework files. In this early stage of development, the application object is merely an application shell responsible for all the events surrounding the beginning and end of an application. We will be adding functionality to our application object as we progress through the book.

Folder structure

Organizing the files that comprise the application will help to reduce development time, promote reuse, simplify backups, provide flexibility, and facilitate the distribution process. In this section, I will identify the key elements of an organized folder structure and describe (or propose) a way to set up a folder structure.

The following list of requirements further define what it means to work on multiple projects:

- Changes to the framework affect all projects that share the framework.

- Application developers must have the ability to change behavior at the framework or project level.

- A change in one project does not affect the framework.

- A change in one project does not affect other projects under development.

The term "project" here refers to each application under development. Do not confuse the term "project" with the Visual FoxPro project manager. A project manager is (in FoxPro) a tool that organizes the files in your project and facilitates the compilation and distribution process.

Reviewing the requirements document, the following requirements affect how the file folders should be organized:

- Developers should have the option of sharing the framework between multiple projects.

- Changes to the framework affect all projects that share the framework.

Separating framework files from application files

Providing the ability for projects to share the framework folder means that users of your framework will have one or more projects pointing to the framework folder. **Figure 1** shows how this might be arranged.

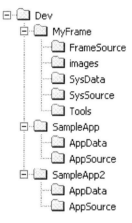

Figure 1. *An example of how your framework and project folders might be arranged.*

I like storing all of my work under one folder, "Dev." This is a personal preference and one you do not need to follow. The important point of this illustration is that there is one framework folder with a separate folder for each project. Each application sharing the framework files points to the MyFrame folder. The relative structure, that is, each application existing on the same level as MyFrame, should not change.

 MyFrame is not required to exist on the same level as the applications. It can exist anywhere you prefer. However, once you decide on a relative structure, adhere to it. Changing the relative structure will break existing applications expecting to find the MyFrame folder in a certain location.

Later in this chapter when I discuss creating the startup routine, I'll explain how the application "points" to the framework. If the concept of relative structures is unclear to you now, review this again after reading that section.

 It is not required that each application in the Dev folder be associated with the framework. You or other developers may have other projects that are not based on MyFrame.

Configuring the application folder

A second requirement is to have the ability to switch between one or more data sets—for example, live and test data. Stated differently, users of your framework should have the ability to run against a variety of data sets. The least complicated way to provide this ability is to keep source code separate from test data. **Figure 2** shows application data and source code in separate folders.

Figure 2. *Separating source code from data.*

Having the ability to run the application against a variety of data sets provides a number of advantages. In practice you'll want to provide the application developer with the ability to use at least three sets of data: pristine, test, and live. With test data, developers or end users can freely enter data as they test the application. Pristine data is a clean set of data used to begin all testing. After each test is completed, the test data can be "reset" back to the pristine state, making it ready for the next set of tests.

Another advantage to keeping application data separate from source code is that it is simpler and faster to back up projects, transfer them between developers, and so on, without having to move large volumes of test data.

A final benefit may be realized when it comes time to distribute your applications. If you have not been through the distribution process, one of the steps is to separate the files you want to distribute from those that you do not. Some developers prefer to generate the data files programmatically as part of the installation or as part of the initial application startup. Others prefer to distribute the data files directly. If you intend to distribute the data files directly, but not the source code, separating the data files throughout development ultimately makes the distribution process smoother.

Configuring the framework folder

The data and source code for the framework are also separated. However, the reasons are different. Your framework will store certain types of information common to all applications. Assume you have a table, AppData.dbf, which contains AppName, CustName, and so on. Each application gets its own discrete copy of the data. At the start of each new application, a copy of this data is placed in the AppData folder. I'll refer to this type of data as "system data."

One other folder rounds out the discussion of the framework folders: Tools. The Tools folder holds files that are used by the framework but never become part of the final application. For example, the sample framework accompanying this book has programs that create your framework base classes, create framework business objects, and programmatically subclass the framework base classes at the start of a new project.

The Tools folder also stores forms and templates used in some of the builders presented in Chapter 17, "Developer Tools." **Figure 3** illustrates the configuration of the framework folder.

Figure 3. *The folder structure for the MyFrame folders.*

Project manager

The project manager is an essential tool when compiling applications. Although it is not required for development, using the project manager simplifies many tasks throughout the development cycle. The source code accompanying this book has four projects. MyFrame.pjx is provided to work with the framework files. The Examples project contains the chapter samples. The Hello World project is a simple example of how to create an application, while the SampleApp project contains a more detailed example of creating a framework application. The sample application is presented in detail in Chapter 19, "Sample Application."

Framework and application files

In this section I discuss an organized approach to storing your source code. I'll explain the types of code that go into each file, some rules associated with the code, and where the file is stored on disk.

Where possible, try to keep similar types of code in the same file. The application developer should be able to quickly and easily find source code. For example, store all of the framework functions you provide in a file called FrameProc.prg. Source code and additional files will be added in subsequent chapters.

.\Tools\GenProc.prg

Most developers have a set of generic procedures they would have included in the language had they been Calvin or Dr. Dave.

 Calvin refers to Calvin Hsia, lead developer for Visual FoxPro. Dr. Dave refers to David Fulton, who joined Microsoft in June 1992 when Fox Software merged with Microsoft.

Generic functions can be described as extensions to the language and are useful in a variety of situations. As a rule, they should be self-contained, relying on no other procedures. If a case arises where one procedure is dependent upon another, the called procedure should exist in this file as well. A rule of thumb is that a developer should get the benefit of any function provided in this file with a single SET CLASSLIB TO. A sample of a general procedure is shown here.

```
*===========================================================
*|  Purpose......Return only the integers in a string
*|  Author.......K.Chazotte
*|  Created......June 28, 2002
*|  About........
*|  Mod List.....
*===========================================================

FUNCTION JustDigits(tcString)
      LOCAL lcNewString
   lcNewString=""
   FOR lnI=1 TO LEN(tcString)
      IF ISDIGIT(SUBSTR(tcString,lnI,1))
            lcNewString=lcNewString+SUBSTR(tcString,lnI,1)
      ENDIF
   ENDFOR
   RETURN lcNewString
ENDFUNC
```

.\Tools\DevProc.prg

Developer procedures are useful to the developer and generally are not included in the application. The documentation header shown in the previous example was created by a procedure stored in DevProc.prg.

```
#DEFINE DeveloperName  "K.Chazotte"
FUNCTION DocumentationHeader()
   KEYBOARD ''CLEAR
   KEYBOARD '*==========================================='+CHR(10)
   KEYBOARD '*|  Purpose......'+CHR(10)
   KEYBOARD '*|  Author.......'+ DeveloperName +CHR(10)
   KEYBOARD '*|  Created...... '+ MDY(DATE())+CHR(10)
   KEYBOARD '*|  About........'+CHR(10)
   KEYBOARD '*|  Mod List.....'+CHR(10)
   KEYBOARD '*=============================  =============='+CHR(10)
   KEYBOARD '{UPARROW}{UPARROW}{UPARROW}{UPARROW}{UPARROW}{END}'
   KEYBOARD '{UPARROW}'
ENDFUNC
```

.\FrameSource\FrameProc.prg

Similar to generic procedures, framework procedures also serve as extensions to the language. The attribute that sets them apart from general procedures is that they are framework specific. Taken outside the context of the framework, they would probably be of little use.

Functions programmed in this file can safely operate under the premise that all features of the framework are available.

.\AppSource\AppProc.prg

This file is similar to frame procedures, except that it contains application-specific procedures. There's a trick here: The framework should not call any application-specific functionality. This file is provided as a courtesy for the application developer. As a framework developer, you should not place any code in this file.

.\FrameSource\MyFrame.h and .\AppSource\MyApp.h

Maybe it's because I got scarred as a little developer, but I don't use include files. With the introduction of IntelliSense, I don't even feel the guilt for not having some really crafty way of remembering MessageBox() parameters. However, this is an example of where it is helpful to develop your framework with others in mind.

 When using include files in conjunction with relative paths, as I do in this framework, you must set the path prior to rebuilding a FoxPro project. If you don't, you'll get an error even if the include file is included in the project. The path is set as part of running the main program.

All joking aside, include files and predefined compile-time constants do provide specific benefits. Among them are improved performance and a centralized point to change values system wide. Provide two files for predefined constants: one for the framework, and one for the application. Here are two examples of predefined constants:

```
#DEFINE BOOK_NAME "Build Your Own Framework"
#DEFINE APP_NAME "Chapter 04"
```

.\AppSource\Config.fpw

FoxPro provides a slew of commands that enable you to configure the development environment. Oddly, there are not as many commands as there are settings. From the config file, you can specify where FoxPro does some of its processing work or whether the background screen is displayed when your compiled application runs.

Consult the Help file to see which commands are available. As the framework developer you should provide a single config file per application as a courtesy for the application developer.

.\FrameSource\MyFrame.vcx

MyFrame.vcx holds the class definitions for all the classes provided as part of the MyFrame framework. Chapter 6, "Creating a Class Library," is devoted entirely to developing the classes in this file.

.\SysData\AppData.dbc

AppData.dbc is the template database used as the starting point for each new application.

Starting a FoxPro application

Each application has a single starting point—a single routine where the developer establishes the application environment and launches the application. The startup program is referred to as the "main" program. Likewise, each time an application closes, FoxPro provides a single place for the developer to take any actions necessary before closing the application and also to close the application. FoxPro does not require that you place the shutdown actions in the main program. However, keeping the startup routine and the shutdown routine in the same file is more intuitive for the application developer. Here are the types of activities that occur in the startup and shutdown sequence:

List of activities performed on application startup

- Set the default directory

- Set the search path

- Check the machine capacities

- Save the current environment

- Show the splash screen

- Set the application environment

- Load the class libraries

- Load the procedure files

- Open the data

- Load the framework components

    - Security (login screen)

    - Messaging module

    - Forms manager

    - Error handler

    - Location manager

- Assign keypad functionality

- Launch a menu

- Set the wait state

List of activities performed on application shutdown

- Clear the wait state

- Close any open forms

- Save/revert any buffered data

- Release any objects in memory

- Restore original settings

As mentioned previously, FoxPro allows you to configure the application environment at any time. However, in practice, there is a reason why you load all your application files in the startup routine, and there's a particular order in which the startup and shutdown activities should occur.

Loading files into memory and setting the application environment takes time. End users expect an application to take a few seconds to start and are relatively patient during this time.

When end users experience delays, even minor delays, at various times while using an application, it causes a feeling of frustration.

A second reason to load all the files at the beginning of the application is that developers should not have to be concerned about whether a particular library or database has already been loaded. Each piece of functionality you provide should be available once the startup routine is complete.

Finally, FoxPro allows files to be opened in any order. However, in practice, there is a definite sequence in which startup activities should occur. Passive events are those where no subsequent activity may occur. For example, when loading a procedure file using SET PROCEDURE TO, there isn't an opportunity for any other code to execute. Conversely, loading a database is an active event. As of version 7.0, code may execute when issuing the OPEN DATABASE command. If you have SET DATABASE EVENTS ON, two events fire when a database opens: OpenData and Activate.

This leads me to a point where I can define a few rules for the startup sequence…

- RULE: All activities associated with starting an application must occur in the startup program.

- RULE: Passive events must occur before active events.

- RULE: If any of the startup events fail, tell the user a problem exists and the nature of the problem, and then exit the application.

…and for the shutdown sequence.

- RULE: Before closing the application, the user must have the opportunity to complete any pending entries. The user must have the ability to cancel the closing sequence if edits are still pending.

Your role as a framework developer is to provide a way to incorporate each of the activities and rules associated with starting and closing an application into the startup and shutdown routines, while making it easy for developers to tailor these routines to fit their applications. Using a class, in conjunction with template methods, to control application activities offers the framework developer the most control while providing the end developer with the most flexibility. In the next section, I'll create a class, "aApplication," to handle these responsibilities.

The "template method" (Gamma et al.) is a pattern designed to specifically handle situations where the structure of an event sequence is known, but the steps in each event are unknown—as is the case with the startup and shutdown sequences. As defined in *Design Patterns* (Gamma, Helm, Johnson, Vlissides; Addison-Wesley, 1995), the intent of the template method is to "Define the skeleton of an algorithm in an operation, deferring some steps to subclasses. Template method lets subclasses redefine certain steps of an algorithm without changing the algorithm's structure." In the context of the framework, create two template methods, LoadApp() and OnShutDown(), to handle the starting and closing of the application.

Refer back to the list of events associated with starting and closing an application. Add a separate method to aApplication for each activity in the list. The template methods control the sequencing of the method calls. The application developer can customize the startup routine by overriding specific methods.

aApplication

Let's start by taking a look at the class definition in its entirety. (For the sake of saving space, empty methods are not listed.) A summary review explaining some of the more important aspects of the class follows.

```
DEFINE CLASS aApplication AS SESSION

    PROTECTED lDevMode, lOKToLaunch, ;
        cAppName, cFramework, nSplashDelay
    lDevMode = .F.
    lOKToLaunch = .F.
    cAppName = ""
    cFramework = "Build Your Own Framework"
    nSplashDelay = 5000

    FUNCTION INIT()

        IF ! THIS.LoadApp()
            THIS.OnShutDown()
            RETURN .F.
        ENDIF

    ENDFUNC

    FUNCTION DESTROY()
        THIS.OnShutDown()
    ENDFUNC

    PROTECTED FUNCTION LoadApp()

        WITH THIS

            DO CASE
                CASE !.OnSetDevMode()
                CASE !.OnShowSplash()
                CASE !.OnCheckMachine()
                CASE !.OnSetEnvironment()
                CASE !.OnLoadProcedures()
                CASE !.OnLoadLibraries()
                CASE !.OnSetAppKeyPad()
                CASE !.OnLoadData()
                CASE !.OnLoadComponents()
                CASE !.LoadMenus()

                OTHERWISE

                    IF .lDevMode
                        .lOKToLaunch = .OnSetDevEnvironment()
                    ELSE
                        .ReleaseSplash()
                        .ShowScreen()

                        IF .OnLoadSecurity() AND .onLaunchApp()
                            .lOKToLaunch = .T.
                        ELSE
                            THIS.OnShowAppFailedMessage()
                        ENDIF
                    ENDIF
```

```
                    .ShowStatus("")
        ENDCASE

        RETURN .lOKToLaunch

    ENDWITH
ENDFUNC

FUNCTION OnShutDown()

    WITH THIS
        IF .CloseAllForms()
            .ReleaseObjects()
            .RestoreEnvironment()
            .RestoreMenu()
            .ClearKeys()
            .CloseAllData()

            ON SHUTDOWN

            IF THIS.lDevMode
                *--Do nothing
                *) At this point, the framework classes are released
                *) and the development environment is returned to
                *) the state it was in before starting the
                *) framework.
                *) However, if you really want to exit FoxPro,
                *) uncomment the next line

                * QUIT
            ELSE
                CLEAR EVENTS
            ENDIF

            RELEASE THIS
            RELEASE goApp
        ELSE
            RETURN .F.
        ENDIF
    ENDWITH
ENDFUNC

ENDDEFINE
```

This code, even without documentation, is clear and easy to follow. Adhering to the conventions, all places where a developer can place code begin with "On," "Is," or "Get," clearly identifying which pieces of functionality can be modified and which should not. You will see, when setting up the sample application for the chapter, that this structure also "hides" the complexity of the startup and shutdown processes from application developers. In fact, they won't be required to know the difference between active and passive code. Their concern will be to know only where to place the application code.

Declaring the function LoadApp() as protected prevents other classes that are not subclasses of aApplication from calling this function. One of the basic principles in object-oriented programming is that the interface of a class is defined by its public, or exposed, properties, events, and methods. LoadApp() is not a method we want to expose as part of the interface for this class.

As a developer, you may say, "I would never call the LoadApp() function from somewhere else in my code." And, that may be true. But when developing for others, it is best to specifically state that the LoadApp() and OnShutDown() methods should not be called directly.

```
PROTECTED FUNCTION LoadApp()
```

The CASE statement evaluates a series of logical expressions. If the expression evaluates to True, the code directly beneath the CASE statement is executed. Each CASE statement is evaluated in sequence. If none of the expressions has evaluated to True, the code in OTHERWISE is executed.

Developers equate a logical value of True with success, and False with failure. When reading through and developing code for any of the called methods, the application developer would expect a return value of True to indicate the step completed successfully. The logical .NOT. operator "!" is used to reverse True and False, satisfying the requirements for the CASE statement and meeting the application developer's expectations.

Beginning with OnCheckMachine() and ending with OnLoadAppMenu(), each method is executed in sequence. Only when all methods complete successfully are we ready to load the application.

```
DO CASE
    CASE !.OnCheckMachine()
    CASE !.OnSetEnvironment()
    CASE !.OnShowSplash()
    CASE !.OnLoadProcedures()
    CASE !.OnLoadLibraries()
    CASE !.OnSetAppKeyPad()
    CASE !.OnLoadData()
    CASE !.OnLoadComponents()
    CASE !.OnLoadAppMenu()
    OTHERWISE
     *--Load the application as illustrated above
     *) If the application or development environments
     *) are successfully loaded, .lOKToLaunch will be .T.

ENDCASE

RETURN .lOKToLaunch
```

If the application loaded successfully, no action is taken. If any of the load steps failed, the user is shown a message indicating that the enriching user experience they were about to enjoy could not be completed for some (specified) reason. In the case of failure, the LoadApp() method is terminated and returns a value of False.

As a developer not familiar with the framework, I would read the code below as "Each time the class aApplication is instantiated the application is loaded. If the application does not load properly, shut it down." Perfect! That is exactly what is happening. This code is self-documenting. Calling LoadApp() from the Init() method also follows a general rule of object-oriented programming: Never place procedural code directly in an event.

```
FUNCTION INIT()
     IF ! THIS.LoadApp()
        THIS.OnShutDown()
        RETURN .F.
     ENDIF
ENDFUNC
```

If the application could not load successfully, the class representing the application shouldn't exist either. A value of False returned from the Init() method of any class in FoxPro prevents the class from loading.

Enabling the developer to determine if the application is started in "development mode" provides developers with a way to load special tools while developing, and to configure the environment differently while developing, yet quickly switch to "run mode," simulating the application's behavior when compiled. A subtle point is that the following code executes after the run environment has been established, enabling the developer to overwrite application settings.

```
IF .lDevMode
  .lOKToLaunch = .OnSetDevEnvironment()
ELSE
  *--Load the application
ENDIF
```

When closing the application, first check to make sure any open forms closed successfully. If each form does not close successfully, the application won't close. Notice that the CloseAllForms() method does not begin with "On" or "Is." I'll develop the code for this method in Chapter 13, "Data Entry Forms."

If CloseAllForms() is successful, the remainder of the method proceeds with shutting down the application and restoring the original environment.

```
FUNCTION OnShutDown()

    WITH THIS
        IF .CloseAllForms()

            .ReleaseObjects()
            .RestoreEnvironment()
            .RestoreMenu()
            .ClearKeys()
            .CloseAllData()

            *-- Always clear the existing shutdown handler.
            ON SHUTDOWN

            IF THIS.lDevMode
                *--Do nothing
            ELSE
                CLEAR EVENTS
            ENDIF
```

```
                RELEASE THIS
                RELEASE goApp

          ENDIF
      ENDWITH
ENDFUNC
```

Creating the main programs

The bulk of the work in starting a FoxPro application has already been accounted for with the class aApplication. The main programs really boil down to stub programs that perform a few tasks. They are:

- Set the default path.

- Set the search path.

- Add include files (optional).

- Create an instance of the application object, aApplication.

In the next two sections I'll create two main programs, one to load the framework files and one to start the application.

Main_Frame.prg

When working on the framework, you'll want to load only the framework files. In practice, when developing applications, Frame_Main merely serves as the container for the class aApplication. The class definition is not repeated again here. In the source files provided, the class definition begins after the line oApp.SetRead().

Refer back to the requirements document. One requirement is that the application must run wherever launched. FoxPro provides us with a system function that returns a value specifying in which directory a program was started. Using JUSTPATH() returns the path portion of the start directory.

```
    SET DEFAULT TO JUSTPATH(SYS(16,0))
```

The search path is set using relative paths. Again, the ability to start the application wherever launched is not compromised. Another key point is that none of the application folders are loaded here. Main_Frame should only be run while working on the framework.

```
SET PATH TO ";
.\,;
.\Meta\ ,;
.\FrameSource\ ,;
.\SysData\,;
.\Test\,;
.\Tools\ ;
```

Following is the code of the main program in its entirety.

```
*-- First Task, set default directories and search path
SET DEFAULT TO JUSTPATH(SYS(16,0))

SET PATH TO ";
.\,;
.\Meta\ ,;
.\FrameSource\ ,;
.\SysData\,;

.\Test\,;
.\Tools\ ;

#include MyFrame.h

RELEASE goApp
PUBLIC goApp AS aApplication

ON SHUTDOWN goApp.OnShutDown()

goApp = CREATEOBJECT('aApplication')
IF VARTYPE(goApp) = 'O'
    goApp.SetRead()
ENDIF

*-- End of Frame_Main
```

Main.prg

The program required to start an application is similar to the one for the frame. Some differences exist. The differences are listed here and are explained following the code.

- Path

- An extra include

- Declare oApp as aApp

- Set procedure to framework main

```
*Main - Application

SET DEFAULT TO JUSTPATH(SYS(16,0))
SET PATH TO ";
.\,;
.\appSource\,;
.\appData\ ,;
..\MyFrame\,;
..\MyFrame\FrameSource\,;
..\MyFrame\Images\,;
..\MyFrame\Tools\;
"
#include MyApp.h
#include MyFrame.h

SET PROCEDURE TO "Main_Frame.prg" ADDITIVE
```

```
RELEASE goApp
PUBLIC goApp

ON SHUTDOWN goApp.OnShutDown()

goApp = CREATEOBJECT('smpApplication')
IF VARTYPE(goApp) = 'O'
    goApp.SetRead()
ENDIF


DEFINE CLASS smpApplication AS aApplication OLEPUBLIC

    cAppName = "Hello World"

    FUNCTION OnLaunchApp()
        MESSAGEBOX("Hello World",0, APP_NAME + ' of ' + BOOK_NAME)
        *  Return .f. &&For testing. Returning False will close the app.
    ENDFUNC

ENDDEFINE
```

The SET PATH statement is similar to the one found in Main_Frame except that the framework folders SysData and SysSource are no longer included in the search path. Instead, the search path includes the application folders AppData and AppSource. Notice that by changing the search path, you can change the data used by the application. Changing the search path is one way to switch between pristine, test, and live data as mentioned earlier in the chapter.

A second difference is that the application's main program is creating an object defined in a separate program file, Main_Frame.prg. Before you can instantiate the application object, Main_Frame must be loaded into memory. This is the only file ever loaded outside of the aApplication or smpApplication classes.

```
SET PROCEDURE TO "Main_Frame.prg" ADDITIVE
```

Placing the ON SHUTDOWN call inside the application class works. However, a dependency exists between ON SHUTDOWN and CREATEOBJECT, namely that both rely on the presence of goApp. Don't set a trap for application developers who want to use a different variable name for goApp (for example, oApp).

```
ON SHUTDOWN goApp.OnShutDown()
```

A sample application (the obligatory "Hello World") has been included for this chapter. It illustrates how to use the OnLaunchApp() method of the application class to start an application. Notice that I used the application object properties cAppName and cFramework to build the MessageBox() caption.

```
FUNCTION OnLaunchApp()

    MESSAGEBOX(THIS.cAppName,0, THIS.cFramework)
    *  Return .f. &&For testing. Returning False will close the app.

ENDFUNC
```

Overwriting the default behavior of OnLaunchApp() is an example of how you can tailor the aApplication class to meet the needs of the application developer.

Summary

Much has gone into the setup of this framework. The benefit of your hard work is that the application developer has a well-defined, flexible approach with which to begin each application. Flexibility is easily obtained by subclassing aApplication and overwriting or extending the methods provided. If further modifications are required, I have provided two template methods that are clear and easy to comprehend.

> Updates and corrections to this chapter can be found on Hentzenwerke's Web site, **www.hentzenwerke.com**. Click "Catalog" and navigate to the page for this book.

Chapter 6
Creating a Class Library

A class library is a set of reusable classes, programs, and functions. It is the foundation—the lowest level on which your framework is built. Factors to consider when structuring your class library include creating a single point of entry into the framework, understanding the role inheritance plays in extending behavior, and giving the application developer the ability to tap into the power of your class library. This chapter illustrates how to properly structure your class library.

You start the process by creating a set of base classes. Visual FoxPro 8.0 provides 43 classes for you to build upon (Textbox, Label, Custom, Session, and so on). Each subclass of the FoxPro base classes is the most general and least specialized class in your class hierarchy. Consider the text box, which is a general tool for collecting and presenting data. It does not know which data format to use, whether the data entered into it is valid or when it is appropriate for users to view the data it contains. A text box is not a specialized class.

In this chapter, you will learn how to apply the concept of inheritance to your class structure. From your base classes you begin the process of specializing each class by further subclassing your base classes. You will learn where to add functionality; that is, methods (behavior) and properties (state) in your class structure to maximize the benefits of inheritance while minimizing some of the risks associated with a poorly designed inheritance structure.

This chapter illustrates these concepts with detailed examples. The final segment of this chapter concludes with a review of how your class design affects the application developer and a recommendation of the approach you should consider.

Base classes
Your base classes are subclasses of the FoxPro base classes. They act as a buffer between the framework and the classes provided by FoxPro.

For example, in previous versions of FoxPro, you accessed each page in a page frame using the Pages collection. Each option button in an option group could be accessed using the Buttons collection. In FoxPro 7.0, this approach was standardized with an Objects collection. In this case, FoxPro retained compatibility with prior versions and did not remove the Pages or Buttons collections. But what if they had removed them? Code that relied on the native Fox Pages or Buttons collections would break. On the other hand, if you subclassed them properly, and made an intermediary layer between your framework and the FoxPro classes, you would be able to fix this problem by changing the code in your base class rather than in every form that used a page frame or an option group.

Your base classes also serve as an entry point into your framework. If you prefer all your text boxes to have a yellow background and pink borders, changing your base Textbox class would carry that stunning combination throughout the application. **Figure 1** and **Figure 2** show the base classes in the Class Browser and document window, respectively.

Figure 1*. The visual base classes for MyFrame.*

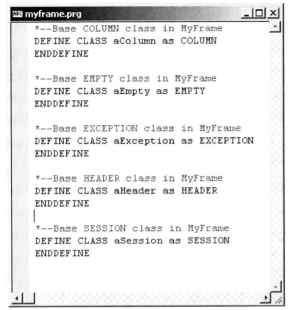

Figure 2. The nonvisual classes for MyFrame.

MyFrame.vcx is the file in which the visual classes are stored, while nonvisual classes are stored in MyFrame.prg. Each class at the base class level is an abstract class and is never used directly in the application. As dictated by the MyFrame standards, all abstract classes are prefixed with an "a."

Notice there is not a nonvisual Custom base class. Custom is a visual class and was defined with the visual classes. Do not create two versions of your base classes—one for programmatic definitions and one for visual definitions. Remember, the point is to have one place where you can access *all* custom classes.

You can still use aCustom, or any other visual class, in programmatically defined classes. The following code illustrates that you can base a nonvisual class on a visual class.

```
DEFINE  CLASS MyCustomNonVisualClass as aCustom
ENDDEFINE
```

A simple class library

Think of a class library as normalized code. Just as each non-key field in a database is unique to that database, each property or method should be unique to the class library. A general rule of thumb is that if you are changing behavior, and have to do it in more than one place, you have done something wrong. How you approach the organization of each class line differs depending on the classes under consideration. The results, however, are the same: classes related in such a way that only one implementation of each feature exists.

I mentioned that building a framework is an iterative process. The same is true of structuring your class library. This is your first iteration. Focus on inheritance and the relationship between classes. Do not rush to add every feature you want as part of your library in this pass. Instead, work deliberately and build up your class library in layers. The way you implement a specific feature in a framework may not be the same as if you were implementing the feature in isolation.

The requirements for the visual controls will state that each control must respect the state of the form: edit mode, read-only, styles, and so on; and any security settings. Because you haven't created any forms yet or implemented the security module, it's impossible to implement how controls integrate with forms or security at this point in your development.

During the beginning stages of development, your only concern is to define the major roles each class will play and to add functionality that is isolated to the specific class. The only relationship between classes you should be concerned with at this time is the inheritance relationship. Stated differently, you are defining the classes you need and their lines of inheritance, and implementing some basic functionality.

Understand the roles of your classes. The base classes contain common framework code. If you intend to specialize a class beyond the common code, create a subclass.

How classes integrate with other classes is not your concern … on this pass. And that's a key point. This is just one pass. Don't create a hierarchy 20 levels deep. Keep it shallow and broad at the start. In subsequent passes, you'll have the chance to extend and specialize.

Approach the "normalization process" starting with the most general and working toward the most specialized, and then again from specialized to general. Your base classes are general classes. For example, the Textbox class contains certain functionality that is common to all text boxes. Users see a text box and expect to be able to enter information into it. That is a common characteristic of text boxes, regardless of the type of data displayed. A specialized text box might be one that formats numerical data similar to a calculator, with numbers greater than 0 scrolling from the right. This feature is not suitable for all text boxes; it is a feature for a special text box.

Next, repeat the process in the reverse order. In other words, work back through your class structure from the specialized classes to the most general class. This time you are looking for common features that could be moved up in the class structure.

In practice, the approach you start with is a matter of preference and circumstance. The key point is to make a minimum of two passes. The best way to illustrate these concepts is through examples. I'll start with labels.

Labels
Labels display information throughout an application. Labels can also convey information to developers; these labels never appear in the completed application. For example, I often use a Label class rather than a Custom class because I can use the Caption property to display some meaningful information. For example, in Chapter 8, the Framework collection classes are based on the label. When I add a label to a form, I can use the caption to indicate why the collection is on the form.

In these situations, I want the caption to appear during development, and not in the final application. An invisible label (invisible to the user) with automatic word wrap is perfect for a purpose such as this.

First pass
We have identified that labels can be captions on a form or they can be a utility for developers. Consider each purpose. Can the caption be specialized further? Sure. I usually display a title on each form and occasionally a subtitle or two. And each form control usually has a prompt associated with it. Okay, I've identified three additional potential classes.

Repeat the process. Can a title be further specialized? Depending on your situation, sure. However, your job as a framework developer is to provide a class structure that can accommodate as many styles as are needed by the application developer—not to define the styles themselves. Be careful not to create classes "in case" you need them. Without a clear reason to provide specially formatted labels, stop the specialization process here, for the same reasons the SubTitle and Prompt classes are also not extended further.

Evaluate the use of labels as a developer's utility. Can the Label Utility class be further specialized? Sure, and I'll expand on that later. For now, let's just create the aUtilitylbl class.

Okay, we have identified the following classes of labels: Caption, Title, SubTitle, Prompt, and Utility. Ask yourself if each class is useful on its own or if it is provided as a starting point for others. Title, SubTitle, and Prompt are useful in their own right and are preceded by the framework prefix of "my."

The other classes are abstract classes meant to be further specialized (subclassed) before use. According to the MyFrame standard, they are prefixed with an "a." The resulting class hierarchy is shown in **Figure 3**.

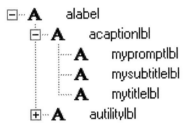

Figure 3. *The Label class hierarchy.*

Second pass

Reverse the process used in the first pass and evaluate each class, starting with the most specific classes and working back to the most general. When working from specific to general, look for commonalities between classes. If a property or event exists in two classes, move the definition of that class or property up to the parent.

Start with myTitleLbl. Is there any behavior you want for myTitleLbl? Yes, as a matter of preference, my titles have the following settings:

```
BackStyle = 0 && Transparent
FontSize = 14
FontBold = .T.
AutoSize = .T.
```

Move on to the next class, the SubTitle. Is there any behavior you want for all subtitles in the framework? Yes, and they are:

```
BackStyle = 0 &&Transparent
FontSize = 11
Fontbold = .T.
AutoSize = .T.
```

And for each Prompt:

```
BackStyle = 0 &&Transparent
FontSize = 11
Fontbold = .T.
AutoSize = .T.
```

Well, wait a minute. The only differentiation between these classes is the font size. Rather than setting each property (BackStyle, FontBold, and AutoSize) in each of the classes, set the value for these properties once in the class aCaptionLbl. In other words, do not set the BackStyle property to 0 in the class myTitleLbl; let it inherit the value of that property from its parent class. Setting a property once at the parent-class level allows the application developer to change properties in aCaptionLbl and have those changes reflected in all classes based on aCaptionLbl. Are there any other changes we want to make to aCaptionLbl? Not at this time.

Before moving up to aLabel, evaluate other classes on the same level as aCaptionLbl. In this example, only one class exists on this level: aUtilityLbl.

Are there any specialized characteristics we want for aUtilityLbl? Yes, the user should not see this control. So you have a choice here. You could simply set the Visible property to False (.F.), allowing the developer to see it only at design time, and requiring the developer to change the property to .T. if he or she wants to see the control on a form. Alternatively, you could use a bit of code to conditionally allow the developer to see the control.

```
IIF(VARTYPE(goApp)='O' AND Pemstatus(goApp,'ShowDevTools',5),
goApp.ShowDevTools(),.F.)
```

 The application object has a public property, IDevMode, that could be used as the condition for showing developer tools. However, running in development mode is not the same thing as wanting to see developer tools. A better approach is to add a new method, ShowDevTools(), to the aApplication class defined in Chapter 5. The default behavior of ShowDevTools() is to return IDevMode. By providing a separate method to retrieve this value, the application developer can overwrite this method as desired in the application subclass pApplication.

Are there any other characteristics that aUtilityLbl should have? Yes, AutoSize should be set to True (.T.) and BackStyle to 0 (Transparent). Now that all classes have been evaluated at this level in the class hierarchy, move up to the parent aLabel.

aUtilityLbl and aCaptionLbl have two properties, AutoSize and BackStyle, that are the same for each class. aUtiltiyLbl and aCaptionLbl represent all the classes directly subclassed from aLabel. Evaluate whether you want to change the parent class, aLabel, rather than set AutoSize and BackStyle directly in each of the subclasses. In this case you want to move the setting of these properties to aLabel.

The Label class is a good example of how you define the inheritance relationship between classes. Several properties (FontBold, AutoSize, BackColor) appeared to belong to one class, but because of inheritance were best implemented in another class.

Command buttons

Command buttons are controls provided to users so they can execute an action. In the labels example, my analysis went from general to specific and back again. In the command button example, I'll start with a list of specific items and work back toward a general parent common to all buttons. After reaching the general class, I'll reverse the process and work from the general to specific.

Here is a list of typical specific actions:

- Delete

- Edit

- New

- Undo

- Save

- Find

- FindFile

- GoBottom

- GoTop

- Next

- Previous

- Close

What are the requirements for the command buttons in MyFrame? You should expect that each button will invoke form methods in a uniform manner. Ideally, you should be able to specify which control should receive focus after the button's Click() event fires. Finally, each button should be able to display a picture, text, or both.

First pass

Keep in mind, this is the first pass, and you're not looking to define or implement code that interacts with other classes. With that in mind, ask yourself, "Are there any attributes (properties) shared by these buttons that could be 'moved up' the class hierarchy?" At this time the answer is "No."

Categorizing similar classes provides a single point of access to subsequent classes. You can categorize the buttons based on the functionality they'll provide. New, Undo, Delete, Edit, and Save (NUDES) are all data-manipulation functions. Similarly, GoTop, GoBottom, Next, and Previous are record-based navigation functions. The Close button does not have any commonalities of function with the other buttons. Leave it. Similarly, the Find and FindFile buttons do not have anything in common with the other classes. Leave them alone as well.

Although I may be getting a bit ahead of myself, each of these buttons, with the lone exception of MyGetFileCmd, calls methods on a form. However, that is not true of all command buttons. Adding an abstract class to handle the code associated with calling a form method gives you one place to concentrate your code for calling form methods. The name of this class is aFormCmd. The new structure is shown in **Figure 4**.

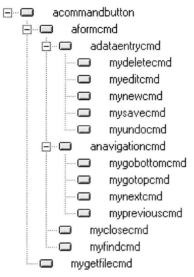

Figure 4. The completed Command Button hierarchy.

Second pass

Evaluate the class structure from general to specific. Beginning with aCommandButton, ask yourself, "Is there any behavior all command buttons should have?" In this case, the answer is yes. One of the requirements states that all command buttons should be able to display a picture, a caption, or both. Ideally, the user would have the ability to specify which "mode" is used on each form. Because you have not defined how the user can set personal preferences or create the classes that implement this behavior, the best you can do at this point is to define the method that implements this behavior, ConfigureDisplay(), and implement a simplified version of the code that will later comprise this method. Later, you'll come back to this class and enable users to customize their display settings.

For now, the nDisplayType property controls whether the command button displays the caption or picture, or both the caption and the picture. The default setting is to display the command button caption. To implement this, call the ConfigureDisplay() method from the Init() method.

The programmatic class definition of aCommandButton appears as follows:

```
DEFINE CLASS acommandbutton AS commandbutton

    *-- 1 = Text, 2 = Picture, 3 = Both
    nDisplayType = 1

    Caption = "Command"
    Name = "acommandbutton"
```

```
PROCEDURE Init
    IF DODEFAULT()
        THIS.ConfigureDisplay()
    ENDIF
ENDPROC

PROCEDURE configuredisplay
    DO CASE
        CASE THIS.nDisplayType = 1 &&Text
            THIS.PICTURE=""
        CASE THIS.nDisplayType = 2 &&Picure
            THIS.CAPTION = ""
        CASE THIS.nDisplayType = 3 && Both
            *--Do nothing
        OTHERWISE
            ASSERT .F. MESSAGE "Unhandled Case"
    ENDCASE
ENDPROC

ENDDEFINE
```

The only thing you're going to implement at this time is the ability to configure the button display. Continue applying the question "Is there any behavior all command buttons should have?" to each button as you work toward the top of the hierarchy.

The next class in the hierarchy is aFormCmd, in which you should implement behavior that is common to all form command buttons. In this case, that is a common way to call form methods and to set focus to a control after the click.

To accomplish this, I have added the following properties to the aFormCmd class:

```
DEFINE CLASS aformcmd AS acommandbutton

    cSetFocusTo = ""

    cMethod = ""
    Parm1 = .NULL.
    Parm2 = .NULL.
    Parm3 = .NULL.

    Name = "aformcmd"

ENDDEFINE
```

Let's take a look at these properties, and the behaviors they control, in order.

The cSetFocusTo property and the SetFocusTo() method manage which control receives focus after the button is clicked. The SetFocusTo() method is a custom method that grabs the value in the cSetFocusTo property and uses macro substitution to get a reference to the specified control. If the control has a SetFocus() method, a call is made to set focus to that control. Here's the code for SetFocusTo():

```
PROCEDURE setfocusto
    LOCAL lcControl, loControl
    IF ! EMPTY(THIS.cSetFocusTo)
        lcControl = THIS.cSetFocusTo
        loControl = &lcControl
        IF PEMSTATUS(loControl,'SETFOCUS',5)
```

```
                loControl.SETFOCUS()
            ENDIF
        ENDIF
    ENDPROC
```

The next properties are cMethod, Parm1, Parm2, and Parm3. The cMethod property allows you to standardize the way in which form methods are called. The Parm properties hold parameters that can be passed to a form method. Here's the Click() method that calls the form method.

```
PROCEDURE Click
    LOCAL lcMethod
    lcMethod=THIS.cMethod
    IF EMPTY(lcMethod)
        *--Continue as normal
    ELSE
        IF      TYPE('_screen.activeform')='O'       AND ;
                ! ISNULL(_SCREEN.ACTIVEFORM)         AND ;
                pemstatus(_SCREEN.ACTIVEFORM,THIS.cMethod,5)

            *--Call the method
            WITH THIS

          DO CASE
              CASE ISNULL(.Parm1) AND ISNULL(.Parm2) AND ISNULL(.Parm3)
                      _SCREEN.ACTIVEFORM.&lcMethod.()

              CASE ISNULL(.Parm2) AND ISNULL(.Parm3)
                      _SCREEN.ACTIVEFORM.&lcMethod.(.Parm1)
              CASE ISNULL (.Parm3)
                      _SCREEN.ACTIVEFORM.&lcMethod.(.Parm1,.Parm2)

              OTHERWISE
                      _SCREEN.ACTIVEFORM.&lcMethod.(.Parm1,.Parm2,.Parm3)

          ENDCASE

            ENDWITH
        ENDIF
    ENDIF

    this.SetFocusTo()

ENDPROC
```

This may seem like a lot of work just to call form methods in a uniform way. One benefit to this approach, however, is that you can also control when the button is enabled or disabled. The following code in the Refresh() method enables or disables the button depending on whether the ACTIVEFORM has the method defined in the cMethod property.

```
    PROCEDURE Refresh
        IF      TYPE('_screen.activeform')='O'       AND ;
                ! ISNULL(_SCREEN.ACTIVEFORM) AND ;
                PemStatus(_SCREEN.ACTIVEFORM,'cMethod',5)
```

```
        IF ! EMPTY(THIS.cMethod) AND ;
               PemStatus(_SCREEN.ACTIVEFORM,THIS.cMethod,5)
           DODEFAULT()
        ELSE
           THIS.ENABLED=.F.
        ENDIF

     ENDIF
ENDPROC
```

Note that _SCREEN.ACTIVEFORM is used rather than THISFORM. Using _SCREEN.ACTIVEFORM allows the code to work, without change, whether the button is located in a toolbar or placed directly on a form.

The remaining controls have no additional code associated with them. You can implement all the required behavior by setting a few properties. Rather than list the class definition for all the controls, I'll just present the Delete button class.

```
DEFINE CLASS mydeletecmd AS adataentrycmd

     Picture = "..\images\delete.bmp"
     Caption = "\<Delete"
     ToolTipText = "Delete"
     cmethod = "Delete"
     Name = "mydeletecmd"

ENDDEFINE
```

One final point to note is that the hot keys and captions for each command button have been set. Working with the entire group helps you ensure that each button receives a unique hot key.

 Developers often build their names from the common to the specific—for example, myCmdEdit, myCmdNew, and so on. If you are one of these developers, you may want to reconsider this convention. IntelliSense has made me much more aware of how many letters must be typed to reach a point of differentiation. For example, when typing "MyCmd_" the sixth character is the point of differentiation vs. "My_" where the third character is the point of differentiation.

Text boxes

Text boxes display and collect information. As with labels, text boxes can be used as a tool for conditionally displaying information to developers. For example, each table has one row designated as the primary key. As a developer, you'll want to see the value of the primary key and never show it to the end user. The evaluation of text boxes resulted in the hierarchy shown in **Figure 5**.

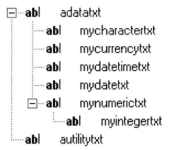

Figure 5. The Textbox class hierarchy.

The approach used to create the Textbox class hierarchy is similar to the command button example. The process started from a list of data types commonly displayed in an application, and a separate class was defined for each type. A common parent, aDatatxt, is defined to provide a single point of entry to each of the data-entry text boxes. No changes are implemented in aDatatxt at this time.

The Textbox class provided by FoxPro has one inconsistency. When the SelectOnEntry property is set to True (.T.), the contents of the text box are selected when the user enters the text box by pressing the Tab key. However, when the user "clicks" on the contents of the text box, the entire text is not selected. I altered the GotFocus() method of aTextbox to change the default behavior. The following code selects the text on entry if the developer has set SelectOnEntry to .T.

```
*--aTextBox.GotFocus()
LOCAL luDefault
luDefault = DODEFAULT()

IF THIS.SELECTONENTRY
    THIS.SETFOCUS()
ENDIF

RETURN luDefault
```

As with aUtilityLbl, aUtilitytxt has its Visible property set to:

```
IIF(VARTYPE(goApp) = 'O' and PemStatus(goApp, 'ShowDevTools',5), ;
    goApp. ShowDevTools(),.F.)
```

Containers

Containers hold objects. However, you generally do not want to see them. To prevent the container from being displayed, I have set the BackStyle property to 0 to make the container transparent and the BorderWidth properties to 0 to suppress the display of the border. The class definition is as follows:

```
DEFINE CLASS acontainer AS container

    BackStyle = 0
    BorderWidth = 0
    Name = "acontainer"

ENDDEFINE
```

Combo boxes

The combo box is an example of a control in FoxPro that does not always bind properly. I use the term "properly" to convey that it does not always bind in the way that I think it should. For example, when binding to an integer field, the control stores the ordinal position (index) of the selection, rather than the value in the bound column.

The solution pursued here is to disconnect the control from its data source and manually read and write information from the cursor at the appropriate times. This is done by saving the value of the ControlSource property to a custom property of the class.

Because I may not want this disconnecting behavior in all of my combo boxes, I have created a subclass of my base combo class (aComboBox) named myDataEntryCbo. MyDataEntryCbo must work with both integer and character data types. I've added two properties to the class to accommodate the "unbinding" process. The properties are _ControlSource and _ControlSourceType, which are used to hold the original control's source and its data type, respectively.

The time to disconnect from the data source is within the Init() method of the class. I have added a separate method, Unbind(), that is called from the Init() method. The Unbind() method checks to see if the control source is empty. If it is not, it saves the value of the ControlSource property to _ControlSource and saves its type to _ControlSourceType.

```
*--MyComboBox.Unbind()
THIS._ControlSource=THIS.CONTROLSOURCE
THIS.CONTROLSOURCE=""
```

After each interactive change, the value in the combo box is written to the underlying cursor as follows:

```
*--MyComboBox.InteractiveChange()
LOCAL lcSource
IF ! EMPTY(THIS._ControlSource)
    lcSource=THIS._ControlSource
    REPLACE &lcSource WITH Str2Exp(THIS.VALUE, this._ControlSourceType)
ENDIF
```

 The function Str2Exp() is a custom function originally published in 1001 Things You Wanted to Know About Visual FoxPro *(Akins, Kramer and Shummer, Hentzenwerke Publishing, 2000). It converts character data into another data type. The code for Str2Exp() is not reprinted here, but is included with the source code accompanying this book.*

To read the value from the control source, you must first check to see if the record pointer is pointing to a record or at the end of file marker. If it is at the end of file, disable the control and set its value to nothing. However, if the record pointer is not at the end of the file, read the value into the control. One note is that the value of a combo box is always stored in character format. So when you read the value in, you force it to data type character.

```
*-aComboBox.Refresh()
DODEFAULT()
*=========================================================
*--If we hava a control source

IF ! EMPTY(THIS._ControlSource)
    *--Store the stored control
    lcSource=THIS._ControlSource

    IF '.' $ lcSource
        lcAlias=JustTable(lcSource)

    *--Check for an end of file situation
        IF EOF(lcAlias)
            THIS.ENABLED=.F.
            THIS.VALUE=str2exp(0,this._ControlSourceType)
        ELSE
            *--Update this value with the value in the table
            lcValue = &lcSource
            THIS.VALUE = ALLTRIM(TRANSFORM(lcValue))
            THIS._ControlSourceType = VARTYPE(lcValue)

        ENDIF
    ENDIF
ENDIF
```

Disconnecting the combo box was necessary to support one of the stated requirements to support character and integer primary keys. If you are set on using character keys only, unbinding the combo control is not necessary.

However, unbinding controls has one other benefit. Sometimes during the data-entry process, a user may change the value of a control and, without exiting the control, change it back to its original value. Well, if you are using buffering, the value of the control may not have changed but the buffer is now "dirty." Unbinding, with the addition of a check to see if the value has changed prior to writing the record, can prevent the user from seeing a message that says information has changed when it really has not.

One benefit of calling the Unbind() method from the Init event is that the value in the control source remains intact at design time. This means that you can continue to use the native drag-and-drop capabilities of the Form Designer without requiring special efforts (of the application developer) to unbind the controls.

Treeview control (MyTreeView)

Microsoft includes the popular treeview control with most of its developer tools. Unlike native FoxPro controls, the treeview does not have built-in data binding capabilities. The changes incorporated into MyTreeView are to add data binding capabilities.

The treeview control is an OLE control that displays hierarchical data as "nodes" of a tree. Each node displays, at a minimum, two types of data: the text of the node and the relationship between nodes. Assuming you let them, users of the treeview control can change the relationship of the nodes in the tree as well as the text in any of the nodes.

To accommodate data binding, I've added three properties to the treeview control: cParentKeyField (to hold the field in which the parent key is stored), cDescriptionField (to hold the field in which the label's text is stored), and lInDragDrop (an internal flag indicating whether a user is in the process of dragging one node onto another).

In the AfterLabelEdit event, the following code transfers the label's text to the underlying cursor.

```
LPARAMETERS CANCEL, newstring

lcDescriptionField = THIS.cDescriptionField
IF ! EMPTY(lcDescriptionField)
     REPLACE &lcDescriptionField WITH newstring
ENDIF
```

Similarly, after one node is dropped onto another node, the following code changes the node's parent and writes the changes to the underlying table.

```
*--MyTreeView.oleDragDrop()
LPARAMETERS DATA, effect, BUTTON, SHIFT, x, Y
LOCAL loNode, lcParentKey

loNode=THIS.hittest(x/96*1440,Y/96*1440)
THIS.lInDragDrop = .T.
IF TYPE("loNode")='O' AND ! ISNULL(loNode)
   THIS.SELECTEDITEM.PARENT= loNode
   IF ! EMPTY(THIS.cParentkeyField)
        lcParentKey = THIS.cParentkeyField
        REPLACE &lcParentKey WITH loNode.KEY
   ENDIF
ENDIF
THIS.lInDragDrop = .F.
```

Highlighting a node as another node is dragged over it makes it clear which node will receive the "drop." The following code uses the HitTest() method of the tree to determine which node is being dragged over, and highlights it using the DropHighlight property.

```
*--MyTreeView.OleDragOver()
LPARAMETERS DATA, effect, BUTTON, SHIFT, x, Y, state
LOCAL oNode
oNode=THIS.hittest(x/96*1440,Y/96*1440)

IF TYPE("oNode")='O' AND ! ISNULL(oNode)
   THIS.drophighlight=oNode
ENDIF
RELEASE oNode
```

Shapes
Shapes are used to visually segregate areas on a form. One popular use of shapes is to set the BorderWidth property to 1 and the SpecialEffect property to 0 – 3D. With these settings the shape appears as shown in **Figure 6**. The resulting shape class structure is shown in **Figure 7**.

Figure 6. MyOutlineShp when viewed on screen.

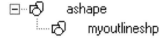

Figure 7. The Shape class hierarchy.

 The highlight effect works only when the border width is set to 1. By setting myOutlineshp's BorderWidth property to 1, the value is "anchored" and is therefore not affected by changes to its super-class aShape.

PageFrame, CommandGroup, and OptionGroup

These controls have had a major enhancement in FoxPro 8.0. You can now specify the controls that populate these containers. So for example, in a PageFrame control you can specify that your framework base class "aPage" is used to create each page in a page frame rather than the FoxPro base class "Page."

Each of these classes now has a MemberClass property, which is where you specify the class to use, and a MemberClassLibrary property, which is the file name of the class library. Although I'm using visual classes here, your class definitions could be in a PRG-based class as well.

Shown here is the PageFrame class definition. The CommandGroup and OptionGroup class definitions are not shown, but their MemberClass properties are set to aCommandButton and aOptionButton, respectively. Both classes are in MyFrame.vcx.

```
DEFINE CLASS apageframe AS pageframe

     ErasePage = .T.
     MemberClassLibrary = "myframe.vcx"
     MemberClass = "apage"
     PageCount = 2
     Name = "apageframe"
     Apage1.Name = "Apage1"
     Apage2.Name = "Apage2"

ENDDEFINE
```

One other point to mention is that the Page class is now visual. Both the OptionButton and CommandButton classes were visually editable in prior versions.

PageFrame

When a form is refreshed, only the active page in a page frame is refreshed. Pages that are not visible when a form is refreshed are not refreshed. This could result in a page that displays the incorrect information when a page is activated.

The page frame's Click event fires as a user clicks on a page to activate it. To ensure that the active page is always refreshed, I have added the following code to the aPageFrame.Click() event.

```
THIS.PAGES(THIS.ACTIVEPAGE).REFRESH()
```

Grids

Like the other container controls, you can now (in VFP 8.0) specify which grid columns are added to a grid by default by setting the MemberClass and MemberClassLibrary properties. The grid column class is still a nonvisual class. Similar to the Grid, PageFrame, OptionGroup, and CommandGroup classes, you can specify the header class added to each grid column by default. Oddly, the makers of FoxPro did not adhere to the nomenclature devised for the other container controls. Instead, the column class has a HeaderClass and a HeaderClassLibrary property.

The class definitions are shown here for the aGrid and aColumn classes. Notice that the grid points to the nonvisual class definition located in MyFrame.prg.

```
DEFINE CLASS agrid AS grid

    MemberClassLibrary = "myframe.prg"
    MemberClass = "aColumn"
    lrefreshonrowchange = .T.
    Name = "agrid"

ENDDEFINE
```

The aColumn class definition includes changes to the HeaderClass and HeaderClassLibrary properties.

```
*--Base COLUMN class in MyFrame
DEFINE CLASS aColumn AS COLUMN
    HeaderClass = "aHeader"
    HeaderClassLibrary = "MyFrame.Prg"
ENDDEFINE
```

You may choose to use the full path (for example, "C:\MyFrame.prg") to reference the HeaderClassLibrary or the MemberClassLibrary properties. However, this presents a problem if you move the project to another directory. I have omitted the file path from the properties to avoid this problem. The drawback to this approach is that FoxPro cannot find the class definition unless MyFrame.prg is in the current search path.

One feature I like in my grids is that the user can sort the columns by clicking on the column header. The following additions to the header class automatically allow you to sort a column if an index tag exists for the field specified in the column's ControlSource property.

The following code uses a custom function, IsTag(), to check whether an index tag exists. It accepts two parameters, the name of the index tag and an alias to search for the tag. The IsTag() function is not illustrated here, but can be found in .\FrameSource\GenProc.prg of the sample framework. The aHeader class definition is shown here.

```
*--Base HEADER class in MyFrame
DEFINE CLASS aHeader AS HEADER
    lAscending      = .F.

    FUNCTION INIT()
        IF istag(JUSTEXT( THIS.PARENT.CONTROLSOURCE), ;
                JUSTSTEM(THIS.PARENT.CONTROLSOURCE))

            THIS.BACKCOLOR= 8421376

        ENDIF
    ENDFUNC

    FUNCTION CLICK()
        WITH THIS.PARENT
            IF ! EMPTY(.CONTROLSOURCE) AND ;
                    IsTag(JUSTEXT(THIS.PARENT.CONTROLSOURCE), ;
                    JUSTSTEM(THIS.PARENT.CONTROLSOURCE))

                IF ! THIS.lAscending
                    SET ORDER TO JUSTEXT(.CONTROLSOURCE) IN;
                            JUSTSTEM(.CONTROLSOURCE) ASCE
                    THIS.lAscending = .T.
                ELSE
                    SET ORDER TO JUSTEXT(.CONTROLSOURCE) IN ;
                            JUSTSTEM(.CONTROLSOURCE) DESC
                    THIS.lAscending = .F.
                ENDIF

                THISFORM.REFRESH()

            ENDIF
        ENDWITH
    ENDFUNC
ENDDEFINE
```

Grid classes have two new properties, MemberClassLibrary and MemberClass, which you can use to set the default custom class for member objects. When these properties are set, new member objects inherit from the specified member class. Column objects have two new properties, HeaderClassLibrary and HeaderClass, which you can set to specify a custom header class.

You can now edit and subclass the Page class in the Class Designer. The CommandButton and OptionButton classes already exist in the Class Designer. However, the Class Designer does not include the column and header classes.

Forms

Chapter 12, "Forms," is devoted entirely to building this particular line of classes. At this point, however, it is worth noting three of the form classes included in the sample framework: aForm, aDialogFrm, and myDataFrm. The aForm class is the lowest-level form class in the framework. Changes that should affect every form in the framework are made to aForm. The aDialogFrm class is an abstract class that is used to create each of the modal forms in the framework, and myDataFrm is the foundation for all data-entry forms. See **Figure 8**.

Figure 8. *The Form class hierarchy.*

Using framework classes in an application

In this chapter I've defined some of the classes that will be used throughout the framework. The question now is, how are they used by the application developer? There are six ways the application developer could use the framework classes. Each approach has strengths and limitations. The approaches are:

- Direct
- Direct Subclass
- CodeBook Style
- Assembled In App
- Rebuild
- Meta

Direct

When using the Direct approach, the application developer does not create subclasses of the framework classes. Instead, the framework classes are used directly. Refer back to the Label class hierarchy. Using the Direct approach, the application developer would drop instances of MyPromptLbl, MySubTitleLbl and MyTitleLbl directly on his or her forms and change the caption as required.

The drawback to this approach is that there is no way to make an application-wide change without changing the framework classes. Changing framework classes directly makes it difficult to upgrade to new versions of the framework. Additionally, all projects sharing the framework would be affected.

On the positive side, if you are developing a framework for your own use, this is the simplest approach to implement, and upgrading to a new version is not a limiting factor.

Direct Subclass

In the Direct Subclass approach, each class you want to provide to the application developer is subclassed and given an application-specific prefix. As a reminder, all of the sample application classes are prefixed with "smp." So a subclass of MyPromptLbl is created and named SmpPrompt. A representation of the Direct Subclass model is shown in **Figure 9**.

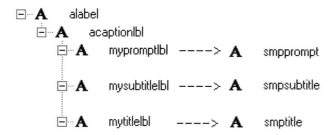

Figure 9. *The Direct Subclass approach.*

The benefit of the Direct Subclass approach is that the application developer has the ability to override or extend the classes you provide on a class-by-class basis. There are two drawbacks. First, the application developer must modify framework classes to realize the benefit of your class hierarchy. Second, it is very time consuming to set up new applications. In Chapter 17, "Developer Tools," you will create a tool that automates this process, dramatically reducing the time it takes to set up a new application.

The concept of losing the benefit of your class hierarchy warrants further explanation. Refer back to Figure 7. Labels are an example of a class in which most of its usefulness is tied to its class structure. One benefit of building a class hierarchy is that a change to aCaptionLbl would result in a change to MyPromptLbl, MySubTitleLbl, and MyTitleLbl. The Direct Subclass approach removes this benefit because the developer cannot make one change (at the application level) to affect all labels without changing aCaptionLbl, which is a framework class.

Losing some of the benefits of the class hierarchy is not always a limiting factor. Consider the class MyGetFilecmd. The main purpose of MyGetFilecmd is to find files on the user's computer. Its ability to open files is contained entirely within its own class definition. MyGetFilecmd relies on no other classes to accomplish its main purpose. The class hierarchy of which it is a part provides only framework services, and those services are not lost using the Direct Subclass method. In other words, providing a direct subclass of MyGetFilecmd does not materially alter the application developer's ability to use the class.

CodeBook Style

Yair Alan Griver introduced this method of distributing inheritance to the FoxPro community in his CodeBook framework. The CodeBook Style approach creates an intermediary layer between each layer in the class hierarchy. Alan prefixes the intermediary layer with an "i." See **Figure 10**.

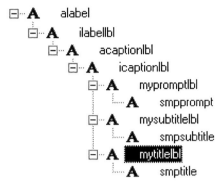

Figure 10. *The Label class hierarchy in CodeBook Style format.*

Using the CodeBook Style approach, you, the framework provider, enter into a contract with the application developer and agree that you will not write over the "i" layer when providing updates to the framework.

The CodeBook Style approach works well to retain the advantage of the class hierarchy. For example, the application developer can alter iCaptionlbl to change the font for all labels in an application—*and* changes to the "i" layer are retained through updates.

The only drawbacks are that it is complicated and adds (a lot) of extra classes to the framework.

> *As class structures grow deep, FoxPro shows almost no degradation in performance. If your class hierarchy is three levels deep, the CodeBook Style approach adds two intermediary levels. If you are a formula person, that's (nIntermediaryLayers = nHierarchyLevels – 1).*

Assembled In App

It is possible to assemble the class hierarchy in the application folder. Consider the Form class hierarchy shown in Figure 8. Using this approach, you would create a subclass of aform called smpForm and save it in the AppSource folder. Then you would build smpSplashfrm, smpModalfrm, and smpDatafrm to inherit directly from smpForm. SmpDialogfrm would also be created and would inherit from smpModalfrm. The benefit is that the application developer has control over the smpForm class and can make one change at the application level to change all forms in the application.

The drawback to this approach is that you, as the framework developer, lose the ability to make changes at the framework level. For example, with the Assembled In App approach there is no longer a MyDatafrm class. To add behavior to the data-entry form class you would have to change the application class smpDatafrm and risk overwriting changes made to that class by the application developer. Additionally, if several projects were based on the framework, each would have to be updated.

Rebuild

I have not yet talked about composite classes. A composite class is one that is made up of more than one class. Consider the class MyDatafrm. One possible subclass could be MyDatafrmWithButtons. An illustration of what that class might look like is shown in **Figure 11**.

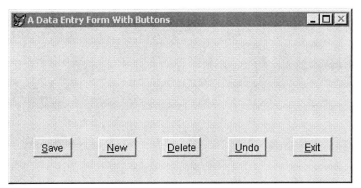

Figure 11. An illustration of a data-entry form with buttons.

The class MyDatafrmWithButtons inherits from MyDatafrm and contains buttons that inherit from MySavecmd, MyNewcmd, MyDeletecmd, MyUndocmd and MyExitcmd. If the application developer subclassed MyDatafrmWithButtons and named it smpDatafrmWithButtons, the buttons are still inheriting from MySavecmd, MyExitcmd, and so on. (For the remainder of this discussion I'll just focus on the Exit button.)

For example, assume the users of a particular application have trouble finding the Exit button. (Yes, it could happen!) The application developer decides to change the ForeColor property to red for all Exit buttons. His or her first inclination might be to subclass myExitcmd, naming it smpExitcmd, and then change the ForeColor property. However, changes to smpExitcmd will not affect the button displayed on smpDatafrmWithButtons because that class points to myExitcmd, not smpExitcmd.

An alternative to subclassing MyDatafrmWithButtons is to create a new class (hence the term "Rebuild"), either manually or programmatically, that inherits from MyDatafrmWithButtons and contains smpExitcmd rather than myExitcmd. The drawback to this approach is that it requires developer intervention (for manual approaches) or a sophisticated class-creation methodology. As a matter of practicality this is not a viable alternative and should not be considered as an option. However, I present it to help illustrate one of the complexities associated with composite classes and how this factor should influence your design decisions.

Meta Data

In the Meta Data approach, a class retrieves information—a property, a class name, or even the code to execute—from a central data store. For example, assume you had a table called AppSettings.dbf and that table had a field called DefaultFont. In the Init() method of the Label classes, this value could be retrieved from AppSettings and applied at run time. A side benefit is that other classes—the Textbox classes, for example—could read the same setting.

The drawback is that this approach could add considerable overhead as each form loads. Another drawback is that it affects how developers work with the classes. It is not intuitive for a developer to have to work with some properties in the design tools and others in the Meta Data tables.

Given these limitations, the Meta Data approach offers a simple, yet powerful way to add flexibility to your applications.

The recommended approach

For a personal framework, I recommend that you keep your class hierarchies shallow and use the Direct Subclass method to distribute the classes to the application developer. As such, that is the primary methodology presented in this book.

Summary

In this chapter, you have created your base classes, begun building your class library, and settled on a primary approach for subclassing your framework classes for each application. The remaining chapters build on the foundation detailed in this chapter.

> Updates and corrections to this chapter can be found on Hentzenwerke's Web site, **www.hentzenwerke.com**. Click "Catalog" and navigate to the page for this book.

Chapter 7
Environments and Sessions

Understanding the concepts of an application environment, data sessions, and data environments is critical to obtaining consistent results throughout your framework. Environments and sessions affect the behavior, and ultimately the design, of your classes. This chapter reviews environments, sessions, and the tools that manage these items in the MyFrame framework.

Data sessions and environments serve distinctly different purposes. Data sessions are a means for accessing data, while the environment controls the behavior of many commands and functions. These concepts are related, however, because each data session has its own environment.

Even if you feel comfortable with the concepts of environments and private data sessions, take the time to read this chapter. Some of the discussion in this chapter is used as the basis for design decisions in later chapters. Besides, you never know, the discussion about how sessions and environments are used in MyFrame may spark some new ideas for YourFrame.

Data sessions

Private data sessions are separate "work areas" that allow you to work with the same table in different ways. Imagine you had two copies of FoxPro open on your machine, and each is using the same table. You could navigate to different records in the table in one instance without moving the record pointer in the other instance. One instance could show deleted records while the other does not.

Private data sessions accomplish that same degree of separation when working with data in one instance of FoxPro. Think of a data session as a separate "space" with its own environment. Tables in one session are not affected by changes in record-pointer position or environment settings made in other sessions. (The concept of an environment and setting the environment are discussed in the next section.)

FoxPro sequentially assigns each data session a numeric ID as each data session is created. The default environment has a DataSessionID of 1. When you create a new data session it is assigned a DataSessionID of 2. The next will be 3, and so on. You can switch between data sessions by issuing the SET DATASESSION TO command.

Creating data sessions

FoxPro provides two ways to create private data sessions: forms and session objects.

Forms

Creating a private data session with a form is as simple as setting a single property. The DataSession property dictates whether a form creates and operates within its own private data session.

The Visual FoxPro Help file states that setting the DataSession property to 1 opens a form in the "default environment." I used the term "default environment" earlier to indicate that the ID of the environment in effect when you open FoxPro has a value of 1. The FoxPro Help is using the term "default environment" to mean that a form with a DataSession of 1 is opened in the same environment in which it was called.

This is an important distinction. When a form has a private data session and opens a second form that is configured to open in the "default environment," the second form will actually open in the same environment as the form that created it.

You can determine the data session a form is bound to by checking the form's DataSessionID property.

The default value for a form's DataSession property is 1.

Session objects

Each Session class has a DataSession and DataSessionID property that behave exactly as they do in the form. The benefit of the Session class is that it allows you to create a private data session without the overhead of a form. Unlike the form, the Session class uses a private data session by default, and therefore has a default DataSessionID of 2.

Object scope

Objects are "bound" to a data session. This means the objects can work only with tables in the data session in which they were created. **Figure 1** depicts a conceptual view of how forms and sessions are bound to separate data environments. You can determine which data session a form or session is bound to by checking its DataSessionID property.

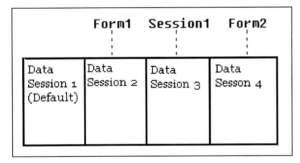

Figure 1. A conceptual view of private data sessions.

Environments

Many FoxPro commands and functions behave differently depending upon the configuration of the environment. For example, issuing the command SET ASSERTS ON and then executing the following line of code would cause FoxPro to suspend program execution and alert the developer that a problem exists.

```
ASSERT 1+1 = 5 MESSAGE "Umm...Houston, we have a problem"
```

However, if SET ASSERTS were OFF, the same line of code would not suspend program execution, and the developer might remain unaware that a problem occurred. In other words, because the environment settings had been changed, the behavior of your code would change even though the code itself did not.

A consistent development environment ensures that your code works as intended. The process of setting the environment is referred to as "configuring" the environment. The section titled "Save, set, and restore the environment" later in this chapter provides an example of how to construct a series of classes for managing the environment.

    The settings selected in the Tools | Options dialog are saved on your machine for your convenience as a developer. These settings have nothing to do with executables that you compile on that machine. When you compile your application, the executable is initialized to FoxPro's default environment configuration—not the environment configuration in effect when you compiled the application. You need to provide a way for developers to specify which environment settings are in effect when they distribute applications.

Data session environments

Each data session operates within a subset of the environment. It is possible to configure the environment of one data session without altering the environment of another. For example, SET EXCLUSIVE ON dictates that FoxPro will open tables exclusively by default, and SET EXCLUSIVE OFF dictates that tables are to be opened for shared use. One data session can be configured for shared use while another can be configured for exclusive use. For this reason, SET EXCLUSIVE is considered "scoped" to a data session. Other commands are not scoped to a data session. For example, SET ASSERTS affects all data sessions and can be considered scoped to the application.

Building on Figure 1, **Figure 2** shows a conceptual view of the environment.

    To see a list of SET commands that are scoped to a data session, see "SET DATASESSION command" in the Visual FoxPro Help file.

Application Environment (Default)	Set Asserts = ON		
	Form1	Session1	Form2
Data Session 1 (Default)	Data Session 2	Data Session 3	Data Sesson 4
Deleted On	Deleted Off	Deleted On	Deleted Off

Figure 2. A conceptual view of the environment.

Objects are bound to the session in which they were created. For example, Form1 is bound to data session 2. Objects created by Form1 also operate within data session 2.

Functions are bound to the environment in which they are called. If Form1 were to call a function, that function would be bound to data session 2.

The fact that objects are bound to the environment in which they were created and functions operate in the environment in which they were called is an important concept that you must fully appreciate before designing generic classes that are affected by data-bound SET commands.

Form1, Session1, and Form2 can communicate—that is, they can call methods and access properties of each other, but they cannot access each other's data directly. For example, assume Form1 opens a table named Customers. The Session1 and Form2 class cannot access the Customers table directly without issuing SET DATASESSION TO. However, Session1 and Form2 can call methods of Form1, which in turn can access the Customers table.

To obtain a complete listing of the values for your environment, follow these steps:

1. On the Tools menu, click Options.

2. Press Shift and then click OK to display the environment SET commands in the command window.

Save, set, and restore the environment

The process of saving, setting, and restoring environment variables is the same whether the command is scoped to the application or a data environment. The following code will save, set, and restore an environment setting.

```
* --Save the current deleted status and set it to ON
LOCAL lcOldDeleted
 lcOldDeleted = SET("Deleted")
SET DELETED ON
* <|  Do some stuff here   |>

*--Restore previous setting
SET DELTED &lcOldDeleted
```

This code works well if you are working within a single method or program. What about the application as a whole? One approach could be to make lcOldDeleted public. The problem with public variables is that they are public. A developer could purposefully or inadvertently change the variable during the span of the application.

A class-based approach

A better approach than the previous one is to use a class that retains the old environment settings as properties. A second property stores the value to which the setting is initialized. When the object is created, the current settings are saved and then set, or initialized. When the object is released, the environment is reset to its former state.

This approach is better for two reasons. First, the properties can be protected and thus would not be subject to changes during the life of the application. Second, the same technique can be used in more than one situation. In other words, you can provide the application developer with a consistent approach for managing all environments.

The approach for saving, setting, and restoring the environment in the MyFrame framework is shown in the following example. Note that only two settings are shown.

```
DEFINE CLASS MySampleEnvironment AS aCustom

   MakeDeleted = "ON"
   MakeExact       = "OFF"

   oldDeleted       = ""
   oldExact       = ""

   FUNCTION INIT()
      THIS.SaveEnv()
      THIS.SetEnv()
   ENDFUNC

   FUNCTION DESTROY()
      THIS.RestoreEnv()
   ENDFUNC

   FUNCTION SaveEnv()
           With this
              .oldDeleted     = SET("Deleted")
              .oldExact       = SET("Exact")
           ENDWITH
   ENDFUNC

   FUNCTION SetEnv()
           WITH THIS
               LOCAL lcMakeDeleted
               lcMakeDeleted = .MakeDeleted
               SET DELETED  &lcMakeDeleted

               LOCAL lcMakeExact
               lcMakeExact = .MakeExact
               SET EXACT   &lcMakeExact
           ENDWITH
   ENDFUNC

   FUNCTION RestoreEnv()
           WITH THIS
                LOCAL lcOldDeleted
                lcOldDeleted = .oldDeleted
                SET DELETED   &lcOldDeleted

                LOCAL lcOldExact
                lcOldExact = .oldExact
                SET EXACT   &lcOldExact
           ENDWITH
   ENDFUNC

ENDDEF
```

To use this class you only need to set the "Make<<SETTING>>" properties to the desired setting. For example, the following class when instantiated would result in SET DELETED ON and EXACT OFF.

```
DEFINE CLASS smpEnvironment as MySampleEnvironment
      MakeDeleted = "ON"
      MakeExact = "OFF"
ENDDEF
```

Environment classes

The environment class structure included as part of the MyFrame framework is shown in **Table 1**. **Figure 3** shows how this class is constructed.

Table 1. Environment classes in MyFrame.

Class	Description
aEnv	The abstract base class for all environments.
MyDataEnv	Implements the SET commands bound to a data environment.
MyCommonEnv	Implements all but a few of the SET commands.
MyAppEnv	Implements settings that may change during the span of the application. For example: SET CLASSLIB, SET PROCEDURE, SET PATH, and so on.
MyDevEnv	A class used to set special developer settings. For example, SET ASSERTS may be off by default, but when running in development mode, asserts should be on.
MySaveEnv	Overwrites the SetEnv() function. In effect, this class will only save the current settings and restore them when released from memory.

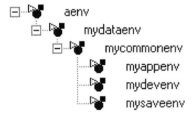

Figure 3. The Environment class hierarchy (MyEnvironments.prg).

aEnv

aEnv is the parent of all environment classes. This class implements the interface. Implementing the interface for the class means to define the methods and properties that are to be used in subclasses.

The Init() and Destroy() methods control the save, set, and restore operations. The class definition is as follows:

```
DEFINE CLASS aEnv AS CUSTOM

   FUNCTION INIT()
      THIS.SaveEnv()
      THIS.SetEnv()
   ENDFUNC

   FUNCTION DESTROY()
      THIS.RestoreEnv()
   ENDFUNC

   FUNCTION SetEnv()

   ENDFUNC

   FUNCTION RestoreEnv()

   ENDFUNC

   FUNCTION SaveEnv()

   ENDFUNC

ENDDEF
```

Data environment class

Application developers probably won't want to use the default configuration for each data session. You must provide them with a way to configure each new environment.

In previous versions of FoxPro, a data session created with a form had an identical configuration to a session created by a session object. In version 8.0, this is no longer true. SET TALK and SET SAFETY are initialized to "ON" when a form creates the data session, and are "OFF" when the data session is created by the Session class.

The approach used in MyFrame is to create a subclass of aEnv named MyDataEnv that saves, sets, and restores settings scoped to a data environment. Following is the "Make" property list for the MyDataEnv class. If the developer wanted to change the default value for SET("Decimals") from 2 to 4, he or she could do so by changing the MakeDecimals property value to 4.

```
MakeAnsi        = "OFF"
MakeAutosave    = "OFF"
MakeBlocksize   = 64
MakeCarry       = "OFF"
MakeCentury     = "OFF"
MakeCollate     = "MACHINE"
MakeConfirm     = "OFF"
MakeCurrency    = "LEFT"
MakeDate        = "AMERICAN"
MakeDecimals    = 2
MakeDeleted     = "ON"
MakeExact       = "ON"
MakeExclusive   = "OFF"
MakeFields      = "OFF"
```

```
MakeFixed          = "OFF"
MakeHours          = 12
MakeLock           = "OFF"
MakeMark           = ""
MakeMemowidth      = 50
MakeMultilocks     = "ON"
MakeNear           = "OFF"
MakePoint          = "."
MakeReprocess      = 0
MakeSafety         = "OFF"
MakeSeconds        = "ON"
MakeSysformats     = "OFF"
MakeTalk           = "OFF"
MakeUnique         = "OFF"
```

 The data environment should be configured before opening any tables.

Common environment classes

Your framework should include a way to initialize application environment settings. Settings scoped to the application are generally initialized once at the start of the application.

MyCommonEnv is used to save, set, and restore most of the settings not scoped to a data session. MyCommonEnv works similarly to MyDataEnv in that a series of Make<<Setting>> properties are used to initialize the environment. One Make<<Setting>> property exists for each SET command. The "Make" settings for MyCommonEnv are shown here:

```
MakeAlternate      = "OFF"
MakeAsserts        = "OFF"
MakeBell           = "ON"
MakeBrowseime      = "OFF"
MakeClock          = "OFF"
MakeCompatible     = "OFF"
MakeConsole        = "ON"
MakeCoverage       = ""
MakeCpcompile      = 1252
MakeCpdialog       = "OFF"
MakeCursor         = "ON"
MakeDebug          = "ON"
MakeDebugout       = ""
MakeDevelopment    = "ON"
MakeEcho           = "OFF"
MakeEscape         = "ON"
MakeEventtracki    = "OFF"
MakeFdow           = 1
MakeFilter         = ""
MakeFullpath       = "ON"
MakeFweek          = 1
MakeHeadings       = "ON"
MakeHelp           = "ON"
MakeHelpfilter     = ""
MakeLogerrors      = "ON"
MakeMackey         = ""
MakeMargin         = 0
MakeMessage        = 57
MakeNotify         = "ON"
```

```
MakeNull          = "OFF"
MakeOdometer      = 100
MakeOleobject     = "ON"
MakeOptimize      = "ON"
MakePalette       = "OFF"
MakePrinter       = "OFF"
MakeReadborder    = "OFF"
MakeRefresh       =  0
MakeResource      = "ON"
MakeSpace         = "ON"
MakeStatus        = "OFF"
MakeStrictdate    = 1
MakeSysmenu       = "AUTOMATIC"
MakeTextmerge     = "OFF"
MakeTopic         = ""
MakeTrbetween     = "OFF"
MakeTypeahead     = 20
MakeUdfparms      = "VALUE"
```

Application environment

Not all settings work in the same way. For example, SET CLASSLIB TO, SET PROCEDURE TO, and a few others are really comma-delimited lists that can be added to throughout the life of the application. Generally, when the list is added to, developers expect the list to remain in effect for the remainder of the application. Rather than include these items as part of the common environment class, the implementation of these items has been deferred to the MyAppEnv class.

The MyAppEnv class is similar to MyDataEnv. The relevant "Make" properties are:

```
oldClasslib  ="" && SET("Classlib")
oldDefault   ="" && FULLPATH(SET("Default"))
oldEventlist ="" && SET("Eventlist")
oldLibrary   ="" && SET("Library")
oldPath      ="" && SET("Path")
oldProcedure ="" && SET("Procedure")
```

Development environment

At times you may want to configure the development environment differently from the completed application environment. For example, you may prefer SET ASSERTS to be ON and SET DELETED to be OFF. MyDevEnv facilitates quickly switching between a design-time configuration and a run-time configuration.

 Of the 100 or so settings, these are some of the ones that application developers will probably use most often.

```
*--Data Environment
MakeCentury    = "" && "OFF"
MakeDeleted    = "" && "ON"
MakeExact      = "" && "OFF"
MakeExclusive  = "" && "OFF"
MakeMultilocks = "" && "OFF"
MakeReprocess  = "" && ""
MakRefresh     = 0 &&nSeconds
MakeSafety     = "" && "OFF"
MakeTalk       = "" && "OFF"
```

```
*--Common
MakeAsserts    = "ON"
MakeDebug      = "" && "ON"
MakeDebugout   = "" && ""
MakeNotify     = "" && "ON"
MakeOptimize   = "" && "ON"
MakeTextmerge  = "OFF"
```

Saving and restoring the environment

At various times it is advantageous to simply save and restore the environment without actually changing any settings. For example, a call to a third-party module or component could change the calling environment. By saving and restoring the environment, the application developer can insulate his or her application from changes that the foreign object might make. Two sample programs, ChangeEnv.app and ChangeEnv.exe, are included in the source code for this chapter to illustrate this point. The following sample code illustrates how to use the environment objects to insulate your applications from foreign code.

```
*--Save environment settings
loEnvironmentSettings = CREATEOBJECT("MyAppEnv")

* <<Launch some foreign app>>

*--Releasing the environment object restores the original settings
RELEASE loEnvironmentSettings
```

Another situation where developers might like a class that saves the environment is when a number of settings must be changed in code. The developers could instantiate a new "Environment Saver" and not have to write the save-and-restore code for each setting. Consider the original illustration for changing an environment setting against this sample:

```
Function SomeFunc()
     Local loTemp
  loTemp = CreateObject("MySaveEnv")
  SET DELTED on
  SET TALK off
  SET ASSERTS on
  *<< Do some stuff here>>

  *--When loTemp goes out of scope, all settings are restored

EndFunc
```

In the following code, the class definition of MySaveEnv overrides the SetEnv() method. The NODEFAULT command prevents the SetEnv() method from executing.

```
DEFINE CLASS MySaveEnv AS MyCommonEnv

   FUNCTION SetEnv()
      NODEFAULT
   ENDFUNC

ENDDEFINE
```

Performance issues

There are approximately 100 different SET commands, and I have chosen to implement almost all of them. The issue with this number of commands is the time it takes to save and restore them. To enhance your performance, you may want to move the code for rarely used settings from MyCommonEnv to MyAppEnv.

An example of a setting you may not want to manage regularly is SET HEADINGS, which is used to format output when the TYPE command is used.

The benefit to moving settings from MyCommonEnv to MyAppEnv is that the settings are not included as part of MySaveEnv. MySaveEnv has the potential to be used frequently throughout an application.

Implementing the environment classes

The purposes of the environment classes are to conveniently save, set, and restore the environment. While you are able to invoke these classes at any time, there are occasions where saving, setting, and restoring the environment is particularly useful—for example, at the startup and shutdown of an application, or each time a private data session is created.

In this section, I'll illustrate how the environment classes are incorporated into the startup and shutdown processes and as data sessions are created using the Session and Form classes.

Changes to Main_Frame.prg

To save and restore the application environment, you must change the main program slightly. As we left the main program in Chapter 5, the first three lines altered the environment by changing the default path and search path, and setting the procedure to Main_Frame.prg. So that these settings can properly be restored when the application closes, I've added three new lines to capture these settings before changing them. Here's the new code:

```
gcOldSysDefault = FULLPATH(SET("Default"))
gcOldSysPath = SET("Path")
gcOldSysProc = SET("Procedure")
```

Changes to aApplication

To load the environment classes, you'll need to know the class names to be created and the file in which the classes are located. Three properties store that information: cEnvironmentPRG, cAppEnvClass, and cDevEnvClass. Two additional properties are added to store a reference to the environment objects. Notice the properties oAppEnv and oDevEnv are declared as PROTECTED. This ensures that environment settings are not inadvertently changed during the span of the application.

The following code is added to the properties section of aApplication.

```
PROTECTED cEnvironmentPRG, cAppEnvClass, cDevEnvClass
PROTECTED oAppEnv, oDevEnv

cEnvironmentPRG = "MyEnvironments.prg"
cAppEnvClass    = "MyAppEnv"
cDevEnvClass    = "MyDevEnv"
```

The code for setting the environment instantiates the class specified in cAppEnvClass, saves the current environment settings, and configures the environment. The values of the three variables initialized at the beginning of the main program are then transferred to the appropriate environment properties. Here's the code:

```
PROTECTED FUNCTION OnSetEnvironment()

    SET PROCEDURE TO (this.cEnvironmentPRG) addi
    THIS.oAppEnv = CreateObject(this.cAppEnvClass)

    WITH THIS.oAppEnv
        .OldDefault     = gcOldSysDefault
        .OldPath        = gcOldSysPath
        .oldProcedure   = gcOldSysProc
    ENDWITH

    *--Clear the environment
        SET PROCEDURE TO
        SET CLASSLIB TO
    SET LIBRARY TO
    CLEAR PROGRAM

ENDFUNC
```

The development environment class is created in OnSetDevEnvironment(), assuming the application is in development mode. OnSetDevEnvironment() runs after OnSetEnvironment(), leaving the development environment settings in effect rather than the application class settings.

Releasing the environment objects triggers them to restore the environment to the state in effect when they were created. The essential point is that the objects must be released in the reverse order in which they were created. This is handled in the RestoreEnvironment() method called as part of the application shutdown.

```
PROTECTED FUNCTION RestoreEnvironment()
    *--Release in reverse order than created
    this.oDevEnv = .null.
    this.oAppEnv = .null.
EndFunc
```

Adding the environment objects to aApplication never sets the default data environment, data session 1. aApplication is based on the Session class and has a private data session. When aApplication is instantiated, it is assigned a DataSessionID of 2. When the environment objects are created, they are actually configuring data session 2, not the default data session (1).

As a developer using the framework, I would find this desirable. Preferences set using Tools | Options are applied to the default data session (1). The framework does not override these settings. If you feel differently, you can change the DataSession property of aApplication to 1 rather than the default value of 2.

Changes to aSession
Each new data session is configured in a similar manner to aApplication. Two properties are added to the class. One property holds the name of the class to load, while the other holds a reference to the instantiated object. The relevant changes to aSession are shown here.

```
cDataEnvClass = "MyDataEnv"
oDataEnvClass = .NULL.

FUNCTION INIT()
   THIS.MakeDataEnv()
ENDFUNC

PROTECTED FUNCTION MakeDataEnv()
   THIS.oDataEnvClass = CREATEOBJECT( THIS.cDataEnvClass )
ENDFUNC
```

Changes to MyDatafrm
Data sessions created by forms are configured in a manner similar to aSession. The one difference is that MyDatafrm.MakeDataEnv() is called from the form's Load() method rather than from the Init() method. This difference is required to configure the data environment prior to opening tables.

Creating a Session class
Framework services often require private data sessions for working with data. A framework class, MySession, creates and configures a separate environment when instantiated, mimicking the ability of the Form and Session classes to create private data sessions.

MySession is a subclass of aUtilityCnt, the base container class for the framework. I've chosen to use the container class so I can use the Visual Designer to drag and drop controls onto the container.

To create a session, MySession calls on the services of the aSession and MyDataEnv classes created earlier in the chapter.

MySession has one factory method, MakeSession, which creates the Session class. If you prefer, you can specify a different session or environment class by changing the value of the cSessionClass or cEnvironmentClass properties to the name of the class or classes you want to use.

Who wins?

The session object can be used in a form or on its own. If the parent object is a form, the responsibility of creating the data session is deferred to the form. However, the data environment still needs to be configured. If the class is instantiated outside of a form, a private data session is both created *and* configured.

Notice the check to see if the object has the FoxPro _Screen as its parent object. You will see some examples at the end of the chapter where it may be beneficial to instantiate a class by using _SCREEN.ADDOBJECT() rather than using CREATEOBJECT. Here's the code:

```
*-- MySession.MakeSession()
IF TYPE('THIS.PARENT')='O' AND ! ISNULL(THIS.PARENT)
   IF UPPER(THIS.PARENT.BASECLASS) = "FORM"
      *--Let the form control the session, create the environment only
      THIS.oSession=CREATEOBJECT(THIS.cenvironmentclass)
   ELSE
      *--Assume this object is part of another business class, let
      *)       that class control all aspects of environment
   ENDIF
ELSE
   THIS.oSession=CREATEOBJECT(THIS.cSessionClass, THIS.cenvironmentclass)
   SET DATASESSION TO THIS.oSession.DATASESSIONID
ENDIF
```

Summary

The concepts of private data sessions and environments are fundamental concepts for designing any Visual FoxPro application. In this chapter, I've reviewed the major issues relating to private data sessions and environments, created framework classes to manage them, and illustrated how they were incorporated into the MyFrame framework.

> Updates and corrections to this chapter can be found on Hentzenwerke's Web site, **www.hentzenwerke.com**. Click "Catalog" and navigate to the page for this book.

Chapter 8
Collections

Collections are common components in most frameworks and class libraries. Although collections are not required for many programming tasks, they are invaluable to a framework developer. In this chapter, you will learn about collections in detail and how to build a Collection class.

New to Visual FoxPro 8.0 is the Collection class. While it is a welcome addition, I find that it is not as powerful as the custom, array-based collection I have been using for years. The material covered in this chapter will give you a better understanding of collections in general and will leave you in a better position to understand the new Collection class.

The first part of the chapter is a primer for collections, providing definitions and some examples. The rest of the chapter walks you through the details of how the collection classes in MyFrame were built.

What is a collection?

A collection is a group of similar yet unrelated items. Consider the _VFP.Projects collection, which is a list of open projects. Actually, the _VFP.Projects collection is a collection of references to projects. Each element in the Projects collection is similar in that it is a reference to a project. The term "unrelated" means that elements in the collection do not reference other elements in the collection.

Collections are often used to work with objects; however, they can be used to manage other types of data, such as strings, integers, and so on. A numeric collection might contain a series of pages to print from a lengthy report or a list of primary keys to be deleted. A collection of strings might include a list of reports to print, a set of instructions to follow, or a history of URLs visited.

Basic operations that you can perform on collections include adding elements, removing elements, and returning a count of the number of elements in the collection.

Accessing elements in a collection

You can access elements of a collection individually or as a group. The _Screen.Forms collection and the _Screen.FormCount property are used in the next few examples to illustrate how elements in a collection can be accessed.

Individually—by position

You can access elements in a collection by their positions in the collection. Assuming the Forms collection contains references to five forms, the following code would display the name of the second form:

```
*--Referencing a form by position
? _SCREEN.FORMS(2).NAME
```

For...Next

To access each element in the Forms collection by using a FOR...NEXT loop:

```
*--For...Next example
FOR lnI = 1 TO _SCREEN.FORMCOUNT
    ? _SCREEN.FORMS(lnI).NAME
ENDFOR
```

Do While

To access each element in the Forms collection by using a DO WHILE loop:

```
*--Do While example
lnI = 1
DO WHILE lnI <= _SCREEN.FORMCOUNT
    ? _SCREEN.FORMS(lnI).NAME
    lnI = lnI + 1
ENDDO
```

For Each

To access each element in the Forms collection by using a FOR EACH loop:

```
*--For Each example
FOR EACH loForm IN _SCREEN.FORMS
    ? loForm.NAME
ENDFOR
```

Types of collections

Now that you are familiar with collections, I'll redefine the definition of "collection" to better illustrate the difference between types of collections. The revised definition of a collection is:

> "An unordered group of similar yet unrelated elements where an element may occur more than once."

The difference in this definition is that it adds the concepts of order and duplicates. This implies that there is a special type of collection that is ordered, which is true. An ordered collection is called a *list*. An unordered collection containing no duplicates is referred to as a *set*.

Stacks and queues

A *stack*, as defined by the National Institute of Standards and Technology, is "a collection of items in which only the most recently added item may be accessed and once it is accessed, it is removed from the stack." The primary difference between a stack and a collection is that the elements of a stack are (generally) not accessible from outside the stack. For example, you typically would not access individual elements or loop through the elements in a stack from outside the stack.

It is common to refer to the ADD operation of a stack as PUSH. Items are PUSHed onto the stack. When items are removed from the stack it is common to say that items are POPped from the stack. A POP is actually two operations in one. The element that is POPped is removed from the stack and returned to the calling program.

An example of a stack in FoxPro is the menu stack. PUSH MENU places menu definitions in the menu stack, while POP MENU retrieves them from the stack.

Another way to think of a stack is based on the accounting concept of Last In First Out, or LIFO. The last item PUSHed onto the stack is the first one POPped off the stack.

Queues are identical to stacks in every way but one. The first item PUSHed onto the stack is the first one POPped off the stack. **Figure 1** illustrates the concepts of a stack and a queue.

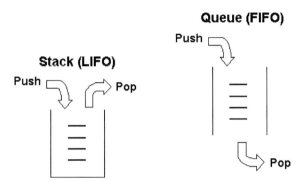

Figure 1. The conceptual view of a stack and a queue.

Using collections

The following example illustrates the difference between the types of collections. The method names used in these examples are based on the classes in MyFrame. However, the names of the methods are similar to most collection classes you might encounter elsewhere.

Assume the following collection of states: {NY, NJ, MA, ME, MA, NY, MA}. When added to the collection classes, GetCount() returns 7. The one exception is the Set class, which returns a value of 4 (duplicates are removed).

To process (and remove) each element by using the stack interface:

```
DO WHILE ! IsDone()
       ? oStack.Pop()
ENDDO
```

A similar traversal could be done using the collection interface. Unlike the stack interface, this traversal could be repeated because the elements are not removed from the collection:

```
oCollection.GoFirst()
DO WHILE ! IsDone()
      ?oCollection.GetCurrentItem()
      oCollection.GoNext()
ENDDO
```

The resulting output from this operation would be different for each class (regardless of which method was used to traverse the collection). A summary of the results would be:

```
List:      {NJ, NY, NY, MA, MA, MA, ME}  && Alphabetic
Queue:     {NY, NJ, MA, ME, MA, NY, MA}  && No change
Set        {NY, NJ, MA, ME}              && Duplicates removed
Stack      {MA, NY, MA, ME, MA, NJ, NY}  && Reverse order
```

The samples for this chapter demonstrate these results.

Design considerations

When constructing your own collection classes, you will most likely use an array to store the elements of the collection. If you decide to use one-dimensional arrays, the examples presented earlier in the chapter will work as intended. If, however, you choose to use two-dimensional arrays, you should consider the following:

A two-dimensional array requires that you specify the column and row of the element you want to access. Refer back to the first example. To reference an element in a collection by position, the line of code presented:

```
? _SCREEN.FORMS(2).NAME
```

becomes

```
? _SCREEN.FORMS(2,1).NAME
```

A second consideration is that the FOR EACH loop processes each element of an array. You cannot use a FOR EACH loop to access only the items in one column of a two-dimensional array.

Collections in MyFrame

Collections are generally based on the concept of a one-dimensional array. The collections in MyFrame are based on a two-dimensional array. The additional column enables you to apply the concept of a collection to a number of different applications.

For example, a set is defined as a collection without duplicates. Refer back to the example where a list of states was added to MySet. GetCount() correctly returned four states in the set. If I knew that seven states were added, and only four made it into the set, I might be curious to know which states were duplicated and the number of times each state was duplicated. In a later section of this chapter, "Implementing MySet," you will see how this can be accomplished.

Another design choice is that all functionality required for the collection classes is implemented in MyCollection (see **Figure 2**). For example, a list is an ordered collection. To place the elements of an array in order, the ASort() function is used. Rather than implementing that functionality in MyList only, the Sort() method is implemented in MyCollection. The only class that uses it directly is MyList, but it is available for all classes.

The Collection classes
Figure 2 illustrates the Collection hierarchy described earlier.

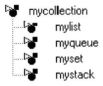

Figure 2. *The Collection class hierarchy.*

Implementing MyCollection
Figure 3 illustrates the public methods common to all collections in MyFrame.

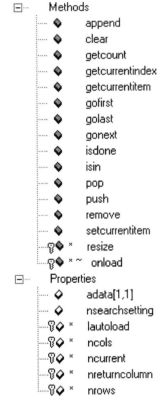

Figure 3. *The PEMS of aCollection.*

Resize()

MyCollection stores information in a two-dimensional array, aData[]. Two properties, nCols and nRows, dictate the size of the array. Therefore, aData[] is nCols wide and has nRows. The initial value of nRows is 0.

The Resize() method re-DIMENSIONs the array as follows:

```
*--MyCollection.Resize()
WITH THIS
   DIMENSION .ADATA(IIF(.nRows=0,1,.nRows),.nCols)
   IF .nRows=0
      .ADATA=.F.
   ENDIF
ENDWITH
```

Notice that when the nRows property is 0 the array is given a value of False (.F.). This is required because an array cannot be dimensioned to 0 rows. If the count goes above 0 and then back down to 0, you must manually remove all elements from the array. This step is especially important when holding objects in the collection. Assigning a value of .F. to the array removes any object references that would otherwise remain in the array.

Append()

To add an element to the collection, Append() accepts one parameter. The size of the array is increased by increasing the row counter nRows by 1 and calling the Resize() method. The element is then assigned to the array and set as the current row.

Here is the code:

```
*--MyCollection.Append()
LPARAMETERS tuItem
WITH THIS
   .nRows=.nRows+1
   .RESIZE()
   .ADATA(.nRows,THIS.nDataColumn)=tuItem
   .nCurrent = .nRows
   RETURN .nRows
ENDWITH
```

Notice that the element is assigned to nDataColumn, which has a default value of 1.

Remove()

Removing items from a collection is little more than a wrapper around the ADEL() function. Remove() optionally accepts the row to delete as a parameter. If a row is not specified, the current row is removed. Once the row has been removed, the nRows property is decremented and aData[] is redimensioned using the Resize() method.

Here's the code for aCollection.Remove().

```
*--MyCollection.Remove()
LPARAMETERS tnRow
LOCAL llSuccess, lnRow
*--Remove the specified or current element
lnRow = IIF(EMPTY(tnRow),THIS.ncurrent,tnRow)
```

```
WITH THIS
    IF lnRow<=.nRows AND lnRow>0 AND .nRows>0
        ADEL(.ADATA,lnRow)
        .nRows=.nRows-1

        .RESIZE()

        *--Make sure we are not past the end of the collection
        IF .ncurrent>.nRows
            .ncurrent=.nRows
        ENDIF
        llSuccess=.T.
    ENDIF
ENDWITH

RETURN llSuccess
```

Contains ()

Contains() returns a numeric value indicating the row number in which the element is located. Contains() accepts three parameters: the value to search for, the column to search in, and a search value for use in the ASCAN function.

ASCAN has been enhanced in FoxPro 7.0 to accept a fourth and fifth parameter indicating which column of the array is searched and which criteria are applied for determining a match. A default value of 15 is stored in the nSearchSetting property. Passing 15 to ASCAN indicates that the search should conduct a case-insensitive search, look for an exact match, and return the row number.

One aspect of ASCAN is that it cannot search for objects. A different comparison is performed when the collection contains object references.

The code for Contains() is shown here:

```
*--MyCollection.IsIn()
LPARAMETERS tuValue, tnCol, tnSearchVal
LOCAL lnCol, lnSearchVal, llFound

lnCol = IIF(EMPTY(tnCol),THIS.nDataColumn,tnCol)
IF THIS.nRows=0
    RETURN 0
ENDIF


WITH THIS
    IF VARTYPE(tuValue) = 'O'
        LOCAL lnI

        FOR lnI= 1 TO ALEN(.ADATA,1)
            IF .ADATA(lnI,lnCol)==tuValue
                llFound=.T.
                EXIT
            ENDIF
        ENDFOR
```

```
        IF llFound
            RETURN lnI
        ELSE
            RETURN 0
        ENDIF

    ELSE

        lnSearchVal = IIF(EMPTY(tnSearchVal),.nSearchSetting,tnSearchVal)
        RETURN ASCAN(.ADATA,tuValue,-1,-1, lnCol ,lnSearchVal )

    ENDIF
ENDWITH
```

The important points about this code are that the column to search and the search setting are optional. The default is to search in the first row, but you can specify a different row. The search is always limited to one row. By default, the search is done using the new ASCAN value of 15, meaning that the search is case-insensitive and SET EXACT is on.

GetCurrrentItem()

GetCurrentItem() returns the value specified in the nReturnColumn of the nCurrent row.

```
*--MyCollection.GetCurrentItem()
LOCAL luReturn
luReturn=.NULL.
WITH THIS
    IF ! .IsDone()
        luReturn = .ADATA[.nCurrent, .nReturnColumn]
    ENDIF
ENDWITH

RETURN luReturn
```

The code for GetCurrentItem() is unremarkable on its own. However, there is an important design concept between Append(), Contains(), and GetCurrentItem(). Both Append() and Contains() use the nDataColumn property to specify the column in which data is stored and searched. GetCurrentItem(), which retrieves elements from the array, uses the column specified in nReturnColumn.

The default setting for nDataColumn, nReturnColumn, and nCols is 1. However, you could change nCols and nReturnColumn to 2 and use the collection to store key/value pairs. This might be helpful, for example, if you wanted to store error message numbers in the first column and the appropriate error message text in the second column.

Push()

PUSHing an item on the stack is identical to APPENDing a new item. However, the Push() method does not duplicate the code for adding an item; it merely forwards the request as shown here:

```
*--MyCollection.Push()
LPARAMETERS tuItem
Return this.append(tuItem)
```

Pop()

The Pop() method retrieves the value of the current item and then removes it from the collection.

```
*--MyCollection.Pop()
LOCAL luReturn
luReturn=.NULL.

WITH THIS
    luReturn = .getcurrentitem()
    .REMOVE(.nCurrent)
ENDWITH

RETURN luReturn
```

GoFirst() and GoNext()

MyCollection has the equivalent of a record pointer. The property nCurrent stores the value of the current row. GoFirst() makes the first element in aData[] active by setting the value of nCurrent to 1. Navigation is simulated by incrementing nCurrent by one. The code for GoFirst() and GoNext() are shown together.

```
*--MyCollection.GoFirst()
IF This.nRows>0
    This.nCurrent=1
ENDIF

*--MyCollection.GoNext()
WITH THIS
    IF .nCurrent<=.nRows
        .nCurrent=.nCurrent+1
    ENDIF
    RETURN .nCurrent
ENDWITH
```

IsDone()

IsDone is the collection equivalent of the EOF() function for tables. IsDone() returns a logical expression, indicating whether the value of nCurrent is greater than the number of elements in the array. The code is shown here:

```
*--Is Done
WITH THIS
    IF .nCurrent>.nRows OR .nCurrent= 0
        RETURN .T.
    ELSE
        RETURN .F.
    ENDIF
ENDWITH
```

Sort()

Sorting the array places the items in the order of the return column. A check is done prior to calling ASORT() to ensure that the column does not contain object references.

```
*--Sort the array
IF THIS.nrows>0 AND ! VARTYPE(THIS.ADATA[1, this.nReturnColumn]) = 'O'
   ASORT(THIS.ADATA, this.nReturnColumn)
ENDIF
```

MyCollection Wrapup

I explained most of the methods and properties for MyCollection, and presented the code for these methods and properties. Those not shown are summarized here.

- GetCurrentIndex() returns the value of nCurrent.

- Destroy() sets the aData[] array to .NULL., removing all object references when the array contains object references.

- Clear() zaps the contents of aData[] by setting the nRows property to 0 and calling the Resize() method. It also sets the value of nCurrent to 0.

- GetCount() returns the value of nRows.

- SetCurrentItem() accepts a row number and sets the value of nCurrent to the row specified. If the row number is greater than 0 and less than or equal to the number of rows, the logical value True (.T.) is returned.

- OnLoad() is an empty hook method. It is provided so that information can be placed into the collection when the class is instantiated. It is called from the Init() method.

Implementing MyStack

MyStack is based on MyCollection. All the functionality that was added to MyCollection is still appropriate for MyStack, with one exception: The Pop() method of MyCollection returns the current element and removes the current row.

A stack, however, moves the last element that was added to the collection. Because Append(), and therefore Push(), always adds a row to the end of the collection, MyStack.Pop() sets the last row in the collection as the current row and then calls the default behavior of the Pop() method as shown here:

```
*--MyStack.Pop()
this.nCurrent=this.nRows
return dodefault()
```

No other changes are required to implement MyStack.

Implementing MyQueue

A queue is similar to a stack with one exception: The first item added is the first item removed from the queue (FIFO). As with MyStack, MyQueue is based on MyCollection, and only the Pop() method needs to be overwritten. The code for MyQueue.Pop is shown here:

```
*--MyQueue.Pop()
IF THIS.SetCurrentItem(1)
    RETURN DODEFAULT()
ELSE
    RETURN .NULL.
ENDIF
```

No other changes are required for MyQueue.

Implementing MyList

A list is an ordered collection with duplicates allowed. To implement the List class, the default behavior of Append() is extended by sorting aData[] after each item is added. The following code added to the Append() method is all that is required to implement the MyList class:

```
*--MyList.Append
LPARAMETERS tuItem

LOCAL luReturn
luReturn = DODEFAULT(tuItem)

THIS.SORT()

RETURN luReturn
```

Implementing MySet

A set is an ordered collection that contains no duplicates. In theory, when adding or removing elements from the collection, you could simply use Contains() to test if an element already exists in the set and return the row number in which it occurs. However, with some additional programming you can track how many times an element occurs in the set. This is not to imply that an element is actually added more than once. Instead, a separate column is added to the array. This extra column is used to store the number of times an element is added to the array.

The list of states used in the example "Using collections" earlier in the chapter is repeated here to illustrate how MySet keeps track of the number of times an element is added to the array. Here's the list of states: {NY, NJ, MA, ME, MA, NY, MA}.

Figure 4 shows the contents of aData after the states have been added.

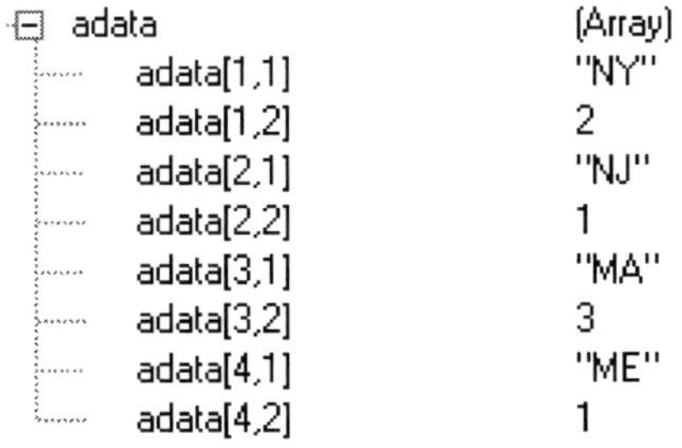

```
⊟ adata                    (Array)
      adata[1,1]           "NY"
      adata[1,2]           2
      adata[2,1]           "NJ"
      adata[2,2]           1
      adata[3,1]           "MA"
      adata[3,2]           3
      adata[4,1]           "ME"
      adata[4,2]           1
```

Figure 4. *The contents of MySet.aData[] with states added.*

As you can see in Figure 4, "MA" was added three times and "NY" was added twice, while "ME" and "NJ" were added only once.

To add the extra column to aData, set the nCols property to 2.

An additional method, GetInstanceCount(), has been added to MySet to return the number of times an element occurs in the collection. To remain consistent with MyCollection, which stores nDataColumn and nReturnColumn as properties of the class, nInstanceCountColumn has also been added to MySet. The value of nInstanceCountColumn is set to 2.

As each element is added or removed, the value in the second column is either incremented or decremented.

The code to append an element is shown here:

```
*--MySet.Append()
LPARAMETERS tuItem

LOCAL lnExistingRow
lnExistingRow = THIS.Contains(tuItem)
IF lnExistingRow=0 && Not in collection
    lnExistingRow=DODEFAULT(tuItem)
    THIS.ADATA(lnExistingRow,.nInstanceCountColumn) = 1
ELSE
    THIS.ADATA(lnExistingRow,.nInstanceCountColumn) =
THIS.ADATA(lnExistingRow,.nInstanceCountColumn)+1
ENDIF

RETURN lnExistingRow
```

Typically sets do not support the stack interface (Push and Pop). However, keeping the Push and Pop methods functional can prove to be beneficial. For example, consider the "Form" pad that appears in the menu bar as you are designing a form. As you open additional forms, additional Form pads do not appear in the menu; and when you close the last form, the Form pad is released.

The Pop() method of MySet is coded to achieve that type of functionality. As each element is added, the instance count is incremented. When an element is popped, the increment counter is decremented. Going back to the Form pad example, you could write code that checks the instance count to see if any remaining references exist. If none do, you can take whatever actions are appropriate. Here's the code for MySet.Pop():

```
*--MySet.Pop()
WITH THIS

    LOCAL lnExistingRow
    lnExistingRow = IIF(EMPTY(tuItem),.ncurrent, .Contains(tuItem))
    IF lnExistingRow>0 AND lnExistingRow<=.nRows

        IF .ADATA(lnExistingRow,.nInstanceCountColumn)=0
            RETURN .NULL.
            *--Set the pointer to 0
            THIS.ncurrent=0
        ELSE
            .ADATA(lnExistingRow,.nInstanceCountColumn)=;
                .ADATA(lnExistingRow,.nInstanceCountColumn)-1
```

```
            IF .ADATA( lnExistingRow,.nInstanceCountColumn) = 0
                THIS.REMOVE(lnExistingRow)
            ENDIF

            RETURN .ADATA[lnExistingRow,.nReturnColumn]
        ENDIF
    ENDIF
ENDWITH
```

GetInstanceCount() accepts an element and finds its location in aData[]. If the element exists in the collection, the instance count is returned. If the element is not in the collection, a value of 0 is returned. The code for GetInstanceCount is shown here:

```
*--MySet.GetInstanceCount()
LPARAMETERS tuItem

LOCAL lnExistingRow
lnExistingRow = THIS.Contains(tuItem)

IF lnExistingRow >0
    RETURN THIS.ADATA( lnExistingRow,this.nInstanceCountColumn)
ELSE
    RETURN 0
ENDIF
```

No other changes are required for MySet.

Example
Here's a simple example and a way to sneak in a function located in GenProc.prg. Collections are used extensively throughout the framework. You will encounter many more examples as you go.

Navigating an object hierarchy
The Visual FoxPro team made some enhancements in FoxPro 7.0 that made it much simpler to navigate object hierarchies. All collection classes now have an Objects collection.

One function, GetObjectList(), recursively navigates an object hierarchy and fills out a "list" of classes contained in the passed object. The "list" is one of the collection classes based on MyCollection.

Here's the code for the GetObjectList() function and an example of how to use the class.

```
*--Located in GenProc.prg
FUNCTION GetObjectList(toObject, toCollection AS MyCollection)

    IF VARTYPE(toCollection) <> "O"
        toCollection = CREATEOBJECT("MyStack")
    ENDIF
```

```
      IF VARTYPE(toObject)='O'
         toCollection.PUSH(toObject)
         IF PemStatus(toObject,'Objects',5)
            FOR EACH loObject IN toObject.OBJECTS
               GetObjectList(loObject,toCollection )
            ENDFOR
         ENDIF
      ENDIF
      RETURN toCollection
ENDFUNC
```

I've prepared a sample for this chapter, titled "Object Traverse Sample." The sample code lists the names of all objects on a form, and the number of instances for each base class. The code is shown here to illustrate how collections and the GetObjectList() function can be used.

```
*--Sample called from a button on a form
ACTIVATE SCREEN
CLEAR

LOCAL loCollection AS MyCollection, loSet as MyCollection
loCollection = CREATEOBJECT("MyCollection")
loSet = CREATEOBJECT("MySet")

GetObjectList(THISFORM,loCollection)

*--Now process the results
? "Your control contains ", loCollection.Getcount(), " controls"

loCollection.GOFIRST()
DO WHILE ! loCollection.IsDone()
   loTemp = loCollection.POP()
   loSet.push(loTemp.BaseClass)
   ? loTemp.NAME
ENDDO
?
?"Base Classes"
loSet.sort()
loSet.GoFirst()
DO WHILE ! loSet.IsDone()
      lcBaseClass = loSet.GetCurrentItem()

      ?loSet.GetInstanceCount( lcBaseClass )
      ?? " are based on "
      ?? lcBaseClass

      loSet.GoNext()
ENDDO
```

Summary

Collections are useful for working with groups of similar, yet unrelated items. In this chapter, I've introduced the MyFrame collection class and several specialized subclasses which include Stacks, Lists, Queues, and Sets.

One example presented in this chapter illustrated how to use collections to store object references to every object on a form. In later chapters, I build on this example and use collections to resize form controls and to implement form-level security.

Having read this chapter, you should have an understanding of what collections are, be familiar enough with them to understand how they are used in later chapters, and have some ideas for how they may be helpful in your framework.

Updates and corrections to this chapter can be found on Hentzenwerke's Web site, **www.hentzenwerke.com**. Click "Catalog" and navigate to the page for this book.

Chapter 9
Cursor and CursorAdapter

Visual FoxPro 8.0 provides the Cursor and CursorAdapter classes to read and write data from a database. These classes represent the data connection layer in a tiered framework. The Cursor class is optimal for accessing FoxPro data, while the CursorAdapter class offers new and exciting ways to work with a variety of data sources. In this chapter, you will extend the Cursor and CursorAdapter classes to create a fully object-oriented approach to working with data.

FoxPro provides the Cursor and CursorAdapter classes to give developers an object-oriented way to work with data. The real power of VFP's cursor classes is how well they integrate with the Form Designer. For example, when you drag and drop fields from a cursor onto a form, FoxPro adds the appropriate control to the form and names the control. If the control is a text box, a label is also added to the form and the label's caption is set to either the name of the field or the value specified in the Field Caption property of the Table Designer.

However, the capabilities of these classes are limited to reading data from a database. In this chapter you will develop the MyCursor and MyCursorAdapter classes to include the basic operations common to working with tables (Add, Save, Delete, and so on). For each operation, I will explain the general aspects of conducting each task, and then give you the method code.

This chapter begins with a review of data buffering and primary keys—two concepts critical for working with data in Visual FoxPro. Next it covers the design guidelines for creating the cursor class for MyFrame, followed by the specific methods. The chapter concludes with an example of MyCursor and MyCursorAdapter.

In the next chapter, you'll create a data environment class that brings all this together.

Data concepts

Visual FoxPro has so many ways to work with data that it can be difficult to decide which is the best approach to use. You need to be aware of two things when creating a table class: buffering and primary keys.

You can write directly to the table or use buffering to hold pending edits in memory prior to updating the table. And if you choose to buffer data (and you should), there are four different buffering schemes to choose from.

A basic tenet of database design is that each record in a table is uniquely identifiable. The unique identifier is known as the "primary key" for the table. The concept of primary keys and database design in general is beyond the scope of this book. However, you must be aware of some general concepts in order to support primary keys as part of your framework.

The next section reviews the concepts of buffering data and working with primary keys.

Buffering

Before writing changes to a record, VFP locks a buffered record to ensure that two users do not write to the same record at the same time. VFP offers two locking schemes that determine the timing of the record lock.

"Pessimistic" locking (or buffering) locks the record once you begin editing it. The lock is maintained the entire time the record is being edited and is removed only when the changes are written to disk or reverted. With pessimistic buffering, two users cannot edit the same record at the same time.

"Optimistic" buffering locks the record just before writing the information to the table. Optimistic buffering dramatically reduces the length of time a record is locked. One drawback to optimistic locking is that two or more people could be editing the same record at the same time.

A second characteristic of buffering has to do with the number of records that may be locked at one time. In VFP, "record buffering" locks only one record at a time. Moving the record pointer or issuing a TableUpdate() writes the changes to disk. "Table buffering" means that more than one record at a time can be held in the buffer. Record pointer movement does not cause the record to be written to disk. Only TableUpdate() can update the cursor when you are using buffering.

The combination of these two schemes results in five possibilities. They are:

- No Buffering (1)

- Pessimistic Row Buffering (2)

- Optimistic Row Buffering (3)

- Pessimistic Table Buffering (4)

- Optimistic Table Buffering (5)

CursorSetProp() is used to set the buffering for a table if you choose to set the buffering mode manually. For example, to set the buffering to Optimistic Table Buffering:

```
CURSORSETPROP('Buffering',5, <TableName>)
```

CursorSetProp() accepts a value of 1 through 5 to set the buffer mode. Passing a value of 1 removes buffering from a table.

Although your framework should support each of the buffering schemes, most developers prefer to use Optimistic Table Buffering.

The approach presented in this chapter works with all the buffering schemes. This is accomplished mainly by ensuring that the record pointer is never moved unless specifically directed by the application developer.

Surrogate primary keys

A surrogate primary key is a field in a table that has no purpose other than to uniquely identify a record in a table. A surrogate key is not based on any information associated with the record it identifies, and its value has no meaning.

It is possible to use more than one field to create a surrogate key. However, because a surrogate key has no meaning, using more than one field in a surrogate key unnecessarily complicates the key and uses unnecessary disk space.

Consider an Employees table that contains the fields First Name, Last Name, and Social Security Number. A surrogate key would be stored in an additional field with a name like EmployeeID. The value of EmployeeID would not be based on any of the information in the other fields. An employee number, however, is not an example of a surrogate key. While it may not be based on other information in the employee record, it does carry a meaning to the organization.

An example of a non-surrogate key would be the combination of First Name, Last Name, and Social Security Number.

Using more than one field to uniquely identify a record is an example of a composite key.

Assuming the combination of First Name, Last Name, and Social Security Number uniquely identified all records in the table, you run into problems when a value of one of the fields changes. For instance, if an employee were to change his or her last name, the unique identifier would also change. In relational databases, changing primary key values can cause a relationship between tables to fail. Surrogate keys are not subject to the same problem. Because surrogate keys are not based on information in the record, they never have a reason to be changed.

Integer or character?

Some developers prefer integer keys while others prefer character keys. Technically, a primary key can be based on any data type other than memo, or general. Yes, you can base a primary key on logical, but then the maximum records you could place in the table would be two—not very useful. Additionally, integer keys offer the best performance.

MyFrame supports integer primary keys, character primary keys, and tables that do not have a primary key. In developing your own framework, I recommend that you choose to use surrogate primary keys and that you standardize on a single data type.

The Cursor object: MyCursor

While the Cursor class is not new to FoxPro 8.0, it is now a visual class. However, there are some shortcomings to the native Cursor class, primarily that it has retained its roots to FoxPro's procedural days. Rather than working with the Cursor class directly, you are still required to issue commands against the underlying cursor. The problem with this approach is that you cannot add behavior to, or override, these actions at the class level. To make the cursor class "objectified," I'll add methods to the framework cursor class.

By creating Save(), New(), Undo(), and Delete() methods, you can tap into the "object model" and take different actions for a given table. For example, some tables may write to auxiliary tables during a save operation (history, backup, data warehouse, and so on). Another example may be that you want to add security to your data layer and open some cursors as read-only. The native cursor class does not have an Open method to which you can add security.

Another limitation is that the Cursor class stores path information to the tables it opens, and the path information cannot be changed at design time. Assume you are working with two sets of data, possibly one for development and one for testing. If you change SET PATH to point to the testing folders, you'll find that your development data is still loaded instead of the test data. As a reminder, in MyFrame, the search path is set in Main.prg.

The framework class MyCursor is used throughout the framework to work with data, replacing the open/close functionality of the native cursor object and adding the capabilities required to manipulate and save data.

Properties

Common information about each table is stored in properties of the class. The relevant properties are:

- CursorSource: The table to open.

- Order: The (index) order of the table.

- Alias: The name of the resulting cursor.

- cPrimaryKey: The primary key of the table.

You can easily set those properties by using the framework builder form in **Figure 1**. The framework builders are explained in detail in Chapter 17, "Developer Tools."

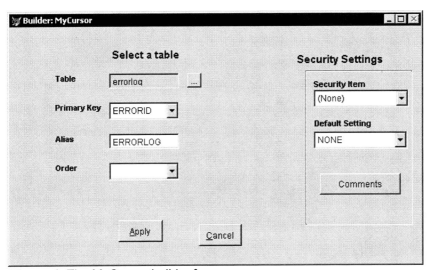

Figure 1. The MyCursor builder form.

Methods

The following methods define the interface of the cursor classes:

- Open: Opens a table.

- Close: Closes a table.

- New: Inserts a new record into a table.

- Delete: Deletes a record.

- Save: Saves all pending changes.

- Undo: Reverts pending changes in one or more records.

- UnsavedChangesExist(): Returns a logical, indicating whether pending changes exist (on buffered tables only).

- SetBufferMode: Changes the cursor's buffer mode.

- Find: Returns the form (class or SCX file) used to conduct a search.

- IsValid(): A place to validate information added or edited.

- Go(): Accepts a primary key value and makes that the current record.

- Set Filter(): Applies a filter to the records in a cursor.

One reason to consider building your own framework is to have the code cater to your preferences. For example, I always use Optimistic Table Buffering. Always, always, always. However, by not presenting the code to update tables with a different buffering scheme or no buffering, the book would not be as informative as it could be. So, you'll see that the implementation for MyCursor works with all buffering modes or no buffering at all.

Each method is broken into several parts. First I present the basic issues surrounding a particular command or commands. Next I present the design objectives for the class, followed by the code. Some methods also include examples of how they can be used to further reinforce what the code is doing.

Design considerations for the MyCursor class
In Chapter 3, "Framework Architecture," I explained that one tier in MyFrame was the data access layer. Well, this is it. The Cursor class knows how to access and write to data. MyCursor is designed specifically for working with FoxPro tables. Also, in this chapter you'll develop a class with a similar interface that knows how to work with client/server data.

In the next chapter, a third class (MyDataEnvironment) knows how to work with data. MyFrame gets its data flexibility by communicating with MyDataEnvironment. Only MyDataEnvironment communicates with the cursors and through the exposed methods of the cursor.

Opening a table
The USE command is used to open a table. For example:

```
USE Customers
```

Issues
The name of the table to open may contain spaces. In order to USE a table with a name containing spaces, the table name must be enclosed in quotation marks. For example:

```
USE "Table Name With Spaces.dbf"
```

The result of issuing the previous command would result in a cursor with an Alias() of "Table_Name_With_Spaces." Notice that underscores have been inserted for the spaces. The name of the table can be in one of several formats, as presented in **Table 1**.

Table 1. Available formats for table names.

Table Name	Example
Just the table name	Customer
Relative path	".\Customer"
Absolute path	"C:\Customer"
Universal Naming Convention	\\127.0.0.1\C$\Customer.dbf or \\Server\Share\Table
Database!Table	AppData!Customer

Design considerations

The name of the table is all that is required to open a cursor. The table name can be in any one of the formats listed in Table 1 and is assigned to the CursorSource property of MyCursor.

Once opened, however, MyCursor no longer works with the value of CursorSource. Instead, it works with the name assigned to the table as defined by its alias. This is an important distinction. As you saw with the spaces example, the name of the table is not guaranteed to be the same as the alias created for it. The developer can also choose to supply an alias if he or she desires. If none is supplied, the name of the table is used by default.

As you will see later in this chapter, in the section about adding a new record, identifying a primary key field enables MyCursor to generate a primary key value. The developer can identify the primary key field in the cPrimaryKey property. However, FoxPro enables you to query information about the table itself. In other words, you can determine the name of the primary key by using a table's metadata. I'll show you some methods that allow you to accomplish this after I review the code for the Open() method.

Finally, as a matter of good housekeeping, if the class opens a table, it should close the table. A test is done to determine if the class truly opened the table or if it was already open before it was called.

Here's the Open() method.

```
*--MyCursor.Open()
LOCAL lcTableToOpen

WITH THIS
    ASSERT ! EMPTY(.CursorSource) MESSAGE "Uh...Need a table here"
    IF EMPTY(.Alias)
        .Alias = JustTable(ALLTRIM(.CursorSource))
        .Alias= STRTRAN(ALLTRIM(.Alias),' ','_')
    ENDIF

    .lCLoseOnExit = IIF(USED(.Alias),.F.,.T.)
    lcTableToOpen = ["]+ALLTRIM(.CursorSource)+["]
    IF .lCLoseOnExit
        USE &lcTableToOpen AGAIN ALIAS (ALLTRIM(.Alias)) IN 0 SHARED
    ENDIF
```

```
      .setorder()
      .SetPrimaryKey()

      RETURN USED( .Alias )
ENDWITH
```

How to use the Open() method
The table to open is specified by filling in the CursorSource property. Although you can set the value in code as shown in this example, you more likely will identify the table to open in the Class Designer at design time.

```
lo = CREATEOBJECT("MyCursor")
lo.CursorSource = "AppCats"
lo.Open()
```

Related methods and functions
Notice how I didn't have to specify the primary key or an alias in the previous example. The Open() method took care of those actions for me. The following functions and methods are related to identifying the primary key and the alias for the table.

Determining a primary key
FoxPro provides a function, Primary(), that returns a logical value indicating whether an index tag is the primary key for the table. To determine the primary key, you need to test each tag until the primary key is found.

In MyFrame, the GetPrimaryKey() function, located in GenProc.prg, is used to determine the primary key of an open table. GetPrimaryKey() returns the name of the primary key if one exists and .NULL. if the key does not exist. The function accepts an alias to search for, and if one is not provided, the currently selected Alias() is used by default. The code for GetPrimaryKey() is shown here:

```
FUNCTION GetPrimaryKey()

    LPARAMETERS tcAlias
    LOCAL lcReturn, lnTagNo, lcAlias
    lcReturn=.NULL.
    lcAlias = IIF( EMPTY(tcAlias), ALIAS(), tcAlias)

    ASSERT VARTYPE(lcAlias)='C'  ;
       MESSAGE 'GetPrimKey(cAlias) accepts only a character parameter'

    IF ! EMPTY(lcAlias) AND USED(lcAlias)

       FOR lnTagNo=1 TO TAGCOUNT(lcAlias,lcAlias)
          IF PRIMARY(lnTagNo,lcAlias)
             lcReturn=TAG(lnTagNo,lcAlias)
             EXIT
          ENDIF
       ENDFOR
    ENDIF

    RETURN lcReturn
ENDFUNC
```

Notice that the record pointer is never moved and that the work area is never switched at any point during this function. I mentioned earlier that part of the strategy for working with a variety of buffering schemes is to make sure the framework never moves the record pointer without being specifically directed by the application developer. This function demonstrates how that concept is applied in practice.

A second function, GetPrimaryKeyValue(), also included in GenProc.prg, returns the value of a primary key. This function is not shown here.

MyCursor.SetPrimaryKey

The SetPrimaryKey() method checks to see if a value has been set for cPrimaryKey. If the name of the primary key is not provided, a custom function, GetPrimaryKey(), is called to identify the primary key for the table.

The GetPrimaryKey function defined earlier could have been called directly from the Open() method. Look at the GetPrimaryKey() function again. It is based on index tags. In some cases, a primary key may not have a tag. Free tables may not have a "primary key tag" but certainly could have a field that uniquely identifies each record in the table. By placing the code for setting the primary key within its own method, it is easier to customize the behavior for setting the primary key without interrupting the rest of the Open() method.

MyCursor.SetPrimaryKey is a wrapper around the GetPrimaryKey() function. The code is shown here:

```
*--MyCursor.SetPrimarykey
IF  EMPTY(THIS.cPrimaryKey)
    THIS.cPrimaryKey=GetPrimaryKey(THIS.Alias)
ENDIF
```

Returning just the table

There is no single function that separates only the table name from each of the formats listed in Table 1. To determine the alias of a cursor, you must be able to separate the table name from the information provided. JustTable(), located in GenProc.prg, returns the name of a table regardless of the format used. Here is the code for JustTable().

```
FUNCTION JustTable()
   LPARAMETERS cString
   *--Check for data
   Assert  VARTYPE(cString)= 'C' and ! EMPTY(cString)

   DO CASE
      CASE AT('\',cString)>0 OR AT('.',cString)>0 or AT('/',cString)>0
         RETURN JUSTSTEM(cString)

      CASE AT('!',cString)>0
         LOCAL nLoc
         nLoc=AT('!',cString)
         RETURN SUBSTR(cString,nLoc+1,LEN(cString))

      OTHERWISE
         RETURN cString
   ENDCASE
ENDFUNC
```

Closing a table

The Destroy() method of the class simply closes the cursor if it was not already open before the class was instantiated. The Destroy() method is shown here:

```
*--MyCursor.Destroy()
IF THIS.lCloseOnExit
    USE IN SELECT(THIS.Alias)
ENDIF
```

Adding a record

You can add records to a FoxPro table by issuing the APPEND BLANK command or the INSERT INTO command. The issues with adding a record have more to do with primary keys and how they are enforced than with the mechanics of adding a record. The issues associated with primary keys are presented prior to the design considerations.

 The issues presented here are common to both surrogate and non-surrogate keys.

Primary keys

Primary keys uniquely identify each record in a table. No two records can have the same primary key value. You can choose to enforce unique values in a field by creating an index on a field and declaring it as the primary index. You can also use candidate index keys to enforce unique values in a field or fields.

There are two issues to consider when using primary keys in FoxPro. First, APPEND BLANK leaves the value of the primary key empty. A subsequent APPEND BLANK command would result in a second empty primary key and would raise an error. To prevent this from occurring, you must assign the primary key a default value from the database. You could choose to assign it immediately after issuing the APPEND BLANK command, but if even one blank primary key sneaks into your table, the effect will be that no one else will be able to add records.

A better approach is to generate the primary key value before adding the record and using INSERT INTO. With this approach the value of the primary key is never blank and thus removes blank primary keys as an issue. One minor drawback with INSERT INTO is that it overwrites a default value generated from the database. However, if you use surrogate primary keys, this is not an issue because you're replacing one meaningless value with another meaningless value.

The second reason primary keys can cause a problem is that deleted records are included as part of the "unique value" test. If you test for the existence of a key using SEEK, for example, and SET DELETED is ON, SEEK will not find the record and could lead you to add a repeated value. Again, an error would be raised.

Generally, this type of error occurs when primary keys have meaning, as would be the case with an employee number. For example, employee 1234 leaves the company and his or her record is deleted from the Employees table. Several months later, a new employee is hired and is assigned 1234 as his or her employee number. To avoid situations like this, I recommend that you use surrogate primary keys and take advantage of the auto-incrementing field added in Visual FoxPro 8.0.

Design considerations

You want the developer to have as much control as possible while adding a record. A number of hook methods have been provided for the application developer to take action before adding a record; once the record is added, the developer is also given a chance to set foreign key values or assign default values by adding code to the OnSetForeignKeys() and OnSetDefaultValues methods.

Immediately after an APPEND or INSERT command is issued, the record pointer is placed on the newly created record. For example, the following line of code would update the time stamp of a newly created record.

```
REPLACE [TableName].TimeStamp with DATETIME()
```

APPEND BLANK is used to add a record when a table does not have a primary key. When a table does have a primary key, a new primary key value is generated and INSERTed into the table.

Notice that the IN clause of APPEND BLANK is used to ensure that the currently selected alias does not change. The INSERT command works regardless of the alias selected when it is called.

Both the INSERT and APPEND commands rely on information contained in properties of the class. This is an essential concept for generic design. Only the value of the properties changes from class to class; the code remains the same.

Finally, the value of the primary key for the new record is returned. Here's the code:

```
*--MyCursor.New()
LOCAL luKey, lcAlias, lcPKField

luKey = THIS.NextID()
lcAlias = THIS.Alias

IF THIS.OnBeforeNew()
    IF ISNULL(luKey)
        APPEND BLANK IN (lcAlias)
    ELSE
        lcPKField = this.cPrimaryKey
        INSERT INTO &lcAlias (&lcPKField) VALUES (luKey)
    ENDIF
    THIS.OnSetForeignKeys()
    THIS.OnSetDefaultValues()
ENDIF

RETURN luKey
```

Deleting a record

You can delete a record by using the DELETE command. There are a few issues with the way FoxPro handles deleted records that you should be aware of; these are explained in the Issues section. The Implementation section contains the code and explains how the code addresses those issues.

Issues

Deleting a record does not physically remove the record from the table. Instead, it simply marks the record as deleted. When SET DELETED is OFF, deleted records are accessible; you can work with them in the same manner as records that have not been deleted. SET DELETED ON prevents deleted records from being displayed.

However, when a record is marked for deletion, the deleted filter is not applied until the record pointer is moved. Therefore, a record can be deleted and still be visible in a screen.

Implementation

The Delete() method accomplishes three objectives: actually performing the delete, saving the deletion, and applying the deleted filter. Hook methods are provided before and after performing the deletion.

The IN clause of the DELETE command is used to avoid unnecessarily changing the work area. Also, notice the DELETE command is tested for success by checking the DELETED() status of the record. Triggers in the database can cause a deletion to fail.

One thing I have noticed is that when users delete a record, they expect the deletion to be persisted. This is particularly true when they have been prompted to confirm a deletion. If MyCursor.lForceDelete is .T., the individual delete is persisted by issuing a TableUpdate(). Notice that the first parameter for TableUpdate is .F. When table buffering is enabled, edits may be pending in more than one record. Passing .F. as the first parameter prevents pending changes in other records from being written to the database.

As a rule, the framework does not move the record pointer unless specifically directed by the application developer. The lApplyDeletedFilter property controls whether the framework moves the record after a successful deletion. The Delete() method is shown here:

```
*--MyCursor.Delete()
LOCAL llOK
WITH THIS
   IF !EOF(.Alias) AND .OnBeforeDelete()
      *--Delete the record
      DELETE IN (.Alias)
      llOK = DELETED(.Alias)

      *--If buffering is on and developer wants to write the delete immediately
      IF llOK AND .lForceDelete AND CURSORGETPROP("Buffering",.Alias)>1
         llOK = TABLEUPDATE(0,.T.,(.Alias))
      ENDIF

      *--If everything's still copasetic
      IF llOK
         IF .lApplyDeletedFilter AND ! EOF(.Alias)
            SKIP IN ( .Alias )
         ENDIF
         .OnAfterDelete()
      ELSE
         .ERROR()
      ENDIF
   ENDIF

ENDWITH

RETURN llOK
```

Saving records

When you access tables without buffering enabled, changes are written to disk as you complete each field. A specific update command is not required. When buffering is enabled, moving the record pointer or issuing TableUpdate() will write the changes to disk depending on the mode of buffering in effect.

Implementation

For non-buffered tables, the Save() method always returns True (.T.). The reason is that non-buffered tables do not contain unsaved changes. Further, because the Save() method didn't actually write the changes to disk, the OnBeforeSave() and Save() methods are called only when buffering is enabled.

The OnAfterSave() hook method is called after a successful save, while the Error() method is called if the save is unsuccessful.

```
*--MyCursor.Save()
Local llOK
llOK = .F.

If CursorGetProp("Buffering",This.Alias)>1 And ;
        this.Validate() And ;
        THIS.OnBeforeSave()

    llOK= TableUpdate(1,.F.,(This.Alias))
    If llOK
        This.onAfterSave()
    Else
        This.Error()
    Endif
Endif

RETURN llOK
```

Reverting pending edits (undo)

TABLEREVERT() "undoes" any pending changes. However, tables that are not buffered don't have any changes. Therefore, the ability to "revert" changes is limited to buffered tables only.

Implementation

The first parameter of TABLEREVERT is logical and indicates whether all changes should be reverted (.T.) or only the current record (.F.). The default is to undo only the current row.

```
*--MyCursor.Undo()
LPARAMETERS tlAllrows
LOCAL llRevertedRecords
llRevertedRecords = 0
IF this.BufferModeOverride>1
    llRevertedRecords =TABLEREVERT(tlAllrows,THIS.Alias)
ENDIF

RETURN llRevertedRecords
```

Checking for unsaved changes

Using a combination of GetNextModified() and GetFldState(), it is possible to determine if unsaved changes exist in a table.

Issues

GetNextModified() returns the record number of the next record that has unsaved changes. Passing a value of 0 in the first parameter instructs FoxPro to begin looking from the first record. If a modified record exists in the table, GetNextModified() returns the record number. If no modified records exist, a value of 0 is returned.

New to FoxPro 7.0 was the ability to suppress database rules from firing. Passing a value of .T. as the third parameter is required to suppress rules from firing. In previous versions of FoxPro, and I suppose the default implementation in 7.0, the record pointer moved as part of the process of checking for unsaved changes.

GetNextModified() works only on tables with table buffering enabled.

GetFldState() evaluates the current record, or field within a record, and returns information about the status of the record or field. The possible return values are shown in **Table 2**.

Table 2. *Return values for GetFldState().*

Value	Description
1	Field has not been edited, or deletion status has not changed.
2	Field has been edited, or deletion status has changed.
3	Field in an appended record has not been edited, or deletion status has not changed for the appended record.
4	Field in an appended record has been edited, or deletion status has changed for the appended record.
.NULL.	At EOF( )

Passing a field name to GetFldState() returns a numeric value from Table 2. Passing –1 to GetFldState() returns a string of information. The first position in the string indicates the deleted status for the record. The remainder of the string is a concatenation of the edit values for each field.

Implementation

You can use GetNextModified() and GetFldState() to do some pretty cool things, such as loop through all edited records and build a comprehensive list of each record that changed. There is a time and place for code like that—error handling and business-rule validation come to mind—but not here.

To determine if a change has been made, I'll just map the appropriate command to the buffer status and get out.

```
*--MyCursor.UnsavedChangesExist()
LOCAL llUnsavedChangesExist, lcModString

DO CASE
    CASE CURSORGETPROP("buffering",THIS.ALIAS)>3
        *--You must force the record pointer to move
```

```
       *) otherwise getnextmodified (with nofires)
       *) does not work.
       *) See the help file. lNOFIRE causes the data
       *) in controls not to be written to disk.
       IF ! EOF(THIS.ALIAS)
           GO (RECNO(THIS.ALIAS)) IN (THIS.ALIAS)
       ENDIF
       IF  GETNEXTMODIFIED(0,THIS.ALIAS,.T.)<>0
           llUnsavedChangesExist=.T.
       ENDIF

   CASE CURSORGETPROP("buffering",THIS.ALIAS)>1
       lcModString = GETFLDSTATE(-1)
       IF ! ISNULL(lcModString)
           llUnsavedChangesExist = !LEN(lcModString) = OCCURS('1',lcModString)
       ENDIF

   OTHERWISE
       *-- Buffering is not enabled, do nothing
ENDCASE

RETURN llUnsavedChangesExist
```

Validating data

Validating data before allowing it into a database is one of the most important aspects of database management. In any framework, the task of validating data is the responsibility of the application developer.

The validation code in MyCursor exists in a method named Validate(). The Validate() method moves the record pointer to each record that has unsaved changes and calls a hook method, IsValid(). The developer can signal that the cursor is not in a valid state by returning a value of False (.F.) from the IsValid() method.

Issues

The number of records that may contain pending edits varies depending on a cursor's buffer mode. Record buffering means that only one record at a time can have pending edits, while table buffering can have multiple records with pending edits. Of course, if buffering is not enabled, no records can contain pending edits.

Using a combination of CursorGetProp() and GetNextModified() it is possible to navigate to any and all records that have pending changes.

Implementation

The means for identifying buffered records varies with the cursor's buffer mode. For table buffering, GetNextModified() identifies the next record in a table where changes are pending. Passing 0 as the first parameter tells GetNextModified() to start searching for changed records from the beginning of the table. GetNextModified() also returns a value indicating in which row the pending change exists. Using a DO WHILE loop, the following code moves the record pointer to each modified record before calling the IsValid() method.

For tables with row buffering, the record pointer can only be on the record with pending edits, so the IsValid() method is called without moving the record pointer. For tables with no buffering, IsValid() is not called because any information in the fields is already written to disk.

```
*--MyCursor.Validate()
NOTE: This method is only called if changes are pending
LOCAL llOK, lnModifiedRecord
llOK = .T.
DO CASE
    CASE INLIST(CURSORGETPROP("buffering",THIS.Alias),4,5)

        lnModifiedRecord = GETNEXTMODIFIED(0,THIS.Alias,.T.)
        DO WHILE lnModifiedRecord<>0
            GO lnModifiedRecord IN (this.Alias)
            llOK = THIS.IsValid()
            IF ! llOK
                EXIT
            ENDIF
            lnModifiedRecord = GETNEXTMODIFIED(lnModifiedRecord,THIS.Alias,.T.)
        ENDDO
    CASE INLIST(CURSORGETPROP("buffering",THIS.Alias),2,3)
        llOK = THIS.IsValid()

    CASE CURSORGETPROP("buffering",THIS.Alias)=1
        *--Buffering Not Enabled
ENDCASE
RETURN llOK
```

The IsValid() method

The IsValid() method is a hook method for developers. It is empty by default. To use this method, just add code that returns a logical value.

As you saw in the previous code, the method is called only when the record pointer is on the record to be evaluated. Also note, however, that the selected work area never changes. To write validation code, you may want to consider always using the "Table.Field" notation. For example, to ensure that the customer's first name is not empty, you could write:

```
*--Validation Sample
IF EMPTY(Customers.FirstName)
    MESSAGEBOX("The customer name cannot be blank")
    Return .F.
ENDIF
```

Setting the buffer mode

CursorSetProp() sets the buffer mode of a cursor. If you allow the data environment to open the cursor, it will set the cursor's buffer mode for you. However, if you overwrite the OpenTables() method of the data environment, or use the table outside of the data environment, you have to set the buffer mode yourself.

The SetBufferMode() method accepts a buffering status. After performing some validations, it sets the buffer mode.

```
*--MyCursor.SetBufferMode()
LPARAMETERS tnBufferMode
WITH THIS
    IF ! EMPTY(tnBufferMode)
        .BUFFERMODEOVERRIDE = tnBufferMode
    ENDIF
```

```
        ASSERT VARTYPE(.BUFFERMODEOVERRIDE ) = 'N'
        ASSERT INLIST(.BUFFERMODEOVERRIDE,3,5)

        IF .BUFFERMODEOVERRIDE >3 AND SET("Multilocks") = "OFF"
            SET MULTILOCKS ON
        ENDIF

        =CURSORSETPROP("Buffering",.BUFFERMODEOVERRIDE ,.ALIAS)

        RETURN CURSORGETPROP("Buffering",.ALIAS) = .BUFFERMODEOVERRIDE

ENDWITH
```

Navigating to a record

To navigate to a particular record, you need to know the value you are looking for and the field or tag in which that value can be found. You can specify the field to search against. If a field or index tag is not specified, the primary key is used (if one exists). If an index tag is available, the SEEK command is used to find the record. If the tag does not exist, the LOCATE command is used instead.

```
*--MyCursor.Go()
LPARAMETERS tuID,tcTag
LOCAL llUseLocate, lcTag, llReturn

IF  EMPTY(tcTag)
      lcTag = THIS.cPrimaryKey
      tuID = str2exp(tuID,this.cPKType)
ELSE
      lcTag = tcTag
ENDIF

IF Empty(lcTag) or IsNull(lcTag) or ! IsTag(lcTag, this.Alias)
      llUseLocate = .T.
ENDIF


ASSERT ! EMPTY(tuID)


IF llUseLocate
    LOCAL lnSaveLoc
    lnSaveLoc=SELECT()
    SELECT (THIS.Alias)

    LOCATE FOR &lcTag = tuID
    llReturn = FOUND()
    SELECT (lnSaveLoc)
ELSE
    llReturn  = SEEK(tuID,THIS.Alias,lcTag)
ENDIF


RETURN llReturn
```

The property .cPKType is a custom property added to the cursor. It exists to support the use of either character or integer data types for primary keys.

Setting a filter

To filter records from a cursor, you can use the SET FILTER TO command. This filter expression can be any expression returning a logical value. To remove a filter, issue the SET FILTER TO command without identifying a filter.

The SetFilter() method of MyCursor accepts a filter condition as a parameter and adds it to the existing filter. Passing an empty string as the filter condition removes the filter entirely. Here's the code:

```
*--MyCursor.SetFilter()
LPARAMETERS tcFilterExp
LOCAL lcFilterExp

IF EMPTY(tcFilterExp)
      this.Filter = ''
ELSE
      this.Filter = tcFilterExp
ENDIF

lcFilterExp = this.Filter

SET FILTER TO &lcFilterExp IN (this.Alias)
```

Working with data objects

At times it is helpful to work with data in an object format. GetCurrentRecord() and SetCurrentRecord() are wrappers around the SCATTER NAME command, and either return a data object or accept a data object and write it to a record.

For example, assume you have a Customers table with 100,000-plus records. Constantly opening and closing the table is a drain on network resources. One alternative is to open the table once and use data objects to pass entire records between objects in different data sessions. An example illustrating this technique is presented after the individual method code.

Returning a data object

To return a record from a table, this framework provides a GetCurrentRecord() function. This method simply retrieves the current record and returns it as a data object. When you use this in conjunction with MyCursor.Go(), you can navigate to a particular record in a table and retrieve its contents. The code for MyCursor.GetCurrentRecord() is as follows:

```
*--MyCursor.GetCurrentRecord ()
LOCAL loData, lnSelect
loData = .NULL.

IF ! EOF(THIS.Alias)
   lnSelect = SELECT()
   SELECT (THIS.Alias)
```

```
   SCATTER MEMO NAME loData

   SELECT (lnSelect)
ENDIF

RETURN loData
```

Writing data object contents to the current record

SetCurrentRecord() accepts a data object as a parameter and writes its values to the current record. While the data object will usually be populated using the SCATTER command, any object with properties matching a table's field names can be used.

```
*--MyCursor.SetCurrentRecord()
LPARAMETERS toData
LOCAL lnSelect, llWritten

IF ! EOF(THIS.Alias) AND VARTYPE(toData) = 'O'
    lnSelect = SELECT()
    SELECT (THIS.Alias)

    GATHER NAME toData MEMO
      llWritten = .T.
    SELECT (lnSelect)
ENDIF

RETURN llWritten
```

Working with data objects—Example

Notice that neither GetCurrentRecord() nor SetCurrentRecord() moves the record pointer. This is in keeping with the philosophy that the framework should never move the record pointer. Used in conjunction with the Go() method, you can navigate to a particular record and retrieve its contents. The following code shows an example of how these two methods could be used. Assume the Customer table has two fields, CustomerID and CustName. As an alternative to using Go(), this example illustrates how you can use New() to add a record to a table, retrieve its contents, assign a customer name, and then save the results.

```
*--Using Data Objects Sample
LOCAL loCustomerObject, loData, lcKey
loCustomerObject = CREATEOBJECT("MyCursor","Customer")

*--Add a new record and assign a primary key
lcKey = loCustomerObject.New()

*--Retreive the record
loData = loCustomerObject.GetCurrentRecord()

*<<Do some processing, move the record pointer, etc.>>

*--Get back to the record
loCustomerObject.Go(lcKey)

*--Assign a name
loData.CustName = "XXXXXXXXXX"
```

```
*--Write the changes
loCustomerObject.SetCurrentRecord(loData)

*--And Save
loCustomerObject.SAVE()
```

Remote data

What's different about client/server applications? Not much, and everything. When you USE a table in FoxPro, you have access to all of the records in the table. In a client/server application, you also have access to all of the data. So what's the difference?

Imagine you have a table that is 1GB in size and is residing on a Local Area Network (LAN). When you USE this 1GB table it appears to open immediately. You can browse it, GO TOP, GO BOTTOM, and everything appears to happen instantly. (And you quietly think to yourself, "Gosh, I love this tool").

Computer network capacities do not magically improve just because you are using FoxPro. Behind the scenes, FoxPro is requesting and retrieving only the portion of the file that you are interested in viewing.

In a client/server application, you are responsible for requesting and retrieving the desired records. You do this by sending an SQL statement to a database server (such as SQL Server or Oracle). The database server processes the SQL statement and returns only the results of the query.

You could access all of the records in the 1GB table by issuing an SQL statement such as this:

```
SELECT * FROM MyOneGigabyteTable
```

And after few minutes or hours you will have access to all the records. Typically you will want to filter the record based on some criteria, such as a primary or foreign key value. For example:

```
SELECT * FROM MyOneGigabyteTable WHERE PK = 1234
```

The result of this statement is that you will see only the contents of the record that has a primary key value of 1234.

Working with remote data is different than working with native data for two reasons. First, FoxPro automatically refreshes data as changes are made to underlying tables, whereas remote data must be refreshed or requeried programmatically. Second, FoxPro cursors are ready to accept input and automatically "know" how to write the changes to the underlying table. Cursors containing remote data must be told specifically how to map the contents of the cursor to its underlying table or tables.

This section, "Remote data," is an overview of the basic concepts for working with remote data—namely, how to make a connection, create a view, and write an SQL statement. I'll also review the new CursorAdapter class that FoxPro 8.0 provided to work with remote data, as well as the framework version of the CursorAdapter.

To learn more about working with remote data and techniques for developing client/server applications, I recommend that you read Client/Server Apps with Microsoft Visual FoxPro and SQL Server, *also from Hentzenwerke Publishing.*

Connecting to remote data

In order to access ODBC-compliant data on a remote database, you must first establish a database connection. To make a connection you have to supply the appropriate connection information: user name, password, database, and so on. Connection information is passed to the ODBC driver as a string. A connection string can contain a variety of information depending on the database to which you are connecting. Here's an example of the connection string used to connect to FoxPro data:

```
DSN=Visual FoxPro Tables;UID=;PWD=;
SourceDB=C:\Dev\MyFrame\AppData\sysdata.dbc;  SourceType=DBC;
Exclusive=No;BackgroundFetch=Yes;Collate=Machine;Null=Yes;Deleted=Yes;
```

Connection information can be stored as a "Named Connection" in a FoxPro database or as a Data Source Name (DSN) stored in ODBC.INI.

 As you can see, the sample code for this book was developed in c:\dev. If you are accessing FoxPro data using a named connection and you copy the files to d:\dev (or any other folder) and then open the project manager, FoxPro prompts you with "Project has been moved. Make d:\dev the new home directory?" Even if you select "Yes," the path in the named connection is not changed. The result: You will no longer be able to open or modify a remote view that uses that named connection.

Accessing remote data using SQL Pass Through

Using SQL Pass Through, you make a direct connection to the back-end database. Once a connection is established, you can begin executing queries or calling stored procedures.

Connecting to data

You can connect to an ODBC-compliant database using SQLConnect() and SQLStringConnect(). SQLConnect() accepts a data source name, user ID and password, or a named connection. SQLStringConnect() accepts only a connection string.

Both functions return a numeric value. A value of −1 indicates that a connection was not successful, while a value greater than 0 indicates a successful connection. Each new connection is assigned a consecutive number: 1, 2, 3, and so on. The number assigned to a connection is referred to as the "connection handle."

Executing a query

SQL Pass Through is as the name implies. An SQL statement is sent (passed through) to the data server using the SQLEXEC() function. SQLEXEC() accepts three parameters: a connection handle, an SQL statement, and the name of the cursor in which the results are stored. For example, to retrieve all customers from a customer table:

```
local lcSQL, lcAlias, lnHandle
lcSQL = "SELECT * FROM CUSTOMERS ORDER BY CustName"
lnHandle = SQLSTRINGCONNECT("<<Long Connection String Here>>")
lcAlias = "Results"
SQLEXEC(lnHandle, lcSQL, lcAlias)
```

It isn't readily apparent in this simple example that the syntax for the SQL statement must be in the syntax of the database on which the query will execute—not FoxPro's syntax. In this example, the syntax for FoxPro and SQL Server are the same.

Updating remote data

Cursors created with SQL Pass Through can be edited, but are not updateable by default. To make a cursor created with SQL Pass Through editable, the following properties must be set using CursorSetProp():

- Tables

- KeyFieldList

- UpdatableFieldList

- UpdateNameList

- SendUpdates

To accomplish this, you set the cursor properties using the CursorSetProp() function. For example, to set the SendUpdates property to True by using CursorSetProp():

```
CURSORSETPROP("SendUpdates",.T.,<<TableName>>)
```

It is possible to write a generic routine to make any remote cursor updateable, assuming you know the tables that comprise the cursor and the primary keys for the table. To do so, you must loop through each field of the cursor and build the UpdateNameList and UpdatableFieldList. The following sample code demonstrates how to assemble the necessary strings and call the appropriate CursorSetProp() functions:

```
*--Sample Code: Formatting a remote cursor to be updateable
lcTable = "<<TableList>>"
lcPrimaryKey = "<<PrimaryKey>>"

STORE '' TO lcUpdateNameList, lcUpdatableFieldList
lnFields = AFIELDS(laFields)

FOR lnI = 1 TO lnFields

   lcUpdateNameList =lcUpdateNameList + IIF(EMPTY(lcUpdateNameList),'',', ')+;
      laFields(lnI, 1)+' '+lcTable+'.'+laFields(lnI,1)+' '

   lcUpdatableFieldList=lcUpdatableFieldList+;
IIF(EMPTY(lcUpdatableFieldList),'',', ')+;
      laFields(lnI,1)

ENDFOR
```

```
DO CASE
   CASE ! CURSORSETPROP("Tables",lcTable)
   CASE ! CURSORSETPROP("UpdateNameList",lcUpdateNameList)
   CASE ! CURSORSETPROP("KeyFieldList",lcPrimaryKey)
   CASE ! CURSORSETPROP("UpdatableFieldList",lcUpdatableFieldList)
   CASE ! CURSORSETPROP("SendUpdates",.T.)

   OTHERWISE
      llFormatComplete = .T.
ENDCASE
RETURN llFormatComplete
```

The results of running this expression on SysCodes, one of the framework tables, results in the following string for the UpdatableFieldList:

```
SYSCODEID, SYSCATID, SHORTDESC, LONGDESC, RETURNVAL, RETURNTYPE
```

Here is the generated UpdateNameList for the same table:

```
SYSCODEID SYSCODES.SYSCODEID, SYSCATID SYSCODES.SYSCATID, SHORTDESC
SYSCODES.SHORTDESC, LONGDESC SYSCODES.LONGDESC, RETURNVAL SYSCODES.RETURNVAL,
RETURNTYPE SYSCODES.RETURNTYPE
```

The CursorAdapter class

The CursorAdapter class is new to FoxPro 8.0. This class "knows" how to access remote data and is loaded with "essential ingredients" necessary to work with a variety of data formats. The examples in this book concentrate on ODBC connections to remote data. However, you could apply the same concepts to the other data formats supported by the CursorAdapter.

The essential properties for working with remote data are KeyFieldList, SelectCmd, Tables, UpdatableFieldList, and UpdateNameList. Notice the similarity between these CursorAdapter property names and the parameters passed to the CursorSetProp() function. The values of the properties are identical as well. Rather than using the previous code to generate the values, FoxPro provides a DataEnvironment builder that enables you to visually build the required property values.

One property that does not map directly between the CursorAdapter and the CursorSetProp() function is the SelectCmd property of the CursorAdapter class. The CursorSetProp() equivalent is the "SQL" parameter. However, the SQL value of the underlying cursor is read-only, whereas the SelectCmd is read/write.

The SelectCmd property determines what information is retrieved each time a call is made to the back-end database. The SelectCmd property contains an SQL statement. For example, the following value for SelectCmd would return all the records from the SysCodes table:

```
SELECT * From SysCodes
```

You call the CursorFill() method of the CursorAdapter class to actually submit the request to the back end.

The CursorAdapter class does not connect to the back-end database directly. The numeric connection handle returned by the SQLConnect() or SQLStringConnect() functions is stored in the DataSource property of the cursor. Setting the UseDataSource property of the CursorAdapter to True indicates that the CursorAdapter obtains the connection handle from the data environment. In the next chapter I'll explain how the new DataEnvironment class manages the connection process.

MyCursorAdapter

Like the native Cursor class, the CursorAdapter class does not provide an object-oriented interface to common data methods. The design objective for MyCursorAdapter is to develop an interface that is similar to MyCursor. In fact, most FoxPro commands and functions work regardless of whether the cursor contains remote or local data. Therefore, most of the commands and methods for MyCursorAdapter are identical to those for MyCursor.

For example, MyCursor.New() inserts a new record into a cursor and assigns a primary key value. MyCursorAdapter.New() also inserts a record into a cursor and assigns a primary key. MyCursor.Go() accepts a key value and makes that record the current record. MyCursorAdapter.Go() also accepts a key value and makes that the current record.

Maintaining a uniform interface between the two classes makes it easier for the developer to learn how to use the classes. Additionally, the DataEnvironment class developed in the next chapter uses the same code whether you are working with local (MyCursor) or remote (MyCursorAdapter) data.

 The CursorAdapter class has a LOT of functionality that I'm not going to explore here. The purpose of this section is to illustrate one approach to using remote data in a manner similar to the approach illustrated with MyCursor.

Methods

Most of the method code in MyCursorAdapter closely resembles the code presented for MyCursor. To avoid redundancy, the code is not repeated here.

There are a few differences worth noting, however; these are explained in the Requery(), Go(), and Open() sections that follow.

Requery()

Retrieving data from a remote database is controlled by the SelectCmd property and the CursorFill() method. The custom Requery() method gathers information from the class to dynamically build an SQL statement prior to calling the CursorFill() method. This allows me to simulate many of the methods for MyCursor, such as SetFilter(), SetOrder(), and Go().

One other aspect of the CursorAdapter class is that you need to capture the data type of the primary key field. This ensures that the primary key generation works properly. The IF statement ensures that the value is set only once, and is not evaluated as part of each Refresh().

```
*--MyCursorAdapter.Requery()
LOCAL lcPKField
WITH THIS
    .SelectCmd = "Select * "+;
        " from " + ALLTRIM(.TABLES)

    IF ! EMPTY(.FILTER)
        .SelectCmd = .SelectCmd + " Where " + .FILTER
    ENDIF
```

```
    IF ! EMPTY(.ORDER)
        .SelectCmd = .SelectCmd + " order by " +.ORDER
    ENDIF

    .CursorFill()

    IF EMPTY(.cPktype)
        lcPKField  = ALLTRIM(.ALIAS)+"."+ALLTRIM(.KEYFIELDLIST)
        .cPktype = VARTYPE(&lcPKField)
    ENDIF
ENDWITH
```

Go()

The Go() method accepts two parameters: the value to search for and optionally the tag to search against. In MyCursor.Go(), a SEEK() or LOCATE moves the record pointer. MyCursorAdapter.Go translates the parameters into a filter expression and calls Requery() to update the cursor.

The code for MyCursorAdapter.Go() is shown here:

```
*--MyCursorAdapter.Go()
LPARAMETERS tuID,tcTag
*--Build a filter string

*--If a tag is not specified, use the primary key
*) identified in .KEYFIELDLIST
LOCAL lcTag
lcTag = IIF(EMPTY(tcTag),THIS.KEYFIELDLIST, tcTag)

*--Convert to correct datatype (Needed for strings passed for numeric info

DO CASE
    CASE VARTYPE(tuID) = 'N' AND THIS.cPKType='C'
        THIS.FILTER = lcTag + [ = '] + Transform(tuID) + [']

    CASE VARTYPE(tuID) = 'N' AND THIS.cPKType = 'N'
        THIS.FILTER = lcTag + [ = ] + ALLTRIM(STR(tuID))

    CASE VARTYPE(tuID) = 'C' AND THIS.cPKType = 'C'
        THIS.FILTER = lcTag + [ = '] + tuID + [']

    CASE VARTYPE(tuID) = 'C' AND THIS.cPKType = 'N'
        this.Filter = lcTag + [ = ] + ALLTRIM(tuID)

    OTHERWISE
        ASSERT .F. MESSAGE "Unsupported Primary Key Type"
ENDCASE

THIS.REQUERY()
```

Open()

Unlike the Cursor class, you cannot open, or USE, a cursor adapter outside of the data environment. Accordingly, MyCursorAdapter does not have an Open() method.

Summary

In this chapter you have learned to create a consistent, object-oriented approach to working with local and remote data. The approach outlined in this chapter considered buffering strategies; populating primary key values; and adding, updating, and deleting records. It also illustrated some of the key differences between remote and local data.

> Updates and corrections to this chapter can be found on Hentzenwerke's Web site, **www.hentzenwerke.com**. Click "Catalog" and navigate to the page for this book.

Chapter 10
Business Objects

Business objects are the "heart" of an application. In practice, business objects are the classes that hold most of the application developer's code. As you can imagine, a business object must be flexible and easy to use. In this chapter, you will learn how to coordinate the mechanics of reading and writing data (presented in the previous chapter) so that developers can focus on the "fun" part of developing an application, namely the application's logic.

In this chapter you will create a business object, which is a composite class consisting of a data environment and one or more of the cursor objects created in the previous chapter.

This chapter begins with an overview of business objects and how to use them in an application. You will then see how to create a class, MyDataEnvironment, which serves as the "super class" that other developers will use to create their business objects. To be clear, MyFrame does not contain a "Business Object" class per se. The application developer subclasses MyDataEnvironment to create application-specific business objects.

Chapter 11, "Framework Services," includes examples of how to create business objects that work independently of forms, while Chapter 13, "Data Entry Forms," shows how to incorporate business objects and forms.

Business objects defined

A business object is a class that application developers use to represent entities, or things, in an application. The developer adds behavior to the business object that further defines that entity. Examples of entities include buildings, customers, assets, and invoices. An application does not contain entities—only the representation of an entity. For example, an application does not contain a building or the physical piece of paper that is an invoice. Instead, the information representing a building or an invoice is stored in your system. You can ascribe actions to business objects; doing so extends the representation of an object beyond its physical characteristics. For example, a physical invoice cannot print, approve, or e-mail itself, but your software representation of an invoice can do these things.

In a three-tier architecture, a business object is the link between the user interface, such as a FoxPro form, and the back-end database. **Figure 1** shows a conceptual model of that relationship.

Business objects have both an internal and an external representation.

Internally

Internally, the information representing an invoice could be modeled as shown in **Figure 2**. As you can see, business objects can be modeled using cursors and relations. However, a business object is more than an arrangement of tables.

The application developer programs business rules into business objects. These business rules define what constitutes a valid entity and how that entity behaves.

For example, one business rule may be that no single invoice may exceed $10,000. Another may be that the LineDesc field cannot be empty. A final example of a business rule might be that when an invoice is added to the system, a journal entry must be created to record the total amount of the invoice.

Externally

Externally, a business object is defined by the properties and methods it exposes. An invoice object would contain methods related to invoices. Examples of some methods an invoice might contain are shown in **Figure 3**.

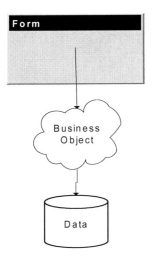

Figure 1. Business objects in a three-tier architecture.

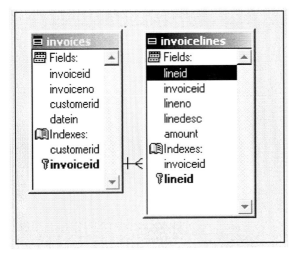

Figure 2. Internal view of a business object.

Figure 3. External view of a business object.

Notice that Figure 3 shows two protected methods, IsValidInvoice() and PostJournalEntry(). Protected methods are not visible to other objects and therefore are not considered part of the external view of a business object.

Whole view

Figure 4 illustrates how you might conceptually think of a business object.

Figure 4 illustrates that a business object is the sum of its internal and external representations. However, it is also more than that.

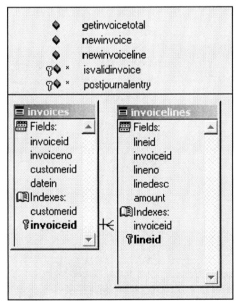

Figure 4. A larger perspective of a business object.

A business object is the central repository for all code related to a particular entity. Using business objects, developers can:

- Map an application's functionality to its data structure.

- Map the data structure of an application to an application's functionality.

- Apply validation code prior to adding information to the database.

- Store special calculations and algorithms.

- Return information about the entity.

  - Use Get() methods.

  - Generate reports.

In short, the Business Object class is responsible for all information coming into or going out of the system for a particular entity.

Creating business objects

By now it should be apparent that much of business object development lies in the hands of those who will use your framework, rather than in your hands as the framework developer. Your job as the framework developer is to provide the tools that are necessary for creating business objects.

In MyFrame, business objects are created using the DataEnvironment class and the cursor classes outlined in the previous chapter. This section illustrates how the data environment is constructed.

Goals for MyDataEnvironment

MyDataEnvironment is the framework class that implements the internal view of the business object. That is, MyDataEnvironment coordinates the Save(), Update(), Undo(), New(), and Delete() methods of its contained cursors.

The ultimate goal of MyDataEnvironment is to provide a class that developers can use to model entities. Included in this section are some additional goals that affect the design of a business object.

Default implementation is generic

The sample invoice object shown in Figure 3 contains two methods for adding a new invoice and invoice line items: NewInvoice() and NewInvoiceLine(). Although the code is not presented, it would be reasonable to assume that these methods result in the creation of an additional record in either the Invoices or InvoiceLines tables.

A more generic approach has to be implemented at the framework level because you don't know which table or tables will be used to model an entity. One method, New(), is provided for adding records to tables. New() accepts a parameter indicating which table should receive the new record. A similar implementation is provided for Undo() and Delete().

Adding a default implementation allows the developer to get a new form or business object "up and running" more quickly. This does not mean the application developer cannot add a New<<Whatever>> method if desired. In fact, you will see several ways to customize business objects later in this chapter and throughout the remainder of the book.

Functional as a form control or standalone

A business object must have the ability to operate on its own or within a form. As such, it must have the ability to optionally create, configure, and operate within a private data environment.

This allows you to use the classes directly. For example, you might access a business object in code as follows:

```
loInvoice = CREATEOBJECT("Invoice")
loInvoice.UseInvoice(4523)
loInvoice.PostTotals()
loInvoice.Print()
```

However, the business object may also be used in a form. When you use a business object in a form, you must defer creation of a private data session to the form.

Developer retains control

This is your first pass at the framework. It is tempting to create a complex validation strategy using collaborative classes or intricate code. Hold off for now. Writing business logic is complicated. Developing a generic approach for handling business logic would probably result in an overly complex approach that still wouldn't properly handle every developer's need.

The approach presented in this chapter is to include many hooks that the developer can take advantage of before, during, or after each step. To make your development efforts as productive as possible, I've provided default implementations for many of the hook methods, but you can override these as your needs dictate. The hooks are clearly marked using the "On," "Is," or "Get" prefixes outlined in Chapter 2, "Project Planning."

Work as middle-tier objects

(Grumble) The business objects in MyFrame are designed to work as middle-tier objects. As such, they cannot communicate directly with the end user. For MyDataEnvironment, that means that messages are not shown to the user, nor are confirmations obtained from the user.

When you need to communicate from a middle-tier object to the user, you do so by passing the message back to the calling routine. Generally, communication from a middle-tier object is restricted to error messages. In MyFrame, error messages are returned from middle-tier objects by passing a message to the error message collection and/or raising an error. Chapter 15, "Error Handling," discusses how this is accomplished, along with error handling in general.

To be clear, labeling MyDataEnvironment as a middle-tier object is a design choice for MyFrame. There is no reason that you cannot display user messages directly from your business objects, if you know in advance that you won't compile them into a DLL or run them on a separate server.

In general, a framework should not assume that nonvisual components won't be compiled as DLLs. Further, making that type of assumption limits the number of ways in which the framework can be used.

MyDataEnvironment

MyDataEnvironment is responsible for applying custom business logic to data and coordinating the Cursor and Relation objects during the data-entry process. In this section I'll present the important aspects of MyDataEnvironment. **Figure 5** shows the entire class definition.

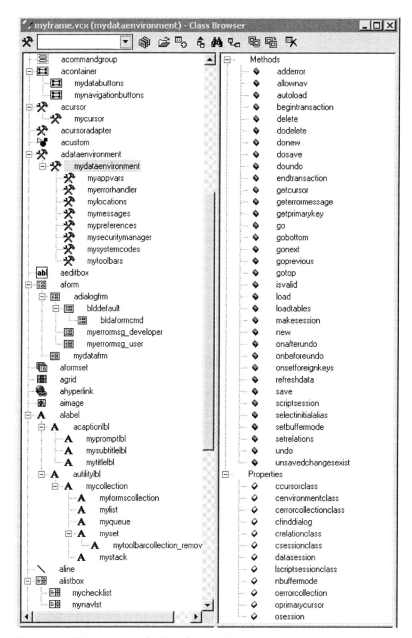

Figure 5. *The class definition for MyDataEnvironment.*

Loading tables

The DataEnvironment class automatically opens your cursors when the AutoOpenTables property is set to True. The process of opening the tables occurs in two steps. First, the BeforeOpenTables() method fires, and then the OpenTables() method fires.

BeforeOpenTables() is a hook method Microsoft provides so that you can insert code before opening the tables. The BeforeOpenTables() method is an ideal place to make any environment settings, such as SET DELETE, and to remove path information from cursors. Setting the environment and optionally creating a separate environment are handled in the MakeSession() method, while path information is removed directly in the BeforeOpenTables() method.

BeforeOpenTables()

The FoxPro Cursor class stores path information in its CursorSource property. Before opening the tables, you can remove the path information by looping through each cursor and replacing the CursorSource with just the file name. However, the Relation class and the new CursorAdapter class do not have a CursorSource property. PEMSTATUS is used to check for the existence of a CursorSource property prior to making the adjustment. Also notice the call to MakeErrorCollection(). I'll illustrate what this method does and how to use it in Chapter 13, "Data Entry Forms."

```
*--MyDataEnvironment.BeforeOpenTables()
THIS.MakeSession()
THIS.MakeErrorCollection()

FOR EACH loObject IN THIS.OBJECTS

    IF PEMSTATUS(loObject, 'CursorSource',5 )
        loObject.CURSORSOURCE = JUSTSTEM(loObject.CURSORSOURCE)
    ENDIF


ENDFOR
```

Creating a separate environment

Forms offer the choice of using a private or public data session by changing the form's DataSession property. I hope by now you are convinced that private data sessions are the way to go and are comfortable with using them.

When creating business objects independently of forms, you must also provide the ability to create private data sessions. The DataEnvironment class does not have a PrivateDatasession property as the form does. To mimic the form, we'll add one, adhering to the convention that a value of 1 indicates to use the default data session, while 2 means to create a separate data session.

When the DataEnvironment is used in conjunction with a form, the MakeSession command instantiates one of the environment classes from Chapter 7, "Environments and Sessions." To review, this class makes all the appropriate environment settings, such as SET DELETED and SET TALK. When the DataEnvironment is created outside of a form, a private data session class is instantiated instead, passing the environment class as a parameter.

```
*--MyDataEnvironment.MakeSession()
WITH THIS
    IF .DATASESSION=1
        *--Let the form control the session, create the environment only
        .oSession=CREATEOBJECT(.cEnvironmentClass)
    ELSE
        *-- Private
        .oSession=CREATEOBJECT(.cSessionClass, .cEnvironmentClass)
        SET DATASESSION TO .oSession.DATASESSIONID
    ENDIF
ENDWITH
```

Saving data

Getting the data structure of an application correct is probably the single most important aspect of building a data-based application. However, even the best data model is meaningless if the quality of the information it contains is erroneous.

The Save() method is a template method that coordinates the application of business rules, transactions, and saving data.

Two hook methods are provided for the developer to save data. IsValid() is an empty hook method that the developer can use to validate data before a transaction starts. If the data is valid, a transaction is started. Another hook method, OnBeforeSave(), offers the developer a chance to take action once the transaction has started. Assuming both hooks complete successfully, the DoSave() method is called.

If DoSave() completes successfully, the transaction ends and the data is refreshed. If DoSave() is not successful, the transaction ends and a value of False is returned.

Here's the code:

```
*-- MyDataEnvironment.Save()
LOCAL llSaveSuccessful, lnSaveLoc
WITH THIS
    lnSaveLoc=SELECT()

    .oErrorCollection.CLEAR()

    IF .isValid()

        .BeginTransaction()
        IF .OnBeforeSave()
            llSaveSuccessful = .DoSave()
            .OnAfterSave()
        ELSE
            llSaveSuccessful=.F.
        ENDIF
        .EndTransaction(llSaveSuccessful)

    ENDIF

    IF llSaveSuccessful
        .RefreshData()
    ENDIF
```

```
EndWith

SELECT(lnSaveLoc)

RETURN llSaveSuccessful
```

The DoSave() method calls the Save() method for each cursor in MyDataEnvironment. Notice the use of the custom function IsType() to check that the cursor object is a framework cursor or a framework CursorAdapter. The code for the IsType() function is shown later in this section.

```
*--DoSave()
LOCAL llSaveSuccessful
llSaveSuccessful = .T.

FOR EACH loObject IN THIS.OBJECTS
        IF IsType(loObject,"MyCursor") or IsType(loObject, "MyCursorAdapter")
            llSaveSuccessful = loObject.SAVE()
            IF ! llSaveSuccessful
                EXIT
            ENDIF
        ENDIF
ENDFOR

RETURN llSaveSuccessful
```

The DoSave() method is an example of generic code that may not be appropriate in all situations. In particular, if the order in which cursors are saved is an issue, this code may not work for you. Consider the invoice example shown earlier. If you choose to enforce referential integrity at the database level, you should commit to the Invoices table before committing to the InvoiceLines table to ensure that the header (parent) record is added to the database before the child records are added.

In cases where the order of the save is important, you can overwrite the DoSave() method. For example, to save the Invoices table before saving the InvoiceLines table, you could overwrite the DoSave() method as follows:

```
*--An example of how to overwrite MyDataEnvironment.DoSave() method
IF THIS.oInvoices.Save() and THIS.oInvoiceLines.Save()
        RETURN .T.
ELSE
        RETURN .F.
ENDIF
```

The Visual FoxPro function ACLASS() accepts an object and creates an array that includes the name of a class and the classes from which that object inherits. The custom function IsType() accepts two parameters: an object reference and the name of a class. The IsType() function scans the array created by ACLASS() and returns a logical value that indicates whether the class is contained in the array. Following is the IsType() function.

```
*--IsType() located in GenProc.prg
FUNCTION IsType(toClass, tcType)
    LOCAL ARRAY laClasses[1]
    ACLASS(laClasses,toClass)
    lnFound = ASCAN(laClasses,tcType,-1,-1,-1,15)
    RETURN lnFound>0
ENDFUNC
```

Using the Save() hook methods

The IsValid() and OnAfterSave() methods are empty hook methods. However, they are particularly significant.

In a large application, you may have dozens or even hundreds of business objects. The intent of these methods is to promote consistency throughout an application. So, if you want to know how something gets validated, look in IsValid(). If a business object has subsequent postings, the code to make the posting will most likely be found in the OnAfterSave() method.

For example, assume you created a second business object, GL, which "knows" how to write journal entries to a general ledger. The IsValid() and OnAfterSave() methods might appear as follows for the Invoices business object.

```
*--Sample Code
*--Invoice Business Object - IsValid()
RETURN ! EMPTY(CustNo)

*--Invoice Business Object - OnAfterSave()
LOCAL loGL
loGL = CREATEOBJECT("GL")
loGL.PostJournalEntry(<<Parameters>>)
RETURN loGL.Save()
```

If the GL business object's Save() method fails for any reason, a value of False is returned from Invoices.OnAfterSave(), which causes the transaction to ROLLBACK. In other words, the invoice is not updated if the appropriate journal entries cannot be created.

Recording validation errors

MyDataEnvironment contains a collection class for collecting error information. Two methods, AddError() and GetErrorMessage(), are provided to add and retrieve information from the Error collection. The collection class is the MyQueue class presented in Chapter 8, "Collections."

The MyDataEnvironment, MyCursor, and MyCursorAdapter classes each contain an IsValid() method in which the developer can insert validation code. From each of these methods you can call the AddError() method of MyDataEnvironment to add validation errors.

AddError()

Each new error is simply added to the Error collection as follows:

```
*--MyDataEnvironment.AddError()
LPARAMETERS tcError,tcAlias, tcField
IF VARTYPE(tcError) = 'C'
    lnRow = THIS.oErrorCollection.PUSH(tcError)
    THIS.oErrorCollection.ADATA[lnRow,2] = tcAlias
    THIS.oErrorCollection.ADATA[lnRow,3] = tcField
ENDIF
```

Here's an example of how to validate information from the MyCursor or MyCursorAdapter classes and pass the message back to the end user. This example tests whether the LastName field is empty. If so, it adds a message, the name of the table, and the name of the field to the Error collection.

```
*--Sample Validation Code for MyCursor.IsValid()
IF EMPTY(Appvars.appvarid)
    THIS.PARENT.AddError("A 'LastName' is needed.","Employees","LastName")
    RETURN .F.
ENDIF
```

GetErrorMessage()
The GetErrorMessage() method is a hook method for the end developer. The default implementation (shown here) constructs an error message by assembling the text of each error message into a string.

```
*--MyDataFrm.GetErrorMessage()
LOCAL lnI, lcReturn

lcReturn = "ERROR:"
THIS.oEerrorCollection.GOFIRST()

FOR lnI = 1 TO THIS.oErrorCollection.GetCount()
    lcReturn = lcReturn + THIS.oerrorCollection.ADATA[lnI,1]
ENDFOR

RETURN lcReturn
```

In Chapter 13, "Data Entry Forms," you'll see that the table and field names are used by the data entry form to alert the user to the control in which the error occurred.

Adding records
The New() method is a template method. Similar to the Save() method, New() directs the action. Notice that the Error collection is cleared, ensuring that any errors that occur were generated while adding the new record. Additionally, the OnBeforeNew() and OnAfterNew() hook methods offer the application developer more control when adding new records.

```
*--MyDataEnvironment.New()
LPARAMETERS tcAlias
LOCAL luPK

THIS.oErrorCollection.CLEAR()

IF THIS.OnBeforeNew()
      luPK = this.DoNew(tcAlias)
      this.OnAfterNew()
ENDIF

RETURN luPK
```

The DoNew() method accepts a parameter indicating which table should be INSERTed INTO. If an alias is not supplied, the alias in cInitialSelectedAlias is used by default. OnNew()

doesn't do the insertion directly. Instead it finds the cursor object responsible for controlling the table and calls its New() method.

```
*--MyDataEnvironment.DoNew()
LPARAMETERS tcAlias
LOCAL lcAlias, loCursor AS MyCursor, luNewPrimaryKey
luNewPrimaryKey = .NULL.

lcAlias = IIF(EMPTY(tcAlias),THIS.cInitialSelectedAlias,tcAlias)
loCursor = THIS.GetCursor(lcAlias)
IF VARTYPE(loCursor) = 'O'
   luNewPrimaryKey = loCursor.New()
ENDIF
RETURN luNewPrimaryKey
```

 The code for the methods Go(), Undo(), and Delete() is not shown because they are similar to the New() method.

Finding a cursor

The GetCursor() method accepts an alias as a parameter, and then loops through the cursors it contains until it finds the cursor tied to the specified alias. If an object is found, it is returned to the calling program.

```
*--MyDataEnvironment.GetCursor()
LPARAMETERS tcAlias
LOCAL loObject AS MyCursor, loReturnObject AS MyCursor
loReturnObject = .NULL.

FOR EACH loObject IN THIS.OBJECTS
   IF IsType(loObject ,"MyCursor")
      IF UPPER(ALLTRIM(loObject.cAlias)) == UPPER(ALLTRIM(tcAlias))
         loReturnObject = loObject
         EXIT
      ENDIF
   ENDIF
ENDFOR
RETURN loReturnObject
```

Connecting to remote data

You must make a connection to the back-end database when working with remote data. The FoxPro DataEnvironment Builder automatically writes the code to make the connection and inserts it into the BeforeOpenTables() method of the DataEnvironment class. **Figure 6** illustrates how to connect to an SQL database using a connection string.

The builder generates code that uses the SQLStringConnect() method to establish a connection with the database. The connection handle is stored in the DataSource property of the DataEnvironment class. Here's a look at the generated code that is inserted into the BeforeOpenTables() method.

```
*** Select connection code: DO NOT REMOVE
set multilocks on
***<DataSource>
This.DataSource = sqlstringconnect([dsn=MyFrame;])
***</DataSource>
*** End of Select connection code: DO NOT REMOVE
```

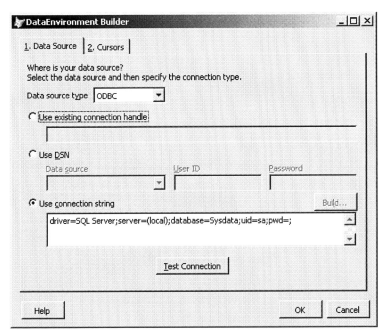

Figure 6*. The DataEnvironment Builder.*

The DataEnvironment class does not open the tables directly. Instead, it uses the CursorAdapter class to retrieve data from a back-end database. Setting the CursorAdapter's UseDataSource property to True causes the CursorAdapter to use the DataEnvironment's connection handle (generated by the previous code) to connect with data.

 In Chapter 9, "Cursor and CursorAdapter," I outlined the mechanics for working with remote data in the section titled "Connecting to remote data."

I have a few issues with the generated code. First, it doesn't contain the DODEFAULT() function. As a result, inherited code will never run. As illustrated earlier in the chapter, the MyCursor class sets its environment from the BeforeOpenTables() method.

Second, the connection string is hard coded into the generated code. What if you had an application with 40 forms and you needed to change the connection string? You'd have to open each form to make the change.

Third, each instance of the DataEnvironment creates its own connection.

A better solution is to create a separate method that is responsible for creating the connection. The original BeforeOpenTables() method has been modified to accommodate remote data as follows:

```
*--MyDataEnvironment.BeforeOpenTables()
LOCAL llConectionEstablished
WITH THIS
    .MakeErrorCollection()
    .MakeSession()


    FOR EACH loObject IN .OBJECTS

        *-- Remove path information from cursor objects
        IF PEMSTATUS(loObject, 'CursorSource',5 )
            loObject.CURSORSOURCE = JUSTSTEM(loObject.CURSORSOURCE)
        ENDIF

        *--Establish a connection once the first
        *) CursorAdapter is identified
        IF !llConectionEstablished AND istype(loObject,'MyCursorAdapter')
            .makeconnection()
            llConectionEstablished = .T.
        ENDIF

    ENDFOR

ENDWITH
```

Many client/server applications use data from only one database. Therefore, that single connection can often be made once, and used for the span of the application. To create the connection at the application level, a MakeConnection() method has been added to the application class as shown here. This allows you to set the connection string once by setting the cConnectionString property.

```
*-- aApplication.MakeConnection()
IF THIS.nConnection=0 AND ! EMPTY(this.cConnectionString)
    THIS.nConnection = SQLSTRINGCONNECT(THIS.cConnectionString)
ENDIF
RETURN THIS.nConnection
```

The default behavior of the DataEnvironment's MakeConnection() method is to call the MakeConnection() method of the application class as follows:

```
*--MyDataEnvironment.MakeConnetion()
IF VARTYPE(goApp) = "O"
    THIS.DATASOURCE=goApp.MakeConnection()
ENDIF
```

This approach is better because you need to change the connection string in only one place (the application object) by default, and you retain the ability to overwrite the MakeConnection() method at the DataEnvironment level.

Summary

In this chapter, you learned how to tailor FoxPro's DataEnvironment class to serve as the template for your business objects. The MyDataEnvironment class developed in this chapter standardizes the approach for working with data while giving the application developer flexibility and control of the entire process.

The next chapter, "Framework Services," illustrates how to use MyDataEnvironment to create nonvisual business objects.

Updates and corrections to this chapter can be found on Hentzenwerke's Web site, **www.hentzenwerke.com**. Click "Catalog" and navigate to the page for this book.

Chapter 11
Framework Services

A framework service is the name I use to refer to classes that exist to service one or more classes in the framework. This chapter looks at some of those services and how they are constructed.

Some features are needed throughout the framework and are useful to more than one class. Examples include remembering object locations and storing user preferences. This chapter focuses on adding features that are useful throughout the framework.

Each framework service presented here inherits from the MyDataEnvironment class developed in Chapter 10, "Business Objects." Framework services illustrated in this chapter are all examples of using the data environment without the form. The examples include an application variable server (myAppVars), a system codes manager (mySystemCodes), a preference manager (myPreferences), a messaging manager (myMessages), and an object location manager (myLocations).

The principles used in this chapter serve as the basis for other framework services. The toolbar manager (Chapter 14), error handler (Chapter 15), and security module (Chapter 16) are each constructed and implemented in a manner similar to the one presented in this chapter. However, these services are more complicated and/or so closely integrated to a particular area of the framework that they are explained in their own chapters.

Framework services can be called from anywhere in the application. That is, a framework service can be invoked from forms, report expressions, methods, menus, stored procedures, and so on.

Here are the characteristics that are common to framework services:

- Not impacted by the calling environment

- Have no impact on the calling environment

- Do not interact with the end user

- Always available

At the end of the chapter, I will review a way to instantiate your framework services once, at the beginning of the application, so they are available throughout the life of the application.

Message services

The framework displays several default messages to the end user. These messages are very generic, such as "Are you sure?", "Press OK to Continue," and so on. Developers and system administrators may want to change the text of a message or how it appears to the user.

The messaging service displays messages using the MessageBox() function by default. However, you can substitute your own class to display the message, as long as it returns a value consistent with the values returned by the MessageBox() function.

Using a data-driven approach (see Chapter 4, "Techniques for Flexibility") for messaging allows system administrators to alter messages at run time, without having to recompile the application. **Figure 1** shows a possible table structure and an example of the data that a record might contain. The data is stored in a table named Messages. **Table 1** presents an example of the data that would go into the table pictured in Figure 1.

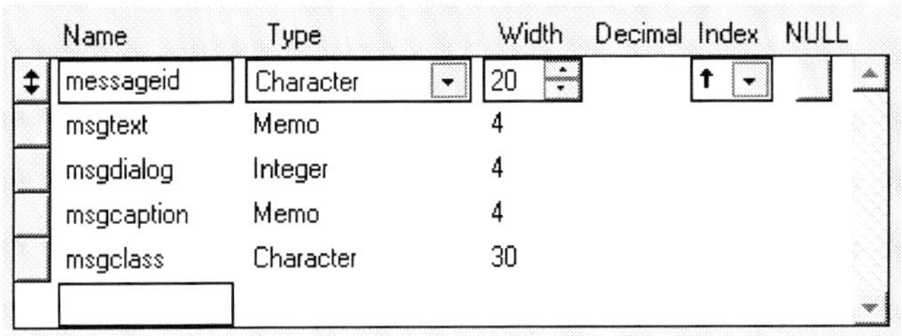

Figure 1. The Messages table.

Table 1. Data that might appear in the Messages table from Figure 1.

Name	Data
MessageID	"ConfirmDelete"
MsgText	"Are you sure you want to delete this record?"
MsgDialog	36 && Yes/No buttons with a question mark
MsgCaption	"Delete Confirmation"
MsgClass	""

Creating the class

The class MyMessages is the first example of how to use a data object, so I'll walk you through the process step by step. The following steps illustrate how to create the class MyMessages.

1. Subclass MyDataEnvironment.

   To create a business object, subclass MyDataEnvironment and name it MyMessages.

2. Add cursor objects.

   Add an instance of MyCursor to MyMessages and name it "oMessages."

   To add an instance, you can select the MyCursor class from the MyFrame project manager and then drag it and drop it onto the MyMessages Class Designer surface.

3. Set the cursor properties.

   Set the CursorSource and Alias properties to "Messages," the cPKType to "C," and the cPrimaryKey to "MessageID."

   By setting the CursorSource and Alias properties, you are indicating that the cursor will open the Messages table. It is not required that you set the cPKType and cPrimaryKey properties if you have specified a primary index for the table.

In Chapter 13, "Data Entry Forms," I will illustrate how you can complete this process programmatically as you build data entry forms.

The property sheet should appear similar to **Figure 2**.

 Figure 2 was prepared by setting the property sheet view to "Non-default properties only."

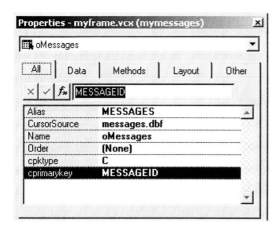

Figure 2. The oMessages as seen in the property sheet.

Add validation
The first piece of code to add is the validation code. Placing the following code in MyMessages.Valid() ensures that the MsgText field is not left empty.

```
*--MyMessages.IsValid()
IF EMPTY(MESSAGES.msgtext)
    THIS.AddError("Message Text is Required!.","Messages","MsgText")
    RETURN .F.
ENDIF
```

Or, you could place similar code in the IsValid() method of the cursor, oMessage.

```
*--MyMessages.oMessage.IsValid()
IF EMPTY(MESSAGES.msgtext)
    THIS.PARENT.AddError("Message Text is Required!","Messages","MsgText")
    RETURN .F.
ENDIF
```

Add behavior
To display the message, add a custom method, ShowMessage(), to MyMessages. The ShowMessage() function accepts the MessageID as a parameter and uses the cursor object, oMessages, to retrieve values from the Messages table. The message is then displayed to the user using the MessageBox() function or a custom display class. Here's the code:

```
*--MyMessages.ShowMessage()
LPARAMETERS tcMessage

LOCAL lnReturn
lnReturn = 0
WITH THIS.oMessages

    IF .GO(tcMessage)

        lcMsgText = .FIELD("MsgText")
        lnDialog  = .FIELD("MsgDialog")
        lcCaption = .FIELD("MsgCaption")

        IF EMPTY(.FIELD("msgclass"))
            lnReturn = MESSAGEBOX( lcMsgText, lnDialog, lcCaption )
        ELSE
            loMsgForm = CREATEOBJECT(.FIELD("MsgClass"))
            lnReturn = loMsgForm.ShowMessage( lcMsgText, lnDialog, lcCaption )
        ENDIF
    ENDIF

ENDWITH

RETURN lnReturn
```

Using the Message class

You can use the Message class to display a message from anywhere in your application as follows:

```
*--Example: Using the message class
loMessage = CREATEOBJECT("MyMessages")
loMessage.Showmessage("ConfirmChanges")
```

You can perform message administration by using the form shown in **Figure 3**. It is available by selecting MyFrame | Messages from the menu provided with the source code accompanying this book.

Application Variables Server (AppVars)

Every application has some values that are relatively constant but may change over time. As mentioned in Chapter 4, "Techniques for Flexibility," you have several options to choose from when deciding how to account for this type of data in your applications. One of the approaches was a "data-driven" approach. A data-driven approach allows you to change the value of application constants without having to recompile the application. The information is stored in a table, AppVars.dbf.

The purpose of the table is to store application variables, or constants, such as Company_Name, and corresponding return values. The AppVars table contains four fields. AppVarID is the primary key for the table, and it contains the application variable. The return value is stored in a memo field, ReturnVal. Because the return value can be of any data type, the ReturnType field indicates the data type of the value in the ReturnVal field. There is also an About field where you can store information about a particular application variable. The structure of the AppVars table is shown in **Figure 4**.

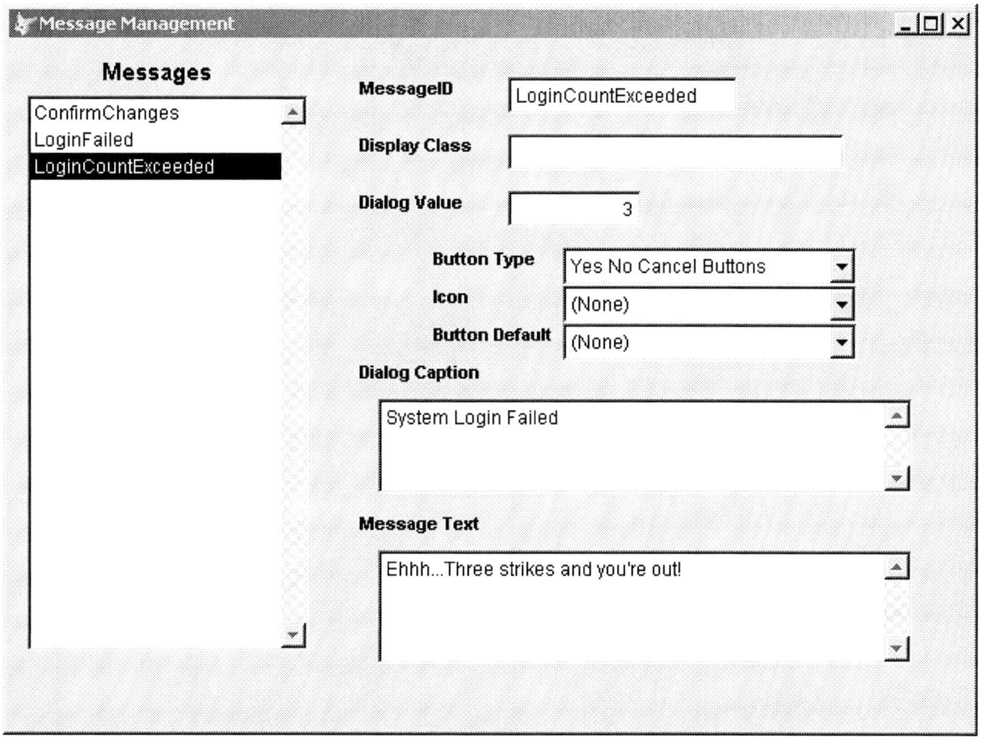

***Figure 3**. The messaging administration form.*

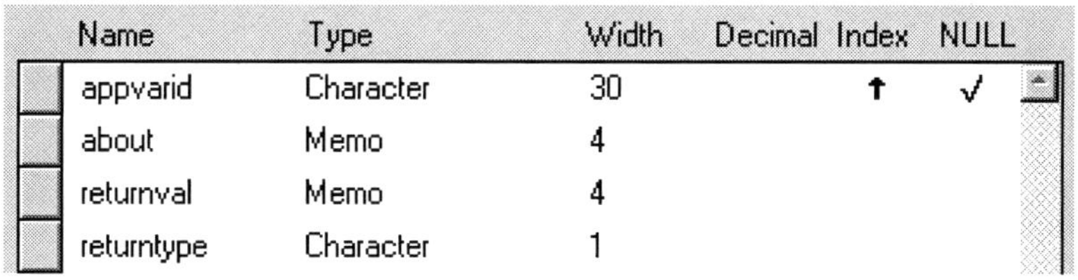

Name	Type	Width	Decimal	Index	NULL
appvarid	Character	30		↑	√
about	Memo	4			
returnval	Memo	4			
returntype	Character	1			

***Figure 4**. The structure of the AppVars table.*

The class MyAppVars is a subclass of MyDataEnvironment. An instance of MyCursor, named oAppVars, is added to access the AppVars table. One method, GetAppVars(), accepts the AppVarID as a parameter and returns the value in the ReturnVal field. Notice that the Str2Expr function is used to convert the return value into its proper data type.

```
*--MyAppVars.GetAppVar()
LPARAMETERS tcAppvar
LOCAL rsAppvars
luReturn = .NULL.
```

```
IF THIS.oAppVars.GO(tcAppvar)
    rsAppvars= THIS.oAppVars.GetCurrentRecord()
    luReturn = Str2Exp(rsAppvars.ReturnVal,rsAppvars.ReturnType)
ENDIF
RETURN luReturn
```

A maintenance form, MyAppVars.scx, as shown in **Figure 5**, allows you to add or remove your own application variables. You can access this form by selecting MyFrame/AppVariables from the menu provided with the source code accompanying this book.

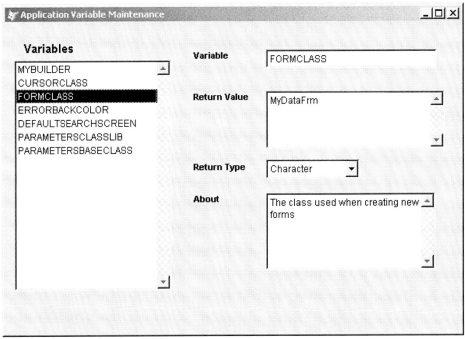

Figure 5. The Application Variable Maintenance form.

System codes

System codes and statuses are common elements in many applications. For example, in a purchasing system, a purchase order may be in any one of several statuses: "Unapproved," "Approved," "Purchased," or "Paid." In a large system, there might be dozens or even hundreds of codes to maintain. Creating a separate table for each code could be a maintenance nightmare.

MyFrame includes a framework service of system codes, which removes the need for many separate "codes" tables. System codes are modeled using two tables: SysCats and SysCodes. SysCats is the parent table that describes the type of code represented—for example, Purchase Order Status, Employee Status, and so on.

The SysCodes table stores the actual codes available for each category. Each system code in MyFrame may be described using a short or a long description. Continuing with the purchase order example, some reports may display the abbreviation "AP" rather than the full description "Approved." Two other fields, ReturnVal and ReturnType, allow you to associate a value with a system code. For example, an error status of "Normal" may contain one set of e-mail addresses, while an error status of "Danger" may contain another.

Sometimes a system code is no longer valid. For example, a change in business rules might dictate that purchases no longer need approval before orders are placed. In that case, "Unapproved" would no longer be a valid selection. However, you cannot just delete the entry, because purchases placed under the old rules still might appear in reports. Placing a value of .T. in the SCObsolete field indicates that a user cannot select the option in a combo box, but leaves the value in the table for reporting purposes.

Finally, a sort code enables you to sort codes non-alphabetically. For example, you may be required to sort AP codes as follows: "Unapproved, Approved, Purchased, and Paid." Placing a value of 1, 2, 3, and 4 in the Sort field enables you to sort the report properly.

The structure of the SysCodes table is shown in **Figure 6**.

Name	Type	Width	Decimal	Index	NULL
syscodeid	Character	10		↑	
syscatid	Character	10		↑	
shortdesc	Character	10			
longdesc	Character	30			
returnval	Memo	4			
returntype	Character	2			
scobsolete	Logical	1			

Figure 6. *The structure of the SysCodes table.*

MyFrame uses a combo box to display the system codes, a business object to process requests for system codes, and a maintenance screen to ... well ... maintain the system codes. The business object is MySystemCodes. It contains two instances of MyCursor named oSysCats and oSysCodes. **Figure 7** shows the MySysCodes class as seen in the Form Designer.

The business object is responsible for retrieving information from the SysCodes table and populating a combo box with the appropriate system codes. The retrieval methods are GetLongDesc(), GetShortDesc(), and GetReturnValue(). So for example, the GetShortDesc() method accepts the primary key of the SysCodes table, SysCodeID, as a parameter and returns the value in the ShortDesc field as follows:

```
*--MySysCodes.GetShortDesc()
LPARAMETERS tcSysCodeID

LOCAL luReturn
luReturn = ""
IF THIS.oSysCodes.GO(tcSysCodeID)
    luReturn = THIS.oSysCodes.FIELD("ShortDesc")
ENDIF

RETURN luReturn
```

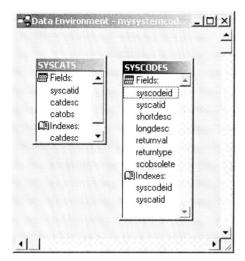

Figure 7. *The SysCodes business object as seen in the Form Designer.*

This type of functionality is very helpful when writing reports. Again, consider the purchase-order codes. Further, assume that you have a table, poheader, with a field, pocode. Retrieving the value of the purchase-order code can be problematic. With only one code, it is hard to imagine how that can be so. However, when you have many different codes in the same table, queries can become complex or slow, or they can require procedural programming to get the correct values to display properly on the report. However, with the SysCodes "Server," the following code snippet in a report will return the proper value without "special programming."

```
goSysCodes.GetShortDesc(poHeader.poCode)
```

The System Codes business object is also responsible for "loading" the combo boxes. In effect, this is a system codes server. The combo box passes a reference to itself as a parameter to the System Code's Populate() method.

To create the combo box class, I subclassed MyDataEntryCbo and named it MySysCodesCbo. Because the class inherits from MyDataEntryCbo, it inherits the improved data-binding capabilities of that class as presented in Chapter 6, "Creating a Class Library." The inheritance hierarchy is shown in **Figure 8**.

The MySysCodesCbo class has a custom property cFieldList that contains the fields displayed from the SysCodes table. Another custom property, cOrder, determines the display order for the values presented in the combo box. And a third, lAllowNone, indicates whether the user can select "None" as an option. The native ColumnWidths property controls the widths of the columns displayed.

The builder for this class, shown in **Figure 9**, helps illustrate the important properties of the combo box as well as demonstrates how the System Codes combo boxes are used. Each of the combo boxes on the builder form is an instance of mySysCodesCbo. The lAllowNone property of the Security Item combo is set to True. The Default Setting combo has cFieldList and cOrder values of "ShortDesc, LongDesc," lAllowNone = .T. and column widths of 50 and 150.

Figure 8. *The inheritance hierarchy for MySysCodesCbo.*

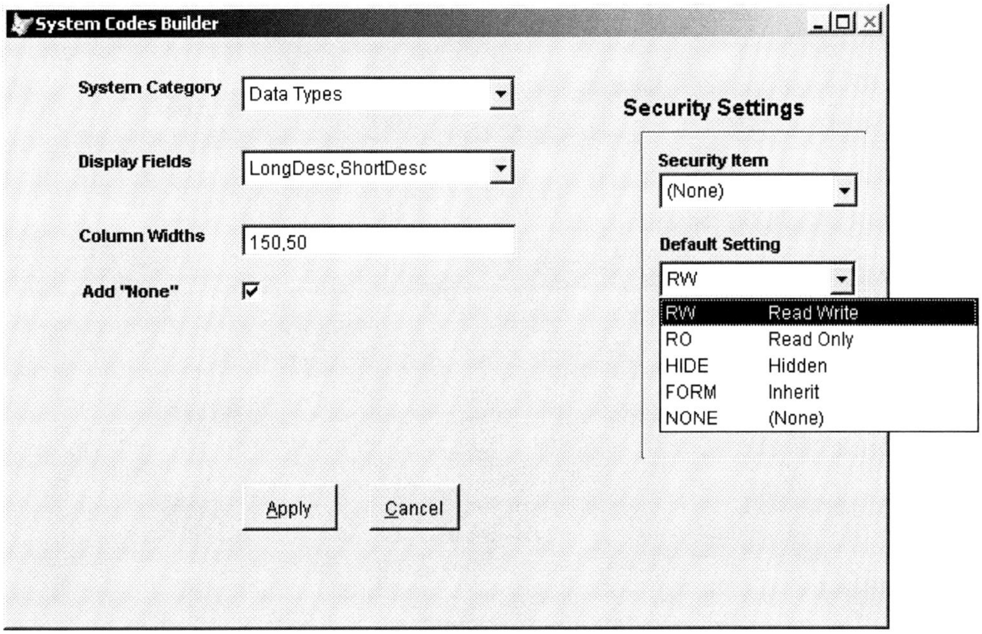

Figure 9. *The builder for MySysCodesCbo.*

Internally, the System Codes combo uses a property array, aData[], to hold the codes that are displayed. The RowSource is set to "THIS.aData" and the RowSourceType = 5 (Array).

The System Codes combo box passes itself to the Populate() method of MySysCodes. The Populate() method then reads the relevant properties of the combo box and populates the aData[] array. Additionally, if the lAllowNone property contains a value of .T., an additional row is added to the results of the query. Here are the relevant portions of the Populate() method.

```
*--MySystemCodes.Populate()
LPARAMETERS toCombo AS mySysCodesCbo

WITH toCombo

    lcFieldList = .cFieldList + ', syscodeid'
    lcOrder = IIF(EMPTY(.cOrder),.cFieldList,.cOrder)

    lcCmd = "SELECT IIF(scobsolete,'\','')+"+ lcFieldList +" FROM syscodes "+;
        " Where SysCatID = '"+ .syscatid +"'"+;
        " ORDER BY " + lcOrder +;
        " INTO ARRAY .aData"
```

```
IF .lAllowNone

    lnCols = ALEN(.ADATA,2)
    lnRows = ALEN(.ADATA,1)+1
    DIMENSION .ADATA[lnRows,lnCols]

    AINS(.ADATA,1)
    FOR lnI = 1 TO ALEN(.ADATA,2)
        .ADATA[1,lnI] = ''
    ENDFOR
    .ADATA[1,1] = "--"
    .NUMBEROFELEMENTS = lnRows
ELSE
    .NUMBEROFELEMENTS = ALEN(.ADATA,1)+1
ENDIF

ENDWITH
```

Remembering object locations

Users will appreciate the ability to visually arrange their most commonly used forms and toolbars in a way that best suits their needs. As a developer, you are probably familiar with the "need" to have the command window, property sheet, and so on, appear exactly where you last placed them.

The same behavior may be required of form controls. Consider a scheduling application where the scheduler can adjust the schedule by moving controls from one location to another.

Each object must be uniquely identifiable in order to save and restore its location. But how can you uniquely identify each control in an application? I guess you could require the developer to assign a unique value to each control, but that would be extremely time-consuming, error-prone, and unacceptable to most developers.

A second alternative, and the one I use in this framework, is to uniquely identify each object based on its position within the containership hierarchy. For example, a button on a page might have the following hierarchy: "Form1.Pageframe1.Page1.cmdSave." However, it is possible to have two Form1's in an application, with each having a page frame and a cmdSave button. (In fact, in a properly designed application, this possibility is likely.) To use the containership hierarchy as an identifier, you must uniquely name each form in your application. For example, Customers.Pageframe1.Page1.cmdSave, or Employees.Pageframe1.Page1.cmdSave.

Multi-user environments offer another wrinkle. Each control must be uniquely identifiable for each user as well. For example, Tom may prefer to see the customer screen in the top left corner, while Jerry may prefer the screen to appear on the right. While you could store the control's data on the user's computer, avoiding the need to accommodate multiple users, all users would lose their settings if they logged in from a different machine.

To uniquely identify each control, I use the combination of the value returned from SYS(1270) and the User ID. FoxPro's SYS(1272) function returns the hierarchy for a specified object. These values, along with the location information, are stored in a single table, Locations.dbf. **Table 2** shows the structure of this table.

***Table 2**. The structure of Locations.dbf.*

Field	Field Name	Type	Width
1	LOCATIONID	Character	10
2	OBJECTID	Memo	4
3	USERID	Integer	4
4	NTOP	Integer	4
5	NLEFT	Integer	4
6	NWIDTH	Integer	4
7	NHEIGHT	Integer	4
8	NDOCKING	Integer	4

Notice that ObjectID is a memo field because SYS(1272) could return a string longer than 100 characters, violating the maximum length for an index. The nDocking field stores the docking status for toolbars. Toolbars have a docking status that determines the location of a toolbar in addition to its Top, Left, Width, and Height properties.

I have created a class, MyLocations, to save and retrieve object location information. To do this, I subclassed MyDataEnvironment, added an instance of MyCursor named oLocations, and set its Alias property to "Locations."

MyLocations "knows" how to find an object in the table and either save or retrieve its locations. The four key methods for this class are GetObjectName(), which returns the name of the object; LocateObject(), which identifies whether this is a new object; SaveLoc(), which writes the control's values to the database; and GetLoc(), which updates the controls with the values in the database.

The GetObjectName() method serves as a wrapper around SYS(1272), returning the name of the object. Creating a separate method accomplishes two objectives. First, GetObjectName is called from more than one place. Providing a separate method avoids duplication of code. In the event that you choose not to use SYS(1272), you would be required to change code only in the GetObjectName() method, rather than in every place the call is made. The second reason is that SYS(1272) does not clearly convey to the reader what the function is being used for. The Visual FoxPro Help file states, "Returns the object hierarchy for a specified object." A developer reading this line of code and subsequently checking the Help file would still have no idea why you are using SYS(1272). Here's the code.

```
*--MyLocations.GetObjectName()
LPARAMETERS toObject
RETURN SYS( 1272,toObject )
```

The LocateObject() method finds the object in the table. The LOCATE command is used because indexes are not allowed on memo fields. The code is shown here.

```
*--MyLocations.LocateObject()
LPARAMETERS toObject
LOCAL lcName, lnUserID

lcName = THIS.GetObjectName( toObject )
lnUserID = goApp.GetUserID()
LOCATE FOR ObjectID = lcName AND USERID = lnUserID
RETURN FOUND()
```

To save an object's location information, a call is made to LocateObject(). If the record is not found, a new one is added as shown here:

```
*--MyLocations.SaveLoc()
LPARAMETERS toObject
LOCAL rsLocations

IF ! THIS.LocateObject( toObject )
    THIS.oLocations.New()
ENDIF

rsLocations = THIS.oLocations.GetCurrentRecord()

WITH rsLocations
    .nTop = toObject.TOP
    .nHeight = toObject.HEIGHT
    .nWidth = toObject.WIDTH
    .nleft = toObject.LEFT
    .USERID = goApp.GetUserID()
    .ObjectID = THIS.GetObjectName( toObject )
    IF UPPER(ALLTRIM( toObject.BASECLASS )) = 'TOOLBAR'
        .nDocking = toObject.DOCKPOSITION
    ENDIF
ENDWITH

THIS.oLocations.setcurrentrecord( rsLocations )
THIS.SAVE()
```

The GetLoc() method retrieves the object's location information and writes it to the appropriate control properties as follows:

```
*--MyLocations.GetLoc()
LPARAMETERS toObject AS TOOLBAR

IF THIS.LocateObject( toObject )
    toObject.TOP = nTop
    toObject.LEFT = nleft
    toObject.HEIGHT = nHeight
    toObject.WIDTH = nWidth

    IF UPPER(ALLTRIM(toObject.BASECLASS)) = "TOOLBAR"
        toObject.DOCK(nDocking)
    ENDIF

ENDIF
```

Saving preferences

Saving an object's location, as outlined in the previous section, is a specialized case of saving property values. However, there are occasions when users may want to set specific property values, such as BackColor, and have that setting remain in effect each time they run the application. For example, if a user wants to change the BackColor property of a form from grey to red, that is a preference for that user.

A generic approach to saving property values is to store the value of each property in a separate record. As described in the section "Remembering object locations," each object must be uniquely identifiable. However, in that section all the values were of integer data type; here, storing and retrieving property values requires that you can accommodate varying data types. **Figure 10** shows the table structure for storing object preferences. As you can see, each property value is stored as a character data type, while its data type is stored in the field PropType.

	prefid	Character	10	↑	▲
	objname	Character	40	↑	
	userid	Integer	4	↑	
	propname	Character	40	↑	
	proptype	Character	1		
	propval	Character	40		▼

Figure 10. *The table structure for storing property values, Prefs.dbf.*

MyPreferences is the name of the class used to save and retrieve data from Prefs.dbf. MyPreferences is a subclass of MyDataEnvironment and contains an instance of MyCursor linked to Prefs.dbf.

MyPreferences contains three methods. GetPreference() returns a single property value in the correct data format. GetPreferences() accepts an object as a parameter and assigns values to the object. NewPreference() accepts three parameters: the name of an object, the property to set, and the value of the property. The object model for MyPreferences is shown in **Figure 11**.

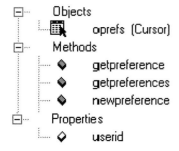

Figure 11. *The object model for MyPreferences.*

The MyPreferences class is used to set preferences for forms and user controls. Examples of how to use this class are included in Chapter 12, "Forms."

Making framework services available

Many of the classes in the MyFrame framework rely on the services presented in this chapter. Like many developers, I like to instantiate frequently used objects at the beginning of an application, thereby reducing the time consumed on each request.

One way to make an object available is to use a public variable. For example, I would have instantiated the class MyMessages as follows:

```
RELEASE goMessages
PUBLIC goMessages
goMessages = CREATEOBJECT("MyMessages")
```

However, with the addition of IntelliSense, I now prefer using _SCREEN.ADDOBJECT(). To understand why, type the following in the command window:

```
goTextBox = CREATEOBJECT("TextBox")
_SCREEN.ADDOBJECT("goTextBox","textbox")
MODIFY COMMAND EraseMe
```

Try typing "goTextBox." in EraseMe.prg and you will see that IntelliSense is not available. However, typing "_Screen.g" does activate IntelliSense as shown in **Figure 12**. One additional benefit is that the _Screen object has only one method or property beginning with the letter G, making it easy to find objects that start with that letter.

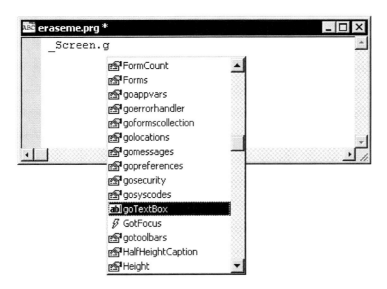

***Figure 12**. Referencing an object added to _SCREEN.*

Instantiating framework services

Framework services are instantiated as part of starting the application and released as part of the application close. In Chapter 5, "Beginning Development," the code for loading and releasing framework components was not completed. The following code has been added to aApplication.

```
PROTECTED FUNCTION OnLoadComponents()
   THIS.ReleaseObjects()

   _SCREEN.ADDOBJECT("goMessages","MyMessages")
   _SCREEN.ADDOBJECT("goPreferences","MyPreferences")
   _SCREEN.ADDOBJECT("goFormsCollection","MyFormsCollection")

ENDFUNC
```

Notice the call to ReleaseObjects(). This prevents classes from being added to the screen when Main.prg is run more than once. Here's the ReleaseObjects() code.

```
PROTECTED FUNCTION ReleaseObjects()

   IF PemStatus(_SCREEN,"goMessages",5)
      _SCREEN.gomessages=.NULL.
   ENDIF
   IF PemStatus(_SCREEN,"goPreferences",5)
      _SCREEN.gopreferences=.NULL.
   ENDIF
   IF PemStatus(_SCREEN,"goFormsCollection",5)
      _SCREEN.goFormsCollection=.NULL.
   ENDIF

ENDFUNC
```

Summary

In this chapter, I illustrated how the Business Object class created in Chapter 10, "Business Objects," can be extended to provide framework services available throughout the framework and applications created with your framework.

The framework services created in this chapter include a number of features you are likely to require in your framework. They include messaging services, application variables management, maintaining system codes, remembering object locations, and tracking user preferences.

Having read this chapter, you should have a better understanding of what framework services are and some ideas for how you can incorporate them into your own framework.

> Updates and corrections to this chapter can be found on Hentzenwerke's Web site, **www.hentzenwerke.com**. Click "Catalog" and navigate to the page for this book.

Chapter 12
Forms

Complicated business logic and pretty reports have little impact on users that work with your systems. To some users, the forms are the application. The application developer is responsible for making the forms aesthetically pleasing. You are responsible for making them functional. This chapter shows you how.

Forms represent a significant portion of the user interface in many applications. Accordingly, developers expect full control over the behavior of the form and require plenty of hooks to extend the functionality you provide. This chapter reviews several different types of forms, beginning with the framework splash screen.

Splash screens add a professional touch to the start of your applications and distract users from the length of time it takes to load the application. Typically, splash screens display information about the application, such as the name of the application or a logo. You can also use the splash screen to inform the user about the progress of the application startup. In this chapter I'll explain how to create a splash screen and incorporate it into your startup routine.

Next, I'll add functionality to the framework form class, aForm, which serves as the parent class for all forms in the framework. Common functionality implemented at this level involves positioning the form properly, resizing controls on the form, and defining a strategy for communicating with toolbars and other forms.

The last topic of this chapter is modal forms, which prevent users from interacting with any other part of the application while the form is active. One of the most common uses of modal forms is to "freeze" an application to collect information from the user and return it to the calling program. In this chapter you'll see some issues you may encounter when developing modal forms for your application, and also some examples of the many ways you can take advantage of FoxPro's modal forms.

Splash screens: MySplash.scx

A splash screen displays information about the application while the application loads. It is common to suppress the title bar, accentuating the contents of the splash screen. **Figure 1** shows an example of a splash screen.

FoxPro does not provide a special "splash screen" form. Any form can appear as a splash screen if you change a few properties. The following settings will make a form appear as a splash screen:

```
AlaysOnTop  = .T.
Caption     = ""
Closable    = .F.
ControlBox  = .F.
MaxButton   = .F.
MinButton   = .F
Movable     = .F.
ShowInWindow = 2
```

Figure 1. *A sample splash screen.*

Design considerations

A splash screen is the first thing a user sees when starting an application. The application developer will want the splash screen to appear in front of the user as quickly as possible to provide immediate feedback that the application is starting. Showing the splash screen before checking machine capacities, loading class libraries, and performing the host of other actions that occur during the start of an application is the fastest way to get the screen in front of the user. You should base the splash screen directly on the FoxPro base controls—rather than on your framework base classes—so you can run the splash screen before loading your class libraries.

The application developer may want to display information about the progress of the application while it is starting. Aside from being informative, visual changes in the screen assure users that the application is not "stuck," because they can see the form is changing.

Displaying information about the application startup has an additional benefit. If the application experiences problems while loading, the step in progress will be displayed on the screen, making it easier for the user to identify at which point the problem occurred.

MySplash.scx

The splash screen included as part of MyFrame is MySplash.scx. You will find it in the .\Meta folder. A copy of MySplash.scx is placed in the .\appsource\ folder at the start of each new project. MySplash.scx is shown in **Figure 2**.

As you can see in Figure 2, MySplash does not have a title set or a picture defined. These are left for the application developer to fill in.

To enable the splash screen to open before you issue any SET CLASSLIB commands, MySplash.scx and the controls it contains are based directly on the FoxPro base classes, rather than the framework classes in MyFrame. Additionally, some functionality has been added to MySplash. Here are the relevant properties and events:

- SetStatus(): This method accepts one character parameter and displays its value in the lower portion of the screen.

- Init(): Optionally accepts a title to display in lblTitle.

- lblTitle: A center-aligned label. To set the title you can either set the caption directly or pass it as a parameter when creating the form.

- Timer1: Releases the splash screen after a period of time has elapsed. The default is 15 seconds.

- AutoCenter: Is set to .T.

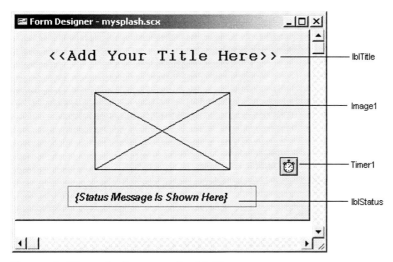

Figure 2. The splash screen for MyFrame.

Adding a splash screen to the startup routine

To incorporate the splash screen into the startup routine, the following properties and methods have been added to aApplication:

- SetStatusText (tcStatusText): Displays a message in the status bar by default. However, if oSplash is an object reference to a splash screen, the request is forwarded.

- cSplashScreen: The name of the form to run.

- nSplashDelay: The length of time (in milliseconds) the splash screen remains open after the application loads.

- oSplash: Holds a reference to the form.

The developer can choose to show a splash screen by filling in its name. Additionally, checks are made to ensure the form exists and that the application is not in development mode. In Chapter 5, "Beginning Development," the code for OnShowSplash() was not completed. Here's the rest of the code:

```
*--aApplication.OnShowSplash()
    PROTECTED FUNCTION OnShowSplash()

        IF ! EMPTY(THIS.cSplashScreen) AND ;
                FILE(THIS.cSplashScreen) AND ;
                ! THIS.lDevMode
```

```
        DO FORM (THIS.cSplashScreen) NAME loSplash
        THIS.oSplash = loSplash

    ENDIF

ENDFUNC
```

A common practice when using splash screens is to suppress the display of the native FoxPro screen while the application is loading. This accentuates the splash screen, because it is the only visible component of the application. To suppress the FoxPro screen, place "Screen = OFF" (without quotes) in the config file. I added a ShowScreen() method and lShowScreen property to aApplication to optionally show the screen. The developer can choose not to display the screen by changing the lShowScreen property of aApplication to False.

```
    PROTECTED FUNCTION ShowScreen()
        IF THIS.lShowScreen
            _SCREEN.WINDOWSTATE = 2   &&Maximized
            _SCREEN.VISIBLE=.T.
        ENDIF
    ENDFUNC
```

When the application finishes loading, the application should remove the splash screen. However, simply releasing the splash screen when the application screen becomes visible gives a "flashing" effect that I find displeasing. Rather than simply releasing the splash screen, I delay closing the splash screen for half a second after the application loads. You can control the delay by adjusting the nSplashDelay property of aApplication. The following method, ReleaseSplash(), has been added to aApplication and is called from aApplication.LoadApp() once the application has finished loading.

```
*--aApplication.ReleaseSplash()
PROTECTED FUNCTION ReleaseSplash()

    IF VARTYPE(THIS.oSplash) = 'O'
        THIS.oSplash.Timer1.INTERVAL = THIS.nSplashDelay
    ENDIF

ENDFUNC
```

Your base form: aForm

The base form is the place to implement characteristics and behaviors you would like all your forms to have. Your framework should have one form that serves as the basis for every form in your framework. In MyFrame, that form is the form class aForm.

This chapter illustrates changes to the aForm class that are representative of changes you might include in your base form. They include identifying the last active form, setting the form's location, setting preferences for the form, providing support for class-based (VCX) forms, and proper positioning and sizing of the form.

Many of the behaviors listed in the previous paragraph rely on framework services described in Chapter 11. In that chapter, you learned how to call those services as the form loads, and release those services when the form unloads. Finally, you'll need to ensure that every form is systematically closed when the user exits the application.

Opening aForm

Each time a form is created, using either CreateObject() or DO FORM, a number of framework activities occur. They are: setting the location of the form, restoring any form preferences the user may have set, loading any appropriate toolbars, adding the form to the form collection, creating a list of objects on the form, recording essential control values, optionally sizing the form to fit the screen, resizing the form, setting security, binding the form controls, and refreshing the screen.

Admittedly, that is quite a bit of activity. To improve the display time of the form, the LockScreen form property is set to True during the Load() method. Setting LockScreen to False suppresses visual updates to the form. Setting LockScreen to True after the form is activated means the form is drawn only once, after all visual changes have occurred.

While it may seem logical to initiate the startup activity from the Init event, the form has not yet instantiated, and an object reference is unavailable. Because many of the framework activities initiated during the startup of a form require an object reference, the Activate event is used instead.

One consideration for using the Activate event, however, is that you don't want the code to fire each time the form is activated. A test is done to ensure that the framework code in the Activate event fires only once. If the Activate event has not fired, the startup sequence is initiated as follows:

```
*--aForm.Activate()
WITH THIS
    IF ! .lActivateFired

        .lActivateFired=.T.
        .SetLocation()
        .GetPrefs()
        .MakeToolbars()
        .AddToFormsCollection()
        GetObjectList(THIS,.oFormControlsCollection)
        .CaptureControlValues()
        .FitToScreen()

        *--This call is after the controls are drawn
        *) and the screen is resized.
        .RESIZE()

        .SetSecurity()
        .BINDCONTROLS=.T.
        .LOCKSCREEN = .F.
    ENDIF
    .REFRESH()
ENDWITH
```

Identifying the last active form

In many cases, it is helpful to have a reference to the previously active form. For example, a generic dialog box can appear "customized" by reflecting some information about the form that called it. For example, "Are you sure you want to save changes for customer <Customer Name>?"

FoxPro's _Screen.ActiveForm property contains a reference to the currently active form. However, _Screen.ActiveForm only references a form once it becomes visible. When a form's

Load() method fires, the form is not visible and is therefore not yet accessible using _Screen.ActiveForm.

However, we can use the form's Load() method to test whether _Screen.ActiveForm contains an object reference. If it does, the reference is to the previously active form.

The following code in aForm's Load() method stores a reference to the previously active form in a property called oPreviousActiveForm.

```
*--Identifying a previously active form
IF TYPE("_Screen.ActiveForm") = 'O' AND ! ISNULL(_SCREEN.ACTIVEFORM)
    THIS.oPreviousActiveForm = _SCREEN.ACTIVEFORM
ENDIF
```

Be sure to remove object references as a form (or any object) is released. Dangling references to objects may prevent objects from releasing properly, or at all, and can cause the dreaded "C5" errors. To make sure there are no dangling object references, the following code is called from a custom method, DoClose(),as the form closes.

```
THIS.oPreviousActiveForm = .NULL.
```

Closing aForm
Some activities should always occur when a form closes. For example, a user should be prompted to save pending changes before closing a data entry form and, if necessary, the framework should prevent the form from closing at all. Other framework activities include conditionally releasing toolbars that support the form, removing the form from the framework Forms collection, and saving the form's location.

Each form in MyFrame has a custom template method, DoClose(), which coordinates these activities. In all cases a form has its Visible property set to False (.F.). This gives the appearance that the form closes immediately, even though some of the framework code that follows may take a few moments.

Notice the conditional release of the form. This step is provided primarily for modal forms where you may prefer not to release the form directly. lReleaseOnClose has a default value of True (.T.) and can be changed in subclasses as needed.

```
*--aForm.DoClose()
WITH THIS
    .VISIBLE=.F.
    .SaveLoc()
    .ReleaseToolbars()
    .RefreshToolbars()
    .RemoveFromFormsCollection()
    .oPreviousActiveForm = .NULL.

    IF .lReleaseOnClose
        .RELEASE()
    ENDIF
ENDWITH
```

There are a number of ways to close a form:

- Clicking the close button (the X on the top right of most MDI windows).

- Clicking the close button of a form.

- Selecting "Close" from the menu on the top left of the form.

- Shutting down the computer.

- Releasing a variable reference to a form.

- Calling the form's Release() method.

The user initiates the first four methods for closing a form, while the developer initiates the last two.

When the user initiates a close, the QueryUnload event occurs and the QueryUnload() method fires.

When a developer closes a form, he or she does so by calling the form's Release() method. However, when the QueryUnload event fires, the Release() method does not. The opposite is also true. This is a good thing, because it gives you a way to distinguish user intent without restricting the developer!

However, the developer still needs a way to simulate the user closing a form—for example, by placing ThisForm.Release() in a command button's Click event from a command button on a form.

One method, Close(), is defined as the way to close the form from within the framework. The QueryUnload() method is redirected to the Close() method. The developer can close the form "framework style" by calling the Close() method or "developer style" by using the RELEASE command. The following code in the form's QueryUnload() method redirects the event sequence to your custom Close() method.

```
*--aForm.QueryUnload()
IF .NOT. THISFORM.CLOSE()
    NODEFAULT
ENDIF
```

Your standard approach to closing a form should separate the process into three parts. First, provide a hook that allows the developer to take action before closing the form. Second, take the steps to actually close the form. Third, provide a hook for the developer to take action once the form is closed.

The approach used in MyFrame is to add four methods to aForm. Close() is a template method that controls the closing process. IsOkToClose() and OnClose() are the developer hooks before and after the form is closed, while DoClose() contains the code to release the form.

IsOkToClose() and OnClose() are the hooks for the application developer and are empty by default. The code for the Close() method is shown here.

```
*--aForm.Close()
WITH THIS
    IF .IsOkToClose() and .DoClose()
        .OnClose()
        RETURN .T.
    ELSE
        RETURN .F.
    ENDIF
ENDWITH
```

For the Close() method to be effective, all objects in the framework that can potentially close a form must call the Close() method. This means that command buttons, menus, toolbars, and so on, call the Close() method.

While developing a form, it is possible that you have some code that erroneously returns a false value from IsOkToClose(). The effect is that the form would never close because the form's Release() method is never called. In this case, you can bypass the Close() method and release the form manually—for example, from the command window.

Working with groups of controls

There are times when it is necessary to work with all the controls on a form. In MyFrame, setting security, resizing a form, and displaying data-validation errors requires access to every control on a form. Continually navigating a form's object hierarchy is inefficient. It is more efficient to navigate the form's hierarchy once and store a reference to each control in a collection.

The collection used to store these references inherits from the MyStack class (see Chapter 8, "Collections") and is named is oFormControlsCollection. At the end of Chapter 8 is an example of how to navigate a form and store a reference to each object in a collection, so I won't repeat it here. However, once the collection is loaded with references to each control on the form, you need to pull some values that are frequently used during some of the framework services listed previously.

Setting the nCols property of oFormControlsCollection to seven (7) indicates that the collection will be seven columns wide. The first column contains a reference to the object itself, the second contains the object's control source (if applicable), and columns 3 through 7 contain the object's original Left, Top, Height, Width, and Fontsize (if applicable) values.

To load these values into the collection, loop through the array, storing the essential values needed in array columns 2 through 7 as shown here:

```
*--aForm.CaptureControlValues()
WITH THISFORM.oFormControlsCollection
    FOR lnI = 1 TO .nRows
        IF PEMSTATUS(.ADATA[lnI,1],'ControlSource',5)
            .ADATA[lnI,2]=UPPER(.ADATA[lnI,1].CONTROLSOURCE)
        ENDIF

        IF      PEMSTATUS(.ADATA[lnI,1],'Width',5) AND ;
                PEMSTATUS(.ADATA[lnI,1],'left',5) AND ;
                PEMSTATUS(.ADATA[lnI,1],'top',5) AND ;
                PEMSTATUS(.ADATA[lnI,1],'height',5)

            TRY
```

```
            .ADATA[lnI,3]  =  .ADATA[lnI,1].LEFT
            .ADATA[lnI,4]  =  .ADATA[lnI,1].WIDTH
            .ADATA[lnI,5]  =  .ADATA[lnI,1].TOP
            .ADATA[lnI,6]  =  .ADATA[lnI,1].HEIGHT

            IF PEMSTATUS(.ADATA[lnI,1],'FontSize',5)
                .ADATA[lnI,7]  =  .ADATA[lnI,1].FONTSIZE
            ENDIF

        ENDTRY

      ENDIF
    ENDFOR
ENDWITH
```

Three activities use the Form Controls collection extensively. Resizing forms is illustrated later in this chapter, in the section titled "Resizing forms and form controls." Chapter 13, "Data Entry Forms," uses the collection to highlight errors detected during data validation. Chapter 16, "Security," uses the collection to apply security settings to each control.

Form location
When you work with FoxPro, you probably have a preference about where the command window should appear the next time you open FoxPro. You have the same expectations for the Properties window, the Trace window, and so on. Users have similar expectations about the forms in their applications. The user should have the ability to arrange multiple forms as desired and have them open where they were last placed.

By default, FoxPro opens each form in the top left corner of the screen. You as the developer can change that, or the user can change that, by repositioning the screen as mentioned earlier. Whether the screen opens in the default location, a developer-defined location, or a user-defined location, another default is that if the user opens a second instance of the same form, it will appear slightly below and to the right of the first form. If the user opens a third instance, it appears slightly below and to the right of the second instance … and so on.

SetLocation() is the form method responsible for setting the form's location. The following approach loops through the _Screen.Forms collection. If another form with the same name is already running, the form is positioned slightly lower and to the right of the existing form. If another form with the same name is not found, a call is made to the framework component responsible for storing and retrieving object locations.

 For information about the mechanics of persisting and retrieving object locations from a table, see Chapter 11, "Framework Services," in the section titled "Remembering object locations."

SetLocation() is called from the form's Load() event. Here's the code:

```
*--aForm.SetLocation()
LOCAL loForm AS FORM, llFound
WITH THIS
    *--Save original form settings for resizing
    THIS.nOriginalWidth  = THIS.WIDTH
    THIS.nOriginalHeight = THIS.HEIGHT
```

```
FOR EACH loForm IN _SCREEN.FORMS
    IF loForm.NAME==.NAME AND ! loForm= THIS
        .TOP= loForm.TOP + .noffset
        .LEFT= loForm.LEFT + .noffset
        llFound = .T.
        EXIT
    ENDIF
ENDFOR

IF .lRememberLocations AND ! llFound AND VARTYPE(goLocations) = 'O'
    _Screen.goLocations.GetLoc(THIS)
ENDIF

ENDWITH
```

Resizing forms and controls

When users resize a form, they generally expect the controls on the form to resize as well. In this section, I will illustrate one way to proportionally resize controls on a form.

To proportionally resize the controls on a form, you need to capture the percent change in the size of the form. If the form height increases by 20 percent, each control's height should also increase by 20 percent.

Determining the percentage change in a form's dimensions requires that you compare the form's original to its current size. In the form's FitToScreen() method, you capture the original size of the form and optionally adjust the form to the size of the screen:

```
*--aForm.FitToScreen()
WITH THIS
    *--Always capture the original height and width
    *) regardless of whether lFitToScreen is .T.
    *) These values are used when resizing the form

    .nOriginalWidth  = .WIDTH
    .nOriginalHeight = .HEIGHT

    IF .lFitToScreen

        .WIDTH=_SCREEN.WIDTH
        .HEIGHT=_SCREEN.HEIGHT
        .TOP=0
        .LEFT=0

    ENDIF
ENDWITH
```

Each time a form is resized, the form's Resize() method fires. The following code in the Resize() method calculates the percent change in the height and width of the form. New values for the control's Left, Width, Height, and Top properties are calculated for each control. Here's the form's Resize() method.

```
*--aForm.Resize()
lnControls = THIS.oFORMCONTROLSCOLLECTION.Getcount()
nWidthChange  = 1+(THIS.WIDTH - THIS.nOriginalWidth )/THIS.nOriginalWidth
nHeightChange = 1+(THIS.HEIGHT - THIS.nOriginalHeight )/THIS.nOriginalHeight

THISFORM.LOCKSCREEN=.T.
```

```
FOR lnI = 1 TO lnControls
    WITH THIS.oFORMCONTROLSCOLLECTION
        loControl = .ADATA[lnI,1]

        IF PEMSTATUS(loControl,'left',5) AND ;
                PEMSTATUS(loControl,'width',5) AND ;
                PEMSTATUS(loControl,'top',5) AND ;
                PEMSTATUS(loControl,'height',5) AND ;
                loControl<>THISFORM

            try
            loControl.LEFT   = INT(.ADATA[lnI,3]* nWidthChange)
            loControl.WIDTH  = INT(.ADATA[lnI,4]* nWidthChange)
            loControl.TOP    = INT(.ADATA[lnI,5]* nHeightChange)
            loControl.HEIGHT = INT(.ADATA[lnI,6]* nHeightChange)

            IF PEMSTATUS(loControl,'FontSize',5)
                lnNewFontSize = INT(.ADATA[lnI,7] * ;
                    IIF(nHeightChange<nWidthChange,nHeightChange,nWidthChange))
                lnNewFontSize = IIF( lnNewFontSize <5,5,lnNewFontSize)
                loControl.FONTSIZE = lnNewFontSize
            ENDIF

            CATCH
            ENDTRY

        ENDIF
    ENDWITH
ENDFOR

THISFORM.CLS
THISFORM.LOCKSCREEN=.F.
```

The Resize() method fires every time the form's size changes. You can control whether a form is resizable by setting its BorderStyle property. The default setting is 3 – Sizable. Settings of 0 – No Border, 1 – Fixed Single, or 2 – Fixed Dialog do not allow the form to be resized.

Form preferences

Preferences are one way for users and developers to customize the forms you provide. For example, a user may prefer to see tool tips while learning how to use a form. Once the user is comfortable with the form, he or she may no longer want to see the yellow tool tips popping up all over the place.

ShowTips is an example of a property that controls form behavior. Allowing users to individually set the value of form properties, such as ShowTips, means that you are giving the user the ability to customize how they view their forms.

Figure 3 shows an example of a preferences screen that allows users to change property values on a form.

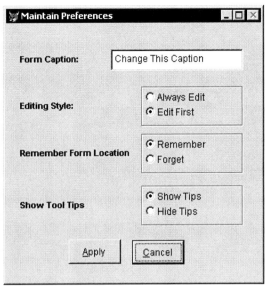

Figure 3. *An example of a preferences screen.*

A factory method is used to create the preferences screen. The aForm class contains one property, cPreferenceScreen, which contains the name of the preferences screen displayed. The factory method MakePrefScreen() instantiates the preference class as follows:

```
*--aForm.MakePrefsScreen()
LOCAL loPrefs
IF ! EMPTY(THIS.cPreferenceScreen)
    loPrefs = CREATEOBJECT(THIS.cPreferenceScreen)
    loPrefs.SHOW(1)
ENDIF
```

Saving and retrieving preferences
The form shown in Figure 3 does two things when a user clicks the Apply button. First, property changes are immediately reflected in the form that called this form. Second, the settings are persisted by calling on the services of myPreferences developed in Chapter 11.

```
*--MyDefaultPreferences.OnApply()
WITH THIS.oPreviousActiveForm

    *--Set the new values
    .CAPTION = THIS.txtFormCaption.TEXT
    .lAlwaysEdit = THIS.opgAlwaysEdit.VALUE = 1
    .lRememberLocations= THIS.opgformLocation.VALUE = 1
    .ShowTips = this.opgShowTips.Value = 1

    _SCREEN.goPreferences.NewPreference(.NAME, "Caption", THIS.txtFormCaption.TEXT)
    _SCREEN.goPreferences.NewPreference(.NAME, "lAlwaysEdit",.lAlwaysEdit)
    _SCREEN.goPreferences.NewPreference(.NAME, "lRememberLocations",.lRememberLocations)
    _SCREEN.goPreferences.NewPreference(.NAME, "ShowTips",.ShowTips)

ENDWITH
```

The preferences class, goPreferences, is also called to retrieve and set preferences as the form loads. The following code is called as the form is loading.

```
*--aForm.GetPrefs()
IF TYPE("_screen.goPreferences") = 'O' AND ! ISNULL(_screen.goPreferences)
     _screen.goPreferences.GetPreferences(this)
ENDIF
```

VCX form support

You can create forms using a screen definition (SCX) or a class definition (VCX). However, creating a class-based form requires a little extra effort. To understand why, it is necessary to review how class-based forms are created.

Class-based forms are instantiated using CreateObject(), which returns a variable reference to the objects it creates. The object is released when the reference is released or goes out of scope. For example, the following code creates a form. However, once the method completes, the variable reference loForm is released. When the variable reference is released, the form is released. The result is that the form is visible for a split second and then disappears.

```
*--SampleMethod
FUNCTION ShowDisappearingForm()
     LOCAL loForm
     loForm = CREATEOBJECT("Form")
     loForm.Visible = .T.
ENDFUNC
```

You need a way to maintain a reference to each form while it is active, and release the reference when the form is closed.

The collection classes created in Chapter 8, "Collections," can be used to "cache" object references. The collection class stores information in a property array, aData[]. Storing an object reference in the collection satisfies the requirement of maintaining a reference to a form after the program or method in which it was created completes.

To use the class, two methods have been added to aForm: AddToFormsCollection() and RemoveFromFormsCollection().

The AddToFormsCollection() method is called from aForm.INIT(). It checks to make sure the Forms collection class is instantiated and then adds itself to the collection. RemoveFromFormsCollection() is called when the form closes. Removing a form from the collection is a two-step process. First, the form finds the row in which its reference is "contained." Second, it "removes" itself from the collection.

The code for each method is shown here:

```
*--aForm.AddToFormsCollection()
IF TYPE("_screen.goFormsCollection") = 'O' AND ;
     ! ISNULL(_SCREEN.goFormsCollection)

     _SCREEN.goFormsCollection.PUSH(THIS)
ENDIF

*--aForm.RemoveFromFormsCollecton()
IF TYPE("_screen.goFormsCollection") = 'O' AND ;
     ! ISNULL(_SCREEN.goFormsCollection)
```

```
      lnRow = _SCREEN.goFormsCollection.Contains(THIS)
      IF lnRow>0
          _SCREEN.goFormsCollection.REMOVE(lnRow)
      ENDIF

ENDIF
```

The Forms collection is a subclass of the MyCollection class created in Chapter 8, "Collections." No special enhancements or modifications are required to make the class functional. However, the entire class definition is shown here:

```
*--MyFormsCollection
DEFINE CLASS MyFormsCollection as MyCollection
ENDDEFINE
```

Modal forms

A modal form suspends program execution, preventing users from working with other forms in an application until the modal form is released or is no longer visible. A modal form can be defined as a class (VCX) or a screen (SCX), and its definition affects the way you call and retrieve values from it.

This section highlights some commonalities as well as some differences between SCX-based and VCX-based forms. The latter part of this section defines the approach used in the sample framework accompanying the book, as well as an example of how to create and use a framework dialog box.

Modal forms (VCX and SCX)

Some behaviors are common to modal forms whether they are SCX-based or VCX-based. For example, you can run any form as a modal form. To do so, instantiate the form without making it visible. For example:

```
*--SCX Version
DO FORM <<FormName>> NAME loForm NOSHOW
*--VCX Version
loForm = CREATEOBJECT(<<ClassName>>)
```

The following line will make any non-visible form modal (regardless of how it was instantiated).

```
loForm.Show(1)
```

Calling the Show() method suspends program execution until the form is released or is no longer visible. However, you may or may not have access to the form depending on which method you choose to close the form. When a form is released, you no longer have access to the form. If, however, you make a modal form invisible, you can still access the form via the variable reference (loForm in the previous example) and therefore can still access properties and methods of the form.

Assuming a form named MyDateRangeForm has two text boxes—txtStartDate and txtEndDate—the following code would display the dates entered on the screen when the form has its Visible property set to False (.F.) and results in an error if the form is released.

```
loForm = CREATEOBJECT("MyDateRangeForm")
loForm.Show(1)
ACTIVATE SCREEN


? 'Start Date = ' + loForm.txtStartDate.Text
? 'nd Date = ' +   loForm.txtEndDate.Text
```

Modal forms (SCX only)

SCX-based modal forms can return a value from the form's Unload() method. To obtain a value from a form in this way, the form must have its WindowType property set to 1 (Modal) and the form must be released to return control to the calling program.

Assume you had a form named frmGetOneDate with a text box named txtDate. The following code in the Unload() method would return a value to the calling program:

```
PROCEDURE Unload()
     RETURN THIS.txtDate.Text
ENDPROC
```

The following code would print the date entered on the screen:

```
DO FORM frmGetOneDate to ldDate
? ldDate
```

As with any method, the Unload() method can return only a single value. However, that value can be an object reference or a property array, which may contain more than one value.

Modal forms (VCX only)

VCX-based forms must be made modal by passing a value of 1 to the Show() method. For example, even if a form's WindowType property is set to 1, the following code will not result in a modal form:

```
loForm = CREATEOBJECT("Test")
loForm.Visible = .T.
```

Instead, you must call the form as shown here:

```
loForm = CREATEOBJECT("Test")
loForm.Show(1)
```

SYS(1272) returns a form's SCX file. SYS(1272) can be used to determine if a form is SCX-based or VCX-based. For VCX-based forms, SYS(1272) returns an empty string.

MyModalFrm

MyModalFrm is a subclass of aForm. It serves as the launching point for all modal forms in the sample framework. It has only one significant change. In support of SCX-based forms, the

WindowState property is set to 1, Modal. However, to use this form as a class, you still must instantiate the form and call its Show() method as described earlier.

MyModalFrm can serve as the parent for VCX-based or SCX-based modal forms. To create an SCX-based form, the developer needs only to write the code that returns a value from the Unload() method. As a reminder, the form's Unload() event fires only when the form is released.

When using VCX-based modal forms to obtain information from the user, you don't want to release the form until you have retrieved the information from it. Instead, you set the form's Visible property to False and then close it after having retrieved the information. To allow the developer to decide whether a form should be released during the close process, I've added a property, lReleaseOnClose. To use the modal form as a VCX-based class, you must change the form's lReleaseOnClose property to False (.F.). I've listed the DoClose() method of aForm again to illustrate how lReleaseOnClose is used.

```
*--aForm.DoClose()
WITH THIS
    .VISIBLE=.F.
    .SaveLoc()
    .ReleaseToolbars()
    .RefreshToolbars()
    .RemoveFromFormsCollection()
    .oPreviousActiveForm = .NULL.

    IF .lReleaseOnClose
        .RELEASE()
    ENDIF
ENDWITH
```

Dialog boxes: aDialogFrm

A common use for modal forms is to create dialog boxes. ADialogFrm is a subclass of MyModalFrm. The 'a' prefix denotes it as an abstract class serving as the basis for other forms. **Figure 4** shows this class in the Class Designer. Notice the Apply and Cancel buttons.

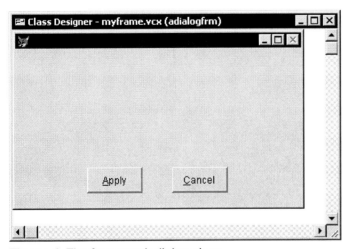

Figure 4. The framework dialog class.

When a user clicks either button, he or she expects the dialog to be released. As a developer, you want to capture which button the user clicked before you close the form.

To coordinate the close, I have added two template methods to the aDialogFrm class: Apply() and Cancel(). Each method sets a form property, lReturnValueFromForm, and calls hook methods that allow the developer to take additional action before releasing the form. The code for the Apply() and Cancel() methods is shown here:

```
*--aDialogFrm.Apply()
This.lReturnValueFromForm = .T.
If This.OnApply()
      This.Close()
Endif

*-- aDialogFrm.Cancel()
This.lReturnValueFromForm = .F.
If This.OnCancel()
      This.Close()
Endif
```

To use this class as an SCX-based modal form, you would place code like the following in the form's Unload() method.

```
If THIS.lReturnvalueFromForm
      <<Return Code Goes Here>>
ELSE
      RETURN .NULL.
ENDIF
```

Summary

In this chapter, you learned how to create a variety of forms for use in your framework, and you learned the differences between SCX-based and VCX-based forms.

At the beginning of the chapter you learned how to create a splash screen. The splash screen illustrates circumstances in which you may choose to include items in the framework that are not based directly on the framework classes.

You also learned how to create a form class that serves as the starting point for other forms in your framework and the types of functionality included in a form at this level. You then learned how to extend your base form by creating a modal form and a dialog box.

Updates and corrections to this chapter can be found on Hentzenwerke's Web site, **www.hentzenwerke.com**. Click "Catalog" and navigate to the page for this book.

Chapter 13
Data Entry Forms

Finding and editing information is essential to a data-based system. This chapter shows how to control when and how users access information, and how to coordinate the editing process.

The funny thing about a data entry form in a tiered framework is that it "knows nothing" about data. There isn't one data entry form for SQL Server data and another for DBFs. Similarly, there is no pessimistic locking form or optimistic locking form. There is only one data entry form class, and in MyFrame that class is MyDataFrm. MyDataFrm coordinates the visual aspects of data entry while passing requests to add, save, and delete records to an instance of the MyDataEnvironment class created in Chapter 10, "Business Objects."

MyDataFrm acts as the coordinator between classes. A change in record pointer position or edit status may require actions in the data connection classes, business objects, form, form controls, and toolbars.

However, there is more to a data entry form than reading and writing data. How do users interact with the entry form? Are they allowed to edit information directly or are they required to click an Edit button first? Are users allowed to move between records while edits are pending? The application developer is responsible for matching the data entry interface with the needs of the end user. It is your job to make sure that your entry forms can accommodate varying needs.

In this chapter, you will see how to create a data entry form that is configurable so that it can meet the majority of situations faced by application developers.

Styles of data entry

Various styles of data entry exist. I'll present a few here to illustrate some differences between them and to serve as the basis for understanding the design of the data entry form class in MyFrame.

Edit First

In the Edit First style of data entry, the user must take some action prior to editing the form. Generally, this involves clicking an Edit button. At that time, text boxes and other controls "magically" come alive and are ready to accept information from the user. **Figure 1** shows an example of a form in Edit First style as it first appears. Notice that the entry controls are disabled and only the New, Edit, Delete, and Close buttons are enabled.

Edit Always

Another approach is to consider the form to always be in edit mode. Each time you navigate to a new record, you can edit immediately without the additional step of clicking an Edit button. A key part of the Edit Always approach is that each record is saved, if changes are pending, prior to moving to another record. In **Figure 2**, notice that the controls are ready to accept data and that each command button is enabled.

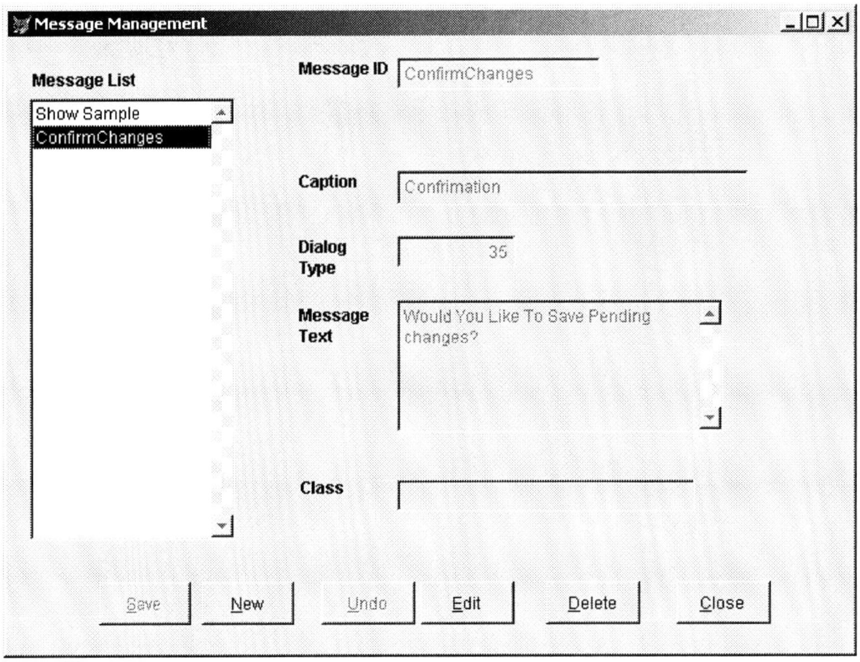

Figure 1*. An example of an Edit First style of data entry.*

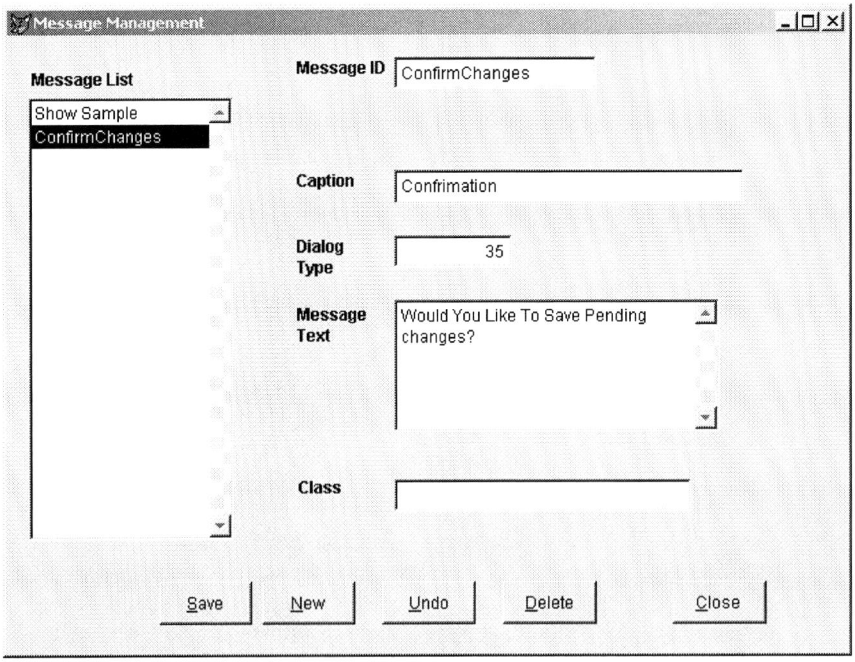

Figure 2*. An example of an Edit Always style of entry.*

One Record

If you limit edits to one record at a time, pending edits are saved or rejected before you add a new record or navigate to another record.

Figures 1 and 2 illustrated examples of "one record" entry forms. In each of these examples, the user has access to only one record at a time. **Figure 3** shows an example of a one-to-many entry form, in which the user is restricted to one record at a time. The Edit Track and Add Track buttons open separate forms in which the user can edit the detail records.

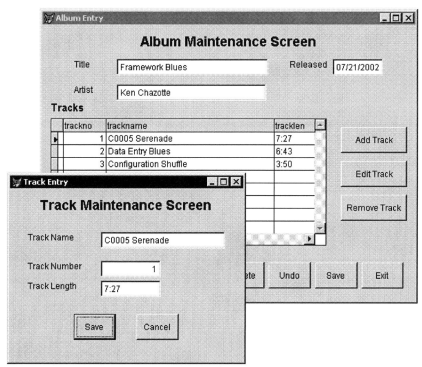

Figure 3. *A one-to-many entry form with a single record entry scheme.*

Multiple Records

If you allow multiple records to be edited, generally users can edit more than one record in one table at one time. A good example of this is a "To Do" list. When adding or editing information in a To Do list, you may want to add or edit a bunch of records before making an update.

Entities

In Chapter 10, "Business Objects," I discussed using business objects to model entities. As a reminder, an entity represents a "thing" such as a building, customer, invoice, or a record album; and an entity might be modeled in more than one table.

Entity maintenance is similar to multiple record updates, in that a user may want to edit one or more records before making an update. Entities are similar to the One Record scenario because the user expects to save pending edits before working with another entity.

Maintaining an entity is unique, however, because pending edits may exist in more than one table at a time and navigation may be allowed in some tables but not in others.

For example, consider an album represented by two tables: Albums and Tracks. The Albums table stores information about an album, while the Tracks table contains a list of the tracks on an album. A user working with the Album Maintenance Screen shown in **Figure 4** considers the album and its tracks as a single entity and is just as likely to change the title (in the Albums table) as well as the name of the track (in the Tracks table).

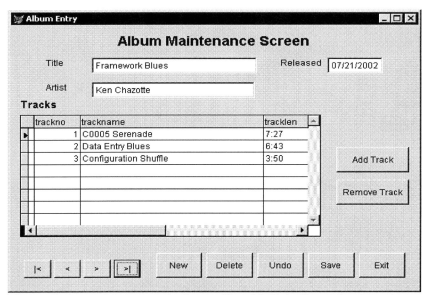

Figure 4. A one-to-many entry form with a Multiple Record entry scheme.

Choosing a data entry style

Each approach to data entry has its own merits and is appropriate in different circumstances. One reason for the One Record scheme is that the grid is a challenging control to work with when the detail table has more than a few fields. Additionally, many developers don't like to allow data entry in a grid. Whatever the reason, your forms should work equally well with either style.

The challenging part of designing a generic data entry form is in accommodating each style of entry. The approach taken in this chapter is configurable and thereby able to accommodate each of the styles presented in this section. Editing information in the Entities style, where multiple records can be edited before an update, is the most complicated of the five approaches. The remainder of this section applies to Figure 4.

One aspect of a generic form is that pending edits must be saved in one entity (Albums) before users can work on another. Moving the record pointer in the Albums table is analogous to changing entities. The record pointer is moved in the Albums table when navigating to another record (SKIP, LOCATE, SEEK, and so on) or when adding a new record (APPEND or INSERT INTO).

Your framework should optionally allow the developer to either save the entry or prevent the action (SKIP, APPEND, and so on) from occurring. Often, all that's required is to inform users that unsaved changes exist and confirm whether they want to proceed. However, the developer may also choose to save the changes automatically, opting to inform users only if the data is invalid.

However, not all record pointer movement should trigger an action. For example, moving the record pointer in the child table (Tracks), either by scrolling through the grid or adding a new Tracks record, does not constitute working with a new entity.

One aspect of data entry forms in general is that, prior to closing a form, pending edits should be handled appropriately. Similar to navigating to a new record, you won't know how the application developer will choose to handle pending edits. In some cases, the edits should be automatically saved; in others, a confirmation process should occur; and in still others, pending changes might automatically be revoked. In a generic solution, you must allow the developer to decide what actions are appropriate.

Finally, a generic solution requires that your solution accommodate multiple tables. For example, consider Figure 4 again. Both the Delete button and the Remove Track button delete records from the Albums and Tracks tables, respectively. While it is possible that the developer of a form like this might add a DeleteAlbum() method and a DeleteTracks() method to the form or to the business class, that solution is not generic. While you are developing the framework data entry screen, you won't know the names of the tables or the names of the methods that will be required in the form.

Avoid creating two methods for adding a new record—for example, creating two procedures such as AddNewParent() and AddNewChild(). Occasions will arise where there are three or more editable tables in the same form. A generic, parameter-based approach for handling multiple tables was presented in Chapter 10, "Business Objects." A similar, parameter-based approach is implemented at the form level as well.

The state of data entry

The responsibility for determining whether a control is enabled or disabled during an edit is divided between the form and the control. The form is responsible for managing the state of a form. Each control is responsible for knowing how to read the form's state and adjust its own display state.

The form's role

The MyDataFrm entry form can be in one of two states. A form is either ready to accept edits, or it isn't ready to accept edits. When the form is ready to accept edits, the form is in "edit mode" and its lEditMode property is set to True (.T.). When a form is not ready to accept edits, lEditMode is False (.F.).

However, one of the styles mentioned earlier indicated that a form might always accept edits. In effect, the lEditMode property will always be True. A second property, lAlwaysEdit, indicates that the form should always remain in a state where edits are allowed. The SetEditMode() method of MyDataFrm controls how the lEditMode property is set. Other methods pass a value to SetEditMode() indicating whether editing is enabled or disabled as follows:

```
*--MyDataFrm.SetEditMode()
LPARAMETERS tlMode
IF THIS.lAlwaysEdit
   THIS.lEditMode = .T.
ELSE
   THIS.lEditMode = tlMode
ENDIF
```

The control's role

Each control is responsible for "knowing" how to read the form's state—that is, a form's lEditMode and lAlwaysEdit properties.

Each control has a property, lEnabledInEditMode, that dictates whether the control is enabled or disabled during an edit.

The following code placed in a control's Refresh() method results in the proper display after each refresh:

```
*--The Refresh() method for all form controls.
IF    TYPE('_screen.activeform')='O'    AND ;
         ! ISNULL(_SCREEN.ACTIVEFORM) and;
         pemstatus(this,'ENABLED',5) and;
         ! this.lSecurityControlled

   IF ! _SCREEN.ACTIVEFORM.lAlwaysEdit
      THIS.ENABLED = THIS.lEnabledInEditMode = _SCREEN.ACTIVEFORM.lEditMode
   ENDIF

ENDIF
```

Notice that when the form is in the Always Edit style of entry, the control is not enabled or disabled. However, when the form is in the Edit First style of entry, the enabled property is set each time a form refresh occurs.

Another point to mention is that "_Screen.ActiveForm" is preferred over "Thisform." This allows your code to work equally well whether the control is on a form or in a toolbar.

Benefits of this approach

The first benefit of this approach is that the form does not need to "know" which controls will be placed on it. If you have ever written code like this …

```
    IF THISFORM.lEditMode
         THISFORM.txtFirstName.ENABLED = .T.
         THISFORM.txtLastName.ENABLED = .T.
    ELSE
         THISFORM.txtFirstName.ENABLED = .F.
         THISFORM.txtLastName.ENABLED = .F.
    ENDIF
```

… you know that you'd have to amend the code each time you added a new control.

There is a second benefit as well. The user can (optionally) be given control of the lAlwaysEdit property using the preferences screen presented in Chapter 12, in the section titled "Form preferences."

Prompting the user

I've taken special care not to prompt the user directly from the data classes. The form class, however, does communicate with the user. Just as there are varying styles of data entry, there are also various ways to communicate with the user. This section presents some approaches you should consider when designing your form classes.

Hard confirmation

With a hard confirmation, the user is interrupted while trying to take an action. For example, before deleting a record, the system can confirm the user's intentions by displaying an "Are you sure?" confirmation screen.

Soft confirmation

With a soft confirmation, the user is not interrupted during the entry process. For example, consider what happens when you edit a program file in FoxPro. An asterisk (*) appears while edits are pending and disappears when pending edits are saved. The appearance and disappearance of the asterisk is an example of a soft confirmation.

No confirmation

In some situations, you may prefer not to inform the user that a systemic action is about to occur. For example, earlier in this chapter, I presented the Edit Always style of data entry. While moving from one record to another, you may choose to automatically save changes without informing the user.

Confirmation messages in general

Consider a form in which the user has made one or more changes and then clicks the Undo button. You may feel it is appropriate to obtain a hard confirmation from the user—for example, "Are you sure?" However, the application developer may want to display a different message, a soft confirmation such as a WAIT WINDOW that states "Undoing Changes…", or no message at all.

Hook methods offer the most flexibility in situations like this because they allow the developer to customize the action and the message on a class-by-class basis. If you prefer, you can provide default messages, as long as the developer retains control over what is displayed and when (or if) it is displayed.

Common form methods

Separating each task required of the form into its own method results in smaller tasks that are easier to understand, easier to code, and occasionally easier to debug. More importantly, however, many of the steps required during the data entry process are similar. Separating each task into its own method reduces the likelihood of duplicate code.

Locking the form

Locking a form when performing updates can make the updates quicker because FoxPro is not managing the form display while also performing the update.

Complex processes might take a few moments to complete, even while the screen is locked. Changing the mouse pointer to an hourglass visually indicates that a process is in progress. The nMousePointerProcess property is used to control which mouse pointer shape is displayed. The default display is an hourglass. However, you can change nMousePointerProcess to any of the possible mouse pointer settings.

 To see a list of possible mouse pointer settings, see the MousePointer property topic in VFP Help.

OnLockScreen() locks the screen and changes the mouse pointer as shown here:

```
*--MyDataFrm.OnLockScreen()
LPARAMETERS tlLock

IF tlLock
   THIS.LOCKSCREEN = .T.
   THIS.nOldMousePointer = THIS.MOUSEPOINTER
   THIS.MOUSEPOINTER = this.nMousePointerProcess
ELSE
   THIS.LOCKSCREEN = .F.
   THIS.MOUSEPOINTER = this.noldmousepointer
ENDIF
```

Setting focus to a control

Setting focus to a control is accomplished by calling a control's SetFocus() method. The OnSetControlFocus() method of aForm is a hook method. It is called only from the New() method but is broken out into its own method so that it is easier to insert your own code.

I've provided a generic implementation that loops through all the controls on a form and looks for the control with a TabIndex of 1. If the control has a SetFocus() method, it is called.

However, there are cases in which the control you want to set focus to does not have a TabIndex of 1 or is not located directly on the form. For example, it could be on a page of a page frame on the form. I've provided a property, cSetFocusToControl, so you can specify the control that should receive focus. To use this property, you must specify the full path to the control. For example:

```
Thisform.Pageframe1.Page1.Textbox1.
```

As with all hook methods in MyFrame, you may choose to insert your own code rather than accept the default code for OnSetControlFocus(), which is shown next. You may prefer to just set the focus to a control directly. The parameters for the New() method have been passed through to help you determine which control should receive focus and are never used directly by the framework.

```
*--MyDataFrm.OnSetControlFocus()
LPARAMETERS tcAlias, tlIsChildtable
IF ! tlIsChildtable
   IF EMPTY(THIS.cSetFocusToControl)
      *--Set the focus to the first control with an index property of 1
      LOCAL lnI
      WITH THISFORM
         FOR lnI=1 TO .CONTROLCOUNT
            IF pemstatus(.CONTROLS(lnI),'tabindex',5) AND ;
               pemstatus(.CONTROLS(lnI),'SETFOCUS',5)
```

```
               IF .CONTROLS(lnI).TABINDEX=1
                  .CONTROLS(lnI).SETFOCUS()
                  EXIT
               ENDIF

           ENDIF
        ENDFOR
      ENDWITH
   ELSE
      LOCAL lcControl
      lcControl = THIS.cSetFocusToControl
      &lcControl..SETFOCUS()
   ENDIF

ENDIF
```

Data entry methods

The data form class forwards requests to MyDataEnvironment. This is best illustrated by the Save() and New() methods. The other methods—Undo(), Delete(), and Go()—are not covered in this book because they closely resemble either the Save() or the New() method.

Before examining the data methods, however, there is a minor version change that you should be aware of. In Visual FoxPro versions 7.0 and earlier, each form creates a data environment at run time and assigns it the name "DATAEVIRONMENT." Therefore, you could access the data environment of a form programmatically at run time by using the following syntax:

```
THISFORM.DATAENVIRONMENT.AUTOOPENTABLES = .T.
```

This behavior remains unchanged in VFP 8.0 when you use the native data environment.

A feature new to VFP 8.0 is that you can specify the form's data environment. To do this you specify the data environment class and class library in the form's DEClass and DEClassLibrary properties. The change from previous versions is that the custom data environments are not named "DATAENVIRONMENT." Instead, the name of the data environment is the same as the class name. For example, if you have a data environment class named MyAppvars, the resulting name of the data environment is also MyAppvars. You must then reference the data environment in the running form as follows:

```
THISFORM.MyAppvars.AUTOOPENTABLES = .T.
```

The fact that the name of the data environment may change on a form makes it difficult to write reusable code. The solution is to add a property to the form, such as oDE, and link it to the data environment class. The code in the Init() method of a form accomplishes this:

```
*--MyDataFrm.Init()
LOCAL lcDEClass
IF ! EMPTY(THIS.DEClass)
    lcDEClass = THIS.DEClass
    THIS.oDE=THISFORM.&lcDEClass
ENDIF
```

This little bit of code allows you to reference the data environment regardless of the name of the class.

Saving data

The form's Save() method is a wrapper around MyDataEnvironment's Save() method. However, that does not mean that the form does not contribute to the data entry process.

The form's Save() method implements the user interface component of a save. In the case of the Save() method, this means locking the screen and setting the edit mode.

If changes are pending, a hook method is provided for the developer to confirm that a user wants to commit the save. By default, this method is empty, and serves only as a placeholder for the developer.

If a save fails, however, the form obtains the error information from MyDataEnvironment and displays the message.

Finally, the Save() method returns a logical value indicating the success of the save. Here's the code:

```
*--MyDataFrm.Save()
LOCAL llSaved
WITH THIS

    .OnLockScreen(.T.)

    IF .oDE.UnsavedChangesExist() AND .OnConfirmSave() AND VARTYPE(.oDE) = 'O'

        IF .oDE.SAVE()
            .SetEditmode(.F.)
            .REFRESH()
            llSaved = .T.
            .OnSave()
        ELSE
            .ShowError( .oDE.GetErrorMessage() )
        ENDIF
    ENDIF
    .OnLockScreen(.F.)
    RETURN llSaved
ENDWITH
```

Adding a record

The form's New() method is a wrapper around the data object's New() method. The form is responsible for the visual aspects of adding a new record, such as changing the mouse pointer, locking the screen, and so on. The request for adding a new record is passed on to the data object.

The New() method accepts two parameters. The first, tcAlias, is the alias to which the record is appended. The New() method passes the parameter to MyDataEnvironment's New() method. The second parameter, tlOverrideChecks, indicates whether a check for unsaved changes exists before adding the record.

The reason for the override is that in a one-to-many form, for example, you will want the ability to add new child records without forcing a save.

I've provided a hook method, OnConfirmNew(),as a developer hook. It has no default implementation.

Prior to calling oDE.New(), a check is made to ensure that all data has been saved. If unsaved changes exist, the hook method OnChangesVerified() is available to help the developer respond to the situation. OnChangesVerified() has a default implementation that obtains confirmation from the user by default. The OnChangesVerified() method code is shown following the code for the New() method.

After calling MyDataEnvironment's New() method, the form is placed in edit mode and an additional hook method, OnNew(), is called. There is no code in OnNew(); this method has been provided as an opportunity for the developer to take action after a record is added.

Here's the code for MyDataFrm.New():

```
*--MyDataFrm.New()
LPARAMETERS tcAlias, tlOverrideChecks
WITH THIS
    LOCAL llAllowNew, lnNewRecordAdded

    llAllowNew=.OnConfirmNew()
    THIS.Onlockscreen(.T.)

    IF !tlOverrideChecks AND .UnsavedChangesExist()
        llAllowNew=.OnChangesVerified()
    ENDIF

    IF llAllowNew AND VARTYPE(.oDE)='O'

        lnNewRecordAdded=.oDE.New(tcAlias)

        .SetEditMode(.T.)
        .OnNew()
        .OnSetControlFocus(tlOverrideChecks)

        .REFRESH()
    ENDIF
ENDWITH

THIS.Onlockscreen(.F.)

RETURN lnNewRecordAdded
```

The other data-centric methods of MyDataFrm—Edit(), Delete(), and Go()—have similar implementations as New(). The code for these methods is included in the source code that's included with this book.

Verifying changes

A user may try to take an action, such as closing the application, that could result in a loss of data. The framework is responsible for making sure pending edits are not lost or unknowingly committed. Before taking an action that might commit or revert edits, OnChangesVerified() is called, prompting the user to see if changes should be saved.

OnChangesVerified() is a hook method with a default implementation. By default, the user is prompted with the following message: "Would you like to save pending edits?" The user can choose to save the changes, revert the changes, or cancel the operation in progress. Returning a value of False (.F.) indicates to the framework that whatever process called OnChangesVerified() should be halted. Here's the code:

```
*--MyDataFrm.OnChangesVerified()
LOCAL lnResponse, llReturn
#DEFINE BUTTON_YES     6
#DEFINE BUTTON_NO      7
#DEFINE BUTTON_CANCEL 2
#DEFINE SUPRESS_VERIFICATION .T.

lnResponse = _SCREEN.goMessages.showmessage("ConfirmChanges")

DO CASE
   CASE lnResponse = BUTTON_YES
      llReturn = THIS.SAVE()

   CASE lnResponse = BUTTON_NO
      this.UNDO(,SUPRESS_VERIFICATION)
      llReturn  = .T.

   CASE lnResponse = BUTTON_CANCEL
      *--Do Nothing, llReturn is already false.
   OTHERWISE
      ASSERT .F. MESSAGE "This return value is not supported."
ENDCASE

RETURN llReturn
```

Notice that the message is not displayed directly by the form. Instead, the request for a message is passed to the messaging object created in chapter 10, "Business Objects." The result of calling _Screen.goMessages.ShowMessage() is shown in **Figure 5**.

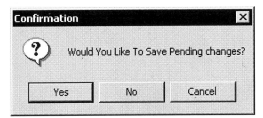

Figure 5. The default confirmation message.

Closing MyDataFrm

Before closing a data entry form, you want to make sure that the user is given a chance to save any pending edits. To accomplish this, the DoClose() method is extended to check for unsaved changes before closing the form.

As a reminder, the DoClose() method is inherited from aForm. In aForm, the DoClose() method does the cleanup work associated with closing a framework form and then releases the form. In MyDataFrm, the DoClose() method is extended using DODEFAULT(); it is not overwritten.

The code for MyDataFrm.DoClose() checks to see if unsaved changes exist. If changes exist and they are not verified, the close operation is canceled by returning a value of False (.F.). Following is the code for closing a form.

The code for OnChangesVerified() was presented earlier in this chapter in the section titled "Verifying changes."

```
*--MyDataFrm.DoClose()
LOCAL llOKToClose

IF THIS.UnsavedChangesExist() AND ! THIS.OnChangesVerified()
   llOKToClose = .F.
ELSE
   llOKToClose = DODEFAULT()
ENDIF

RETURN  llOKToClose
```

Closing all forms

In Chapter 5, "Beginning Development," in the section titled "aApplication," I outlined the application class and the steps that the MyFrame framework would follow as part of the shutdown process.

The first step in the shutdown process is to close all open forms. The CloseAllForms() method of aApplication loops through each form in the framework Forms collection and simply calls the custom Close() method added to all framework forms. For every form in the MyFrame framework, calling the Close() method ensures that the form cleans up after itself before it releases. As I demonstrated in the previous section, data entry forms also check for unsaved changes to ensure that the user does not inadvertently lose pending edits.

At any time during the shutdown sequence, users can prevent the application from closing if they have pending edits. To review, when a user closes a data entry form, and no changes are pending, the form closes. However, when changes are pending, the user has the option to save the changes, to not save the changes, or to cancel the close altogether. The CloseAllForms() method prevents the application from closing if the user cancels the close of any form.

At times, however, it is necessary to "kick out" all the users of an application. For example, some backup systems do not work properly when FoxPro tables are open. Passing a value of True to CloseAllForms() forces the form to revert any pending changes without prompting the user. The CloseAllForms() method is shown here:

```
*--aApplication.CloseAllForms()
FUNCTION CloseAllForms( tlCloseWithForce )

   LOCAL llOK, loForm
   llOK = .T.

   IF  TYPE('_SCREEN.goFormsCollection') = 'O' AND;
       ! ISNULL(_SCREEN.goFormsCollection)

       DO WHILE .T.
          _SCREEN.goFormsCollection.GoFirst()
          loForm = _SCREEN.goFormsCollection.GetCurrentItem()
          IF ISNULL(loForm)
             *--loForm is null when no more forms are left
             *)  in the collection...
             EXIT
```

```
          ENDIF
          IF tlCloseWithForce and PemStatus(loForm,'Undo',5)
              loForm.UNDO(,.T.)
          ENDIF

          llOK = loForm.Close()
          IF ! llOK
              EXIT
          ENDIF

      ENDDO
   ENDIF

   RETURN llOK

ENDFUNC
```

Navigation

FoxPro supports record-based and set-based navigation. The commands SKIP, GO TOP, and GO BOTTOM move the record pointer to a particular record based on its position in the table and are examples of record-based navigation. However, this type of navigation is not appropriate in all situations. Scrolling through 1 million records one at a time is not a practical way for users to find information. In the proper situation, however (read: small tables), it is practical and often desirable to offer record-based navigation. Large tables, however, require that the user be able to search a subset of data to find one or a few records.

All controls must be coordinated in a comprehensive navigation strategy. **Figure 6** illustrates a scenario in which the user can move from one record to another by clicking an item in the list box located on the left side of the form, or one of the VCR buttons located toward the bottom of the form or in the navigation toolbar.

Figure 6 also illustrates that a navigation control can be a member of the form or that it can exist outside of the form. In addition to the toolbars illustrated in Figure 6, navigation may originate from menus, programs, or other forms. VCR buttons, list boxes, combo boxes, search dialogs, and treeviews are all controls that users associate with navigation.

In this section, I'll explain how to navigate from one record to another, describe the framework controls that direct this process, and show you how to coordinate the display of all controls involved.

The form's role

The form class is responsible for accepting navigation requests, forwarding the requests to the appropriate controls, and refreshing the display after the navigation is complete.

In Chapter 10, "Business Objects," I created a business object class called MyDataEnvrionment, which bears the responsibility of moving the record pointer. To accomplish this, I created one method, Go(). The Go() method of MyDataEnvrionment accepts a primary key value and, optionally, an alias in which the navigation should occur.

MyDataFrm also has one method primarily responsible for navigating; it, too, is named Go() and it has the same parameters as MyDataEnvronment.Go(). However, the responsibilities of each class are completely different. MyDataEnvironment.Go() moves the record pointer or retrieves a specific record. MyDataFrm.Go() ensures that all pending edits are saved, notifies the user when a navigation request fails, and refreshes the form when it succeeds.

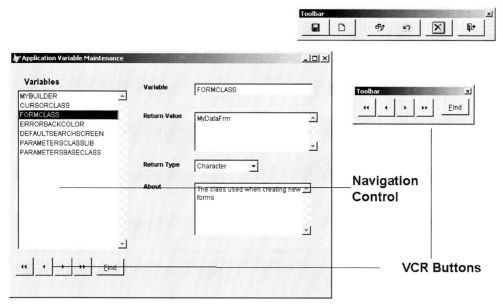

Figure 6. An example of navigation controls.

As mentioned in the previous section, a request for navigation can come from a variety of sources, and each source is different. For example, VCR buttons behave differently than do treeview controls. When a user clicks the Next button, he or she expects to move to the next record. However, for VCR buttons, the next record is generally the next record in the table, while in a treeview control, the "next" record may be the next sibling, which may not be the next physical record in the table.

MyDataFrm has a property, oNavigator, which stores a reference to the navigation control for that form. MyDataFrm forwards requests to GoTop(), GoNext(), GoPrevious(), and GoBottom() to the navigation control rather than overcomplicate the form code to accommodate a variety of navigational scenarios.

When to move

MyDataFrm supports two styles of data entry: Edit First and Edit Always. Examples of these styles were illustrated earlier in the chapter. To review, a form that is in Edit First mode requires that a user click an Edit button prior to editing information. The user is allowed to freely navigate from one record to another when the form has its Edit Mode set to False. However, once edits are pending, the user is restricted from moving to another record until the edits have been committed or reverted.

The user can freely navigate from one record to the next when a form is in the Edit Always style of entry. If edits are pending, the user must commit or revert the changes before moving to another record.

Whether a user is allowed to navigate is controlled by the AllowNav() method of the form. You can force AllowNav() to allow navigation by passing a value of True. You would do this, for example, when moving the record pointer in a child table in a one-to-many relationship. Here's the code for the AllowNav() method:

```
*--MyDatafrm.AllowNav()
LPARAMETERS tlOverride
LOCAL llAllowNav

*--Navigation is not allowed if DE is not a framework de
IF  THIS.HasFrameworkDE()

    IF  tlOverride
        *--Allow navigation in all cases
        *) when instructed to override checks
        llAllowNav = .T.
    ELSE
        IF THIS.lAlwaysEdit
            *--Check for unsaved work
            IF THIS.UnsavedChangesExist()
                llAllowNav=THIS.OnChangesVerified()
            ELSE
                llAllowNav = .T.
            ENDIF
        ELSE
            *--If in edit first mode,
            *) prevent navigation while in
            *) edit mode.
            llAllowNav =! THIS.lEditMode
        ENDIF

    ENDIF

ENDIF

RETURN llAllowNav
```

Notice that if unsaved changes exist, a call is made to verify that the user wants to save changes. This is a call to the same method that is called to verify changes before adding new records. The code for the OnChangesVerfied() method was illustrated earlier in this chapter, in the section titled "Verifying changes."

Record-based vs. set-based navigation
The user can navigate using "record-based navigation" or "set-based navigation." When record-based navigation is in effect, the user can choose "Top," "Previous," "Next," or "Bottom." The MyDataFrm class has a property lAllowRecordBasedNavigation that controls whether record-based navigation is allowed.

This feature is required primarily to keep toolbars from displaying the VCR buttons as enabled. When lAllowRecordBasedNavigation is False, the VCR buttons are disabled.

Moving
The MyDataFrm class does not move the record pointer directly. Instead, it forwards the request to a business object or a special navigation object. For example, the Go() method passes the request to the business object. The form's Go() method is responsible for calling either OnNavigationSucceeded() or OnNavigationFailed(), allowing the application developer to take an appropriate action. If the navigation is successful, the Go() method is also responsible for calling the form's Refresh() method. Here's the code:

```
*--MyDataFrm.Go()
LPARAMETERS tuID, tcAlias, tlOverride

LOCAL llNavigated , llAllowNav

llAllowNav = THIS.AllowNav(tlOverride)

IF llAllowNav
    llNavigated = THIS.oDE.GO(tuID, tcAlias)
    IF llNavigated
        THIS.OnNavigationSucceeded( tcAlias )
        *) Prevent calling the refresh while other controls are
        *) still initializing.
        IF THIS.lActivateFired
            THISFORM.REFRESH()
        ENDIF
    ELSE
        THIS.OnNavigationFailed( tcAlias )
    ENDIF

ENDIF

RETURN llNavigated
```

Like the Go() method, the GoTop(), GoNext(), GoPrevious(), and GoBottom() methods of MyDataFrm forward their requests to the navigation control for the form. For example, the GoTop() method forwards the request as shown in the following code. Note the check for lAllowRecordBasedNavigation. The framework sets this property to True when a framework navigational control is placed on the form.

```
*--MyDataFrm.GoTop()
LOCAL llNavigated

IF THIS.lAllowRecordBasedNavigation
    llNavigated = THIS.oNavigator.GoTop()
ENDIF

RETURN llNavigated
```

The navigation controls

The source code that accompanies this book demonstrates the use of the List Box, Combo Box, Tree View, and Search Form as examples of navigation controls. In this section I'll explain how the List Box control is developed to illustrate the major features of a navigation control.

 The other navigation controls are similarly constructed and are not reviewed in this book. They are, however, included in the source code that accompanies this book.

Figure 7 shows an example of MyNavLst in action, as used in the System Code Management screen. By clicking on one of the possible selections, the underlying record pointer is moved. The grid reflects the information in that record.

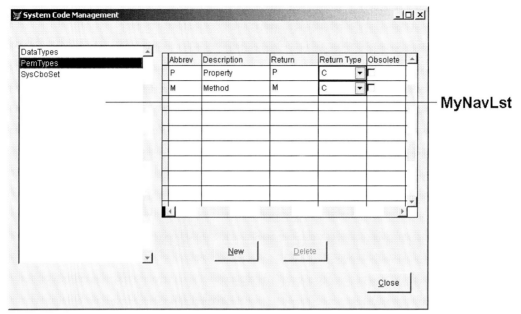

Figure 7. *MyNavLst in action.*

The following code in the Navigate() method is called when the user clicks a selection in the list box or uses the arrow keys to move from one item to the next. The Navigate event calls the form's Go() method, passing the value of the control and, if specified, a target alias. If the navigation is unsuccessful, the control is returned to the previously displayed record, as shown here:

```
*--MyNavlst.Navigate()
LOCAL lAllowMove
IF ! EMPTY(THIS.VALUE)
    IF PEMSTATUS(THISFORM,'go',5)
        lAllowMove = THISFORM.GO(THIS.VALUE, THIS.cTargetAlias)
        IF lAllowMove
            this.cLastID = this.Value
        ELSE
            THIS.VALUE = THIS.cLastID
        ENDIF
    ENDIF
ENDIF
```

The MyDataFrm class passes the request for "Top," "Previous," "Next," or "Last" to the navigation control, and allows the control to "decide" which is the next control. By keeping the determination of which record is "next" or "previous," you can change the behavior of each form by changing the navigation control. For example, VCR buttons may use the order of the table to determine which records are "next" or "previous," while a Web browser uses a history of sites visited to determine which records are "next" or "previous." For this list box, the GoBottom() method is as follows:

```
*--MyNavlst.GoBottom()
IF THIS.LISTCOUNT>0
    THIS.LISTINDEX = this.ListCount
    THIS.Navigate()
ENDIF
```

At times it is necessary to update a navigation control for an action that occurs during data entry. For example, if the user deletes a control, it should no longer appear as a viable selection.

New to Visual FoxPro 8.0 is the BindEvent() method, which gives us the ability to bind events, properties, or methods of one class to events that occur in another. We can use BindEvent() in our list box control to force the list box to Requery() each time a record is deleted. The following code, placed in MyNavList.Init(), binds the list box to the form's data entry methods.

```
*--MyNavLst.Init()
DODEFAULT()
*--PEMSTATUS() is used to ensure that this control
*) only binds if the form method exists.
IF PEMSTATUS(THISFORM,'OnSave',5)
    BINDEVENT(THISFORM,'OnSave',THIS,'OnSave',1)
ENDIF

IF PEMSTATUS(THISFORM,'OnUndo',5)
    BINDEVENT(THISFORM,'OnUndo',THIS,'requery',1)
ENDIF

IF PEMSTATUS(THISFORM,'OnDelete',5)
    BINDEVENT(THISFORM,'OnDelete',THIS,'requery',1)
ENDIF

BINDEVENT(THISFORM,'Init',THIS,'Navigate',1)
```

The benefit of using the BindEvent()method is that you do not need to program each form based on the navigation control it uses. Each navigation control is self-contained, and is ready for use as soon as you drop it on the form.

Building business objects on the fly

By now, you might be thinking to yourself that the data entry and navigation methods just presented will only work with the MyDataEnvironment of MyFrame. And, you would be correct. Chapter 11, "Framework Services," walked you through the process of manually creating a business object. This section shows how to create a business object on the fly using the information (cursors and relations) contained in the form's data environment.

To review, three classes serve as the basis for each business object: data environment, cursor, and relation. It would be ideal if you were able to specify which classes FoxPro used to create these classes. Then, while working in the form's data environment, you could be building framework functionality directly from the Form Designer. But alas, you cannot.

MyDataFrm contains a method, BuildDE(), which is called when the form does not already have a framework data environment. BuildDE() dynamically creates one by adding a cursor or relation class for each cursor and relation in the current DataSession.

The myAppVars framework service illustrated in Chapter 11 contains entries that define the classes used to create the business object. The BuildDE() method first obtains those values and creates a new data environment. Then it adds a cursor object to the data environment for each open table. It also does a second loop, adding a relation class to the data environment for each relation a cursor is engaged in. Here's the code for BuildDE():

```
*--MyDataFrm.BuildDE()
DataEnvironment_Class = _SCREEN.goappvars.GetAppVar("BUSINESSOBJECTCLASS")
Relation_Class        = _SCREEN.goappvars.GetAppVar("RELATIONCLASS")
Cursor_Class          = _SCREEN.goappvars.GetAppVar("CURSORCLASS")

WITH THIS
    .oDE = CREATEOBJECT(DataEnvironment_Class)

    lnSelect = SELECT()
    lnTables = AUSED(laTables)

    *--Set the current alias as the initial
    *) selected alias
    .oDE.INITIALSELECTEDALIAS = ALIAS()

    FOR lnI = 1 TO lnTables

        lcAlias =  laTables[lni,1]

        SELECT(lcAlias)
        lcTable = JUSTSTEM( DBF() )
        lcOrder = ORDER(lcAlias)

        *--Add Cursor Object
        lcObjectName = 'o'+PROPER(lcAlias)
        .oDE.ADDOBJECT(lcObjectName, Cursor_Class, lcTable ,lcAlias)
        .oDE.&lcObjectName..ORDER = lcOrder

        *--While the alias is selected, get all relations
        LOCAL lo AS RELATION
        x= 1
        DO WHILE .T.
            lcForeignCursor = TARGET(x)
            IF  EMPTY(lcForeignCursor)
                *--This alias is not related to another
                *) cursor
                EXIT
            ELSE
                *--Add a relation class...
                lcForeignKey = ORDER(TARGET(x))
                lcParentCursor = lcAlias
                lcParentKey = RELATION(x)
                lcNewRelation = lcParentCursor+"_"+lcForeignCursor
                .oDE.ADDOBJECT(lcNewRelation , Relation_Class )
                *--And set the appropriate properties
                .oDE.&lcNewRelation..PARENTALIAS    = lcParentCursor
                .oDE.&lcNewRelation..RELATIONALEXPR = lcParentKey
                .oDE.&lcNewRelation..CHILDORDER     = lcForeignKey
                .oDE.&lcNewRelation..CHILDALIAS     = lcForeignCursor
            ENDIF

            x = x + 1
        ENDDO
    ENDFOR

ENDWITH
```

Displaying validation errors

Telling users that they have entered information incorrectly, and which information is incorrect, is the "minimum" you should do. A nice feature is to highlight the controls in which an error occurred. The code that provides this functionality relies on the business object's error collection (see Chapter 10, "Business Objects") and the form controls collection (see Chapter 12, "Forms"). After a quick review of these items, I'll demonstrate how to display validation messages and highlight any appropriate controls.

The business object is responsible for validating data before saving it. To record a business logic error, you call the AddError() method of the business object, passing an error message, as well as the alias and field name in which the error occurred. For example, the following code exists in the MyMessages business object and notifies a user that the data in the MsgText field of the Messages table is invalid:

```
*--Sample Code: MyMessages.IsValid()
IF EMPTY(MESSAGES.msgtext)
    THIS.AddError("The 'Message Text' cannot be empty.","Messages","MsgText")
    RETURN .F.
ENDIF
```

The aForm class also contains a FormControlsCollection that stores a reference to every control on a form. The FormControlsCollection is an array-based collection with a reference to the control in the first column, and when appropriate, the ControlSource alias in the second column and the ControlSource field name in the third column.

For each error in an error collection, we can test to see which control is bound to the alias and field in which the error occurs. If the control has a SetErrorState() method, it is called.

```
*--MyDataFrm.ShowError()
LOCAL lcMessage, lnI, lnRow, loControl, loErrorForm
lcMessage = .oDE.GetErrorMessage()

WITH THIS.oDE.oErrorCollection
    lnErrorCount = .GetCount()

    FOR lnI = 1 TO lnErrorCount

        lnRow =
THIS.oFormControlsCollection.Contains(.ADATA[lnI,2]+'.'+.ADATA[lnI,3],2)

        IF lnRow>0

            loControl = THIS.oFormControlsCollection.ADATA[lnRow,1]

            IF PEMSTATUS(loControl,'SetErrorState',5)
                loControl.SetErrorState()
            ENDIF

            *--Set focus to each control that has an error
            IF PEMSTATUS(loControl,'SETFOCUS',5)
                loControl.SETFOCUS()
            ENDIF

        ENDIF
    ENDFOR
ENDWITH
```

```
LoErrorForm = CREATEOBJECT("MyDataEntryErrorList")
loErrorForm.SetErrorText(lcMessage)
loErrorForm.SHOW()
```

An example of the error message displayed to the user is shown in **Figure 8**.

One feature worth noting about the Validation Error form is that it is non-modal. This means that it remains open, but allows users to make corrections based on the error information displayed in the error dialog.

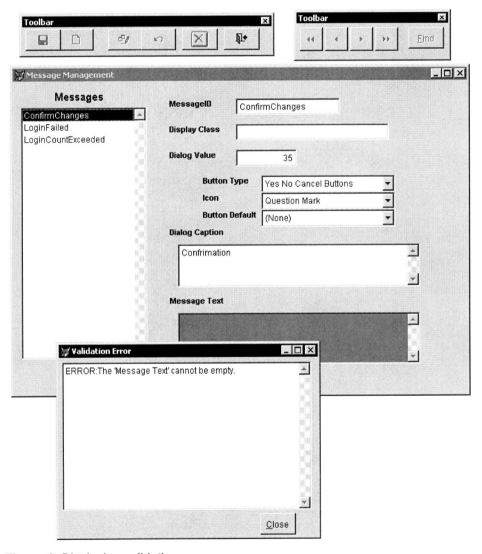

Figure 8*. Displaying validation errors.*

Summary

In this chapter, you learned how to create a flexible data entry form class that supports many different styles of data entry. Each style assures that the user is in control of when pending edits are written to the underlying database.

This chapter also illustrated the concept of separating data entry tasks between classes. The form class, MyDataFrm, is responsible for accepting data entry and navigation requests, then forwarding those requests to the appropriate control. In addition to fulfilling this role as broker, the form class also controls when the form is refreshed.

In conjunction with the previous chapter, this chapter also illustrated how to use the power of inheritance. For example, the mechanics of closing a form are located in aForm, the base form class. MyDataFrm added a check for pending edits to the closing process while retaining the functionality implemented in its parent class.

Having read this chapter and the previous chapter, you should feel comfortable with designing your own form class hierarchy.

Chapter 14
Toolbars

Toolbars are used to manipulate forms and provide easy access to system-level functions. Coordinating the interaction between toolbars and other framework classes can be a bit of a challenge. In this chapter, you will analyze the relationship between toolbars and other framework elements and develop an approach for coordinating their interaction.

The toolbar class included with FoxPro is functional as is. That is, toolbars are dockable, automatically resize to properly display their controls, and cannot be covered by a form. Not included in the standard toolbar class is how it fits into the overall scheme of your framework.

This chapter begins with an overview of some additional behaviors that users generally expect from toolbars. Throughout the chapter you will learn that several framework elements must work together for toolbars to behave as you expect them to behave. Additionally, the toolbar classes rely on many of the services developed in previous chapters. When the toolbar classes collaborate with or rely on the classes developed in previous chapters, I'll refer you back to the chapter in which those classes were developed. However, the association between the toolbar classes and other classes is explained in this chapter.

Having read this chapter you will know how toolbars are incorporated into MyFrame and have a solid understanding of how to include toolbars in your framework.

Expected behaviors

Most applications have a list of toolbars available to the user. For example, the View | Toolbars menu option in FoxPro displays a form in which you can select the toolbars you want to see. Clicking OK results in the creation of selected toolbars. **Figure 1** shows the FoxPro toolbar selection form.

FoxPro "remembers" which toolbars you've selected. The next time you open FoxPro, the toolbars that you have selected are created automatically. Each toolbar also remembers (usually) where it was last situated and whether or not it was docked.

Toolbars are sometimes created as a form opens. For example, when previewing a report, a toolbar appears while the report is open. Once the report is closed, the toolbar is closed as well.

Toolbars are often used as a common control between forms. For example, when editing a form you may prefer to use the Form Controls toolbar. However, editing multiple forms does not result in the creation of multiple Form Controls toolbars. One Form Controls toolbar is created, and can be used for any form that is being edited.

As a user switches between forms, either by opening and closing forms or by switching between open forms, each toolbar reflects the features available for the selected form. For example, when designing a form, the Save button on FoxPro's "standard" toolbar is enabled. If you click on the Project Manager or the command window, the Save button is disabled.

In this chapter you will learn how you can provide the ability for users to select which toolbars they want to view and how to coordinate the interaction between forms and toolbars in your framework.

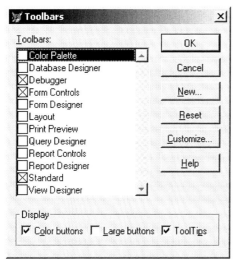

Figure 1. FoxPro's toolbar selection form.

Toolbar Manager

Toolbars can be created when the application starts, as a form loads, or when the user specifically chooses to view them. Toolbars may be released when the user closes the toolbar directly, as a form closes, or when the user closes the application. Rather than placing the code for creating and releasing toolbars in each of these classes, I have created a single class (MyToolbars) responsible for creating and releasing toolbars. MyToolbars is a subclass of MyDataEnvironment. (For more information, see Chapter 10, "Business Objects.")

Each toolbar should be instantiated only once. To limit the number of toolbars created, I have added an instance of the class MySet to store a reference to each toolbar created. MySet is one of the collection classes created in Chapter 8, "Collections." The instance of MySet is named oToolbarCollection.

To review, a set is a collection of items in which no duplicates exist. The "collection" is actually an array property of MySet, aData[]. The collection classes support a stack interface, or the Push() and Pop() methods. As duplicated items are pushed onto the collection, the item is not added to the collection again. Instead, an internal counter is incremented. As an element is removed, or popped from the collection, the counter is decremented. When the counter reaches 0, the row is removed from the collection entirely. When the object, in this case a toolbar, is removed from the collection, there is no longer a reference to the toolbar, and the toolbar closes.

Toolbars are created with CreateObject()—much like the Forms collection presented in Chapter 12, "Forms." The variable reference returned from CreateObject() needs to be stored to keep the variable reference "alive," preventing the toolbar from being released prematurely.

To retain the variable reference returned from CreateObject(), an additional column has been added to MySet. This is accomplished by changing its nCols property from 2, the default value, to 3. MySet uses the first two columns to store the element of the collection and the internal counter, respectively. The third column added to MySet stores the variable reference for each toolbar created.

Figure 2 shows an example of how the array might appear in memory.

aData[]	1	2	3
	Class Name	Instance Count	Object Reference
1	MyDataTlb		3 (Object)
2	MyDevTlb		1 (Object)

Figure 2. *An array for storing toolbar information.*

The Toolbar Manager has six methods: MakeToolbar(), ReleaseToolbar(), RefreshToolbars(), LoadToolbars(), GetPrefs(), and SetPrefs(). These methods are discussed in the sections that follow.

Creating a toolbar

The MakeToolbar() method accepts the name of a toolbar class as a parameter. The class name is added to oToolbarCollection using the Push() method. The Push() method either adds the toolbar class to the array and sets the counter to 1, or it increments the counter by one.

Calling GetInstanceCount() returns the number of outstanding references to the toolbar. If GetInstanceCount() returns 1, there are no outstanding references (other than the one just added), and the toolbar is created.

As each toolbar is created, a reference to the toolbar is stored in the third column of the array. Storing the object reference is required to ensure that the variable reference to the created toolbar does not go out of scope.

Here's the code for creating a new toolbar.

```
*--MyToolbars.MakeToolbar()
LPARAMETERS tcToolbarClass
WITH THIS.oToolbarCollection
    LOCAL lcToolbarClass, lnRow, loToolbar as aToolbar
    lcToolbarClass = ALLTRIM(UPPER(tcToolbarClass ))
    lnRow = .PUSH(lcToolbarClass)

    IF .GetInstanceCount( lcToolbarClass ) = 1
        *--Create the toolbar and add it to the
        *) Third column of the collection
        loToolbar = CREATEOBJECT( lcToolbarClass )
        .ADATA[lnRow,3] = loToolbar
        loToolbar.VISIBLE = .T.
    ENDIF

    RETURN loToolbar
ENDWITH
```

Releasing a toolbar

The ReleaseToolbar() method accepts a toolbar class as a parameter and removes it from oToolbarCollection.

The Pop() method of MySet, the parent class of oToolbarCollection, decrements an internal counter. When the counter equals 0, the row containing the toolbar reference is removed. When the row is removed, the reference to the toolbar is released. When the reference is released, the toolbar is closed. No further action is required. The code for releasing a toolbar is shown here:

```
*--MyToolbars.ReleaseToolbar()
LPARAMETERS tcToolbarClass
THIS.oToolbarCollection.POP( ALLTRIM(UPPER(tcToolbarClass)) )
```

Refreshing toolbars
A simple loop through the collection refreshes all active toolbars.

```
*--MyToolbars.RefreshToolbars()
LOCAL lnRowCount
lnRowCount = THIS.oToolbarCollection.nRows
FOR lnI = 1 TO lnRowCount
    THIS.oToolbarCollection.ADATA[lnI,3].REFRESH()
ENDFOR
```

The Toolbar collection's RefreshToolbars() method is called from the form Refresh(). This refreshes all toolbars each time a user navigates to a new record, deletes a record, activates a new form, and so on. In this way, when the user changes focus from one form to another, for example, the proper toolbars are displayed with the appropriate buttons enabled or disabled.

Loading toolbars at application startup
Providing the ability for users to add toolbars as their application loads adds a professional touch to your application that most users will appreciate. Toolbars.dbf is the table that holds the list of toolbars from which users can select a toolbar to view. **Figure 3** shows the structure for Toolbars.dbf.

The Toolbar Manager class, MyToolbars (based on MyDataEnvironment), contains an instance of MyCursor created in Chapter 9, "Cursor and CursorAdapter." The instance of MyCursor is named oToolbars and is responsible for loading Toolbars.dbf.

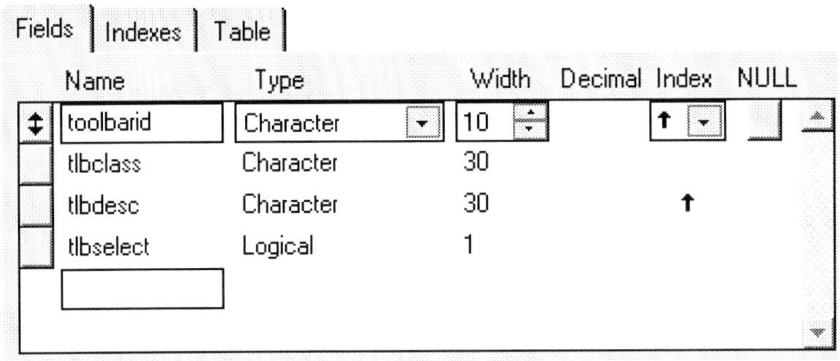

Name	Type	Width	Decimal	Index	NULL
toolbarid	Character	10		↑	
tlbclass	Character	30			
tlbdesc	Character	30		↑	
tlbselect	Logical	1			

Figure 3. The structure of the Toolbars table.

Adding toolbars for selection

Figure 4 shows the Toolbar Manager form, MyToolbarManager.scx, in which you enter the toolbars you want to make available for selection. The Toolbar Manager form is provided for developers to create the toolbar selection list; it's unlikely that you will choose to provide it in a final application. You can access the Toolbar Manager form from the "MyFrame" menu pad provided in the source code accompanying this book.

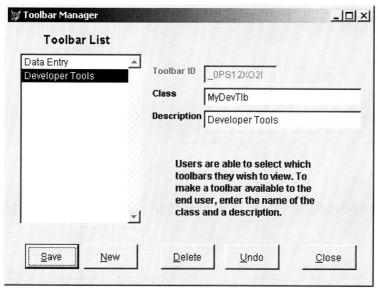

Figure 4. *Adding toolbars for user selection.*

MyToolbarManager.scx is an example of how to use the data entry form class created in Chapter 12, "Forms." It uses the class MyToolbars as its data handler. If you look through the sample code accompanying this book, you will find that MyToolbarManager.scx contains no code. It is a fully functioning data entry form created with classes that were created in previous chapters.

*Toolbars do not need to be in this list to be used throughout the application. This is simply the list of toolbars you choose to allow users to instantiate directly. Users can select which toolbars they want to instantiate using the MyToolbarPreferences form shown in **Figure 5**.*

User selection

Figure 5 shows the toolbar-selection form, MyToolbarPreferences.scx, which is provided for users to decide which toolbars they want to view. MyToolbarPreferences.scx inherits from MyDataFrm (see Chapter 12, "Forms") and uses MyToolbars (based on MyDataEnvironment, described in Chapter 10, "Business Objects") to load the Toolbars table.

Placing a checkmark next to a toolbar, and then clicking Apply, results in the creation of a toolbar if it is not already active. In addition, the toolbar is automatically created the next time the application starts.

Figure 5*. Allowing users to choose which toolbars they prefer to see.*

Loading previous selections

As the name of MyToolbarPreferences implies, the toolbars that a user chooses to load when an application starts is a preference for that user. I mentioned that Toolbars.dbf stores a list of toolbars available for an application. However, in a multi-user environment, a second table is required to store a user's selections.

Rather than create a separate table to store the user's selections, you can take advantage of the MyPreferences framework service instead. The preferences class, MyPreferences, was created in Chapter 11, "Framework Services," in the section titled "Saving preferences."

To load the user's selections for each toolbar, you must scan through each record in Toolbars.dbf and obtain the preferences for that user. The following code in MyToolbars.GetPrefs() obtains the user's toolbar preferences by calling the framework service GoPreferences as follows:

```
*--MyToolbars.GetPrefs()
SCAN
    REPLACE Toolbars.tlbSelect with ;
    _SCREEN.goPreferences.getpreference(Toolbars.toolbarid)
ENDSCAN
```

MyToolbars.GetPrefs() is called from the OnLoad() method of the toolbar selection form, MyToolbarPreferences.scx. Calling GetPrefs() as the form loads results in a checkmark appearing next to the toolbars the user has selected, as illustrated in Figure 5.

Applying changes

When the user clicks the Apply button in Figure 5, the application calls the SetPrefs() method of MyToolbars. To save a user's selections, SetPrefs() loops through each record. A call is made to save the preference and, if the user has chosen to view the toolbar, the MakeToolbar() method is called to create the toolbar. The code for the SetPrefs() method is shown here.

```
*--MyToolbars.SetPrefs()
LOCAL lcClass
SCAN
    _SCREEN.goPreferences.NewPreference(
        Toolbars.toolbarid,"_Toolbar",Toolbars.tlbselect)

    IF Toolbars.tlbselect
        lcClass = ALLTRIM(UPPER(Toolbars.tlbclass))
        _SCREEN.goToolbars.MakeToolbar( lcClass )
    ENDIF
ENDSCAN
```

Changes to aApplication

The Toolbar Manager is instantiated at the start of an application. All the framework elements are loaded in the aApplication.OnLoadComponents() method and are released when the application is closed. To understand why the Toolbar collection is added to the _SCREEN object, see Chapter 11, "Framework Services," in the section titled "Making framework services available."

Creating the Toolbar Manager

The following lines in aApplication.onLoadComponents() instantiate the Toolbar collection.

```
*--aApplication.OnLoadComponents()
.
.
.
_SCREEN.ADDPROPERTY("goToolbars",CREATEOBJECT("MyToolbars"))
.
.
.
```

Loading toolbars at application startup

When the class MyToolbars is instantiated, it calls its LoadToolbars() method, which loops through each toolbar and retrieves the user's preference for the toolbar. If the user prefers to view the toolbar, the toolbar class is passed to the MakeToolbar() method and the toolbar is created. The code for the MyToolbars.LoadToolbars() method is shown here:

```
*--MyToolbars.LoadToolbars()
IF VARTYPE(_SCREEN.goPreferences) = 'O'
    THIS.oToolbars.SELECT()
    SCAN
        llLoadToolbar = _SCREEN.goPreferences.getpreference(Toolbars.toolbarid)
        IF llLoadToolbar
            lcToolbar = ALLTRIM(Toolbars.tlbclass)
            THIS.MakeToolbar(lcToolbar)
        ENDIF
    ENDSCAN
ENDIF
```

Application shutdown

As the application closes, each object created in aApplication.LoadComponents() is released. This action accomplishes two things in the case of the Toolbar Manager. First, the Toolbar Manager is released. Second, as the Toolbar Manager is released, the objects it contains are also released. One of the objects the toolbar contains is oToolbarCollection, which holds the references to each toolbar. When oToolbarCollection is released, the reference to each toolbar is released and any open toolbars are released as well. The following lines, added to aApplication.ReleaseObjects(), result in the release of all toolbars.

```
*--aApplication.ReleaseObjects ()
.
.
.
  IF VARTYPE(_SCREEN.goToolBars) = 'O'
     _SCREEN.GoToolbars=.NULL.")
  ENDIF
.
.
.
```

Synchronizing forms and toolbars

Each form is responsible for "telling" the Toolbar Manager which toolbars it needs. The base form class, aForm (see Chapter 12, "Forms") has a property, cToolbars, that holds a comma-delimited list of toolbars associated with each form. Additionally, aForm has two methods, CreateToolbars() and ReleaseToolbars().

The CreateToolbars() method is called from the form's Load event. It parses the list of toolbars using the new StrExtract() function and calls the Toolbar Manager's MakeToolbar() method.

StrExtract() was new to Visual FoxPro 7.0. It returns the values between two delimiters. In this case the delimiter is a comma, and for StrExtract() to work properly, a comma must appear at the beginning and the end of the string. Rather than requiring the developer to remember to pad the list of toolbars with commas, the commas are added before calling StrExtract().

The CreateToolbars() method of a form is little more than a parsing routine that forwards a request to goToolbars, as shown here:

```
*--aForm.CreateToolbars()
IF ! EMPTY(THIS.cToolBars) AND TYPE('_SCREEN.goToolBars') = 'O' AND !
ISNULL(_SCREEN.goToolbars)

   LOCAL lcToolBars, lcToolBar,lnI

   lnToolBarCount = OCCURS(',',THIS.cToolBars)+1

   *--Add beginning and trailing commas
   lcToolBars = ','+ALLTRIM(THIS.cToolBars)+','

   FOR lnI = 1 TO lnToolBarCount
         lcToolBar = STREXTRACT(lcToolBars, ',', ',', lnI)

      _SCREEN.goToolbars.MakeToolbar(lcToolBar)
   ENDFOR

ENDIF
```

As a form is released, it calls its ReleaseToolbars() method. The ReleaseToolbars() method is not shown here. It contains a similar parsing routine, but passes the name of the toolbar to the goToolbars.ReleaseToolbar() method.

The MakeToolbar() and ReleaseToolbar() methods of MyToolbars were shown earlier in this chapter.

Toolbars and data entry

Toolbars in combination with data entry forms exhibit a "quirky" behavior. For example, suppose you have entered information into a data-bound text box on a form. If you have not tabbed out of the text box before you click on a toolbar, the information in the text box is not written to the underlying table.

This quirk arises because a toolbar is a form, and therefore the text box on the form does not lose focus when you click a control on a toolbar. The value in a text box, or any data-bound control, is written to the underlying table after the control loses focus. The problem is compounded because the Activate() event of the toolbar does not fire either.

On a side note, this problem is most often associated with the relationship between forms and toolbars; this is why I have chosen to address this issue in this chapter. However, if you enter information into a text box and try to close an application by clicking the application's Close button, the data in a bound control is not written to disk either.

To solve this problem, you need to devise a way to ensure that all data is flushed from each control before calling a form method from a toolbar. For example, in Chapter 12, "Forms," I presented MyDataFrm, which is the data entry form for MyFrame. MyDataFrm contains a Save() method. Prior to calling the Save() method from the toolbar, the data in the active control needs to be flushed to its underlying data source. You only need to address the currently selected control because it is the only control that may not have lost focus before a user clicked the toolbar or attempted to close the application.

The question, then, is how to do this. Stepping back from the problem a little, this is not necessarily a form-to-toolbar communication problem. Instead, the problem could be defined as follows: "Prior to performing any data-related functions, a data entry form must ensure that data is flushed from the currently active control."

Defining the problem in this way leads me to add a method to the data entry form class that "knows" how to force the active control to write its data to an underlying table. I have added a method, ForceDataFlush(), to MyDataFrm, which accomplishes just that. The following code checks for an active control, and if one is active, calls its SetFocus() method. The act of calling a bound control's SetFocus() method forces it to write buffered data to its underlying data source. Here's the code:

```
*--MyDataFrm.ForceDataFlush()
IF TYPE('this.ActiveControl') = 'O' AND;
      ! ISNULL(THIS.ACTIVECONTROL) AND;
      PEMSTATUS(THIS.ACTIVECONTROL,'SetFocus',5)

   THIS.ACTIVECONTROL.SETFOCUS

ENDIF
```

A call is made to the ForceDataFlush() method from the data entry form's Save(), New(), Undo(), Delete(), and Close() methods. As a result of this change, the responsibility for flushing data is contained within the data entry form.

Refreshing toolbars

The Toolbar Manager is responsible for refreshing toolbars. However, toolbars need to be refreshed each time a form is activated or released. Toolbars also need to be refreshed each time a data entry form (see Chapter 12, "Forms") changes its edit mode.

In MyFrame, each time a form is activated or has its Edit Mode property changed, the form is refreshed. The following code, called from aForm.Refresh(), ensures that the toolbars are refreshed each time the form is refreshed.

```
*--aForm.Refresh()
IF TYPE('_SCREEN.goToolBars') = 'O' AND ! ISNULL(_SCREEN.goToolbars)
     _screen.goToolbars.RefreshToolbars()
ENDIF
```

Each time a form is closed, the toolbars for a form need to be released. Additionally, any toolbars that remain open need to be refreshed. The DoClose() method of aForm accomplishes this, as shown here:

```
*--aform.DoClose()
WITH THIS
   .VISIBLE=.F.
   .SaveLoc()
   .ReleaseToolbars()
   .RefreshToolbars()
   .RemoveFromFormsCollection()
   .oPreviousActiveForm = .NULL.

   IF .lReleaseOnClose
      .RELEASE()
   ENDIF
ENDWITH
```

The Toolbar class

I mentioned at the beginning of this chapter that the Toolbar class provided by FoxPro is functional as is. And for the most part it is.

One attribute toolbars do not possess is the ability to "remember" where they were last placed. The ability to remember an object's location was implemented in Chapter 11, "Framework Services," in the section titled "Saving preferences." So, for a toolbar to "remember" where it was last, you simply need to call the goLocations object and retrieve the locations. A method, SetLocation(), is added to aToolbars, the base toolbar class. SetLocations() is called from the toolbar's Init() method. The code for SetLocations is as follows:

```
*--aToolbar.SetLocation()
IF VARTYPE(_Screen.goLocations) = 'O'
    _Screen.goLocations.GetLoc(THIS)
ENDIF
```

When a toolbar is released, a similar call is made to goLocations to save its location. However, the Toolbar Manager (developed earlier in this chapter) contains a reference to each toolbar. When the user closes a toolbar directly, by clicking its Close button, the toolbar must make a call to the Toolbar Manager to release it from its collection. The following code in aToolbar.Destroy() saves the toolbar's location and removes it from the Toolbar Manager's collection.

```
*--aToolbar.Destroy()
IF TYPE( '_screen.goToolBars' ) = 'O' AND ! ISNULL( _screen.goToolBars )
   _screen.goToolBars.ReleaseToolbar(THIS.Class)
ENDIF

IF TYPE( 'goLocations' ) = 'O' AND ! ISNULL( goLocations)
   goLocations.SaveLoc(THIS)
ENDIF
```

Individual controls

In Chapter 12, "Forms," and Chapter 13, "Data Entry Forms," you saw how each control is responsible for "knowing" when it should be enabled or disabled. The same approach is taken for toolbars. In other words, the individual toolbar controls are responsible for enabling or disabling themselves each time a toolbar is refreshed.

Summary

In this chapter you learned how to coordinate the interaction between toolbars and other elements in your framework. As you can see, toolbars touch many elements in a framework. Having read this chapter, you should be aware of the issues surrounding toolbars and be able to add toolbars to your application.

> Updates and corrections to this chapter can be found on Hentzenwerke's Web site, **www.hentzenwerke.com**. Click "Catalog" and navigate to the page for this book.

Chapter 15
Error Handling

Unfortunately, errors happen. Worse, you never know when or where an error will happen. After all, if you knew where the error was, you would have fixed it. This chapter presents a generic, customizable error handling routine that you can use as the starting point for your error handler.

New to FoxPro 8.0 is TRY/CATCH error handling, which gives you much greater control over the error handling process than previous versions of FoxPro. However, it is only one piece of an overall error handling strategy.

A robust strategy provides developers with ways to trap for errors, communicate what is happening to the user, record what happened, and handle the situation appropriately while leaving the developer in full control throughout the process.

Maintaining an error log will assist the developer as he or she tries to identify what went wrong. The error log should contain detailed information about the state of the application when the error occurred. Knowing what happened, at which line of code it happened, the events leading up to the error, and the state of the machine at the time of the error, makes it easier to identify a solution. Throughout the chapter, I will review ways to provide as much information as possible to the developer.

Recording the error for the developer is not enough. The end user also needs to be informed about the error in language that is meaningful to him or her and given useful choices afterwards. For example, the following message would mean little to an end user:

```
Invalid seek offset (Error 1103)
```

A more appropriate message may be:

```
<<Application Name>> experienced a problem. If you encounter this error again,
contact your system administrator.
```

How you inform the user that an error occurred depends upon the type of application you are developing. Displaying a dialog may be appropriate in a traditional Windows application. However, it is not possible to display a message in non-visual applications, such as DLLs.

In this chapter, you will learn techniques for developing an error handler for both visual and non-visual applications. Having read this chapter, you will know how to design and implement an error handling solution for your framework.

Error handling in FoxPro—Overview

FoxPro is a mixture of procedural and object-oriented languages. Although error handling is similar between the two parts of the language, there are some differences.

Procedural errors

Procedural, or non-object-oriented code, is located in programs, procedures, menus, reports, labels, and stored procedures. The ON ERROR command specifies what action, if any, should occur when an error happens in your application in any of these places. For example, assume you have placed your error handling code in a program file named TrapError.prg. The following line of code results in TrapError.prg being called each time an error occurs.

```
ON ERROR DO TrapErrors.PRG
```

 The term "default error handler" refers to the error handler named with ON ERROR throughout the remainder of the chapter.

Errors in objects

Each class in FoxPro has an Error event and a corresponding Error() method. When an error occurs in an object, the object's Error event is raised. When the Error event is raised, FoxPro does one of two things. If the Error() method of the class contains code, FoxPro calls the Error() method, passing three parameters: the error number, the method in which the error occurred, and the line number on which the error occurred. If an object's error handler is not equipped to respond to the error (that is, its error method contains no code), the default error handler is invoked instead.

Any code placed in an object's Error() method, even a comment, prevents the default error handler from being called. It's important to note that an object's error handling code may be located in an object's class definition, in an instance of the class, or inherited from another class.

When you view the error method of a class in the Visual Designer, you will see the following default parameters statement:

```
LPARAMETERS nError, cMethod, nLine
```

When you write error handling code for non-visual classes, be sure to always accept these three parameters before writing your error routine. Omitting the parameter statement will result in an error. For example:

```
*--Sample: Trapping for errors
LPARAMETERS nError, cMethod, nLine
DO CASE
CASE nError = 12
    *--Take Some Action
OTHERWISE
*--Unhandled - take some other action
ENDCASE
```

Note that even if you issue a DODEFAULT(nError, cMethod, nLine) in the OTHERWISE clause, FoxPro considers the error handled (whether you have actually addressed the problem or not) and resumes program execution.

TRY, CATCH, and THROW

TRY/CATCH error handling is a new feature of FoxPro 8.0 that lets you trap for errors on a line-by-line basis. Also new to FoxPro 8.0 is the error "exception" object. The exception object stores information about an error as properties of the object. For example, the error object has an ErrorNo property that stores the error number.

To use TRY/CATCH error handling, you wrap a line or lines of code in a TRY/CATCH block. The following code illustrates how TRY/CATCH error handling works. The first line of code simulates the "File Not Found" error.

When an error occurs inside a TRY/CATCH block, the code in the CATCH section executes. This example simply displays the error number and text of the message.

```
*--Sample Code - TRY/CATCH
TRY
    *--Cause an error to occur
    ERROR 1

CATCH TO oError When oError.ErrorNo = 1
      *--Display the results of the error
  ? "Catch Error: ", oError.ErrorNo
  ? "Text: ",oError.Message

FINALLY
  ? "Finally always executes!"
ENDTRY
```

Additionally, TRY/CATCH blocks can be nested. In the event that an unhandled error occurs in one TRY/CATCH block, the THROW clause passes the exception object to the next level in the TRY/CATCH block. The THROW command is commented in the example because the TRY/CATCH block is only one level deep.

Issuing a THROW command that is not "caught" by another TRY/CATCH block raises an error of its own (2059 – Unhandled Structured Exception).

The code in the FINALLY block fires whether an error occurs or not. It is provided for you to place cleanup code associated with the TRY/CATCH block. However, it is equivalent to placing code immediately following the TRY/CATCH block.

Error sequence

FoxPro provides you with three ways to handle errors: TRY/CATCH, Error() methods, and a default error handler. Understanding which error handler is in effect, and the sequence in which it fires, is essential for properly devising an error handling strategy.

The error handling sequence, as you might expect, goes from the most specific to the most general. An error trapped within a TRY/CATCH block is constrained to the TRY/CATCH block. If the TRY/CATCH block exists in an object, and the TRY/CATCH block does not handle the error, the object's Error() method is called. If the Error() method does not contain code, the default error handler is called.

Default error messages

FoxPro makes a slight distinction between errors that occur during development and errors that occur at run time. The dialog shown in **Figure 1** appears when an error occurs during development.

Notice that you have the ability to cancel the program, suspend the program, or ignore the error. In your own error handling routine, you can simulate these results by using the CANCEL, SUSPEND, or RESUME commands.

Figure 2 shows the same error illustrated in Figure 1 when an application is compiled. As you can see, the only significant difference between the two forms is that the Suspend button is not displayed.

For at least two reasons, Figure 2 is not an acceptable dialog to display to end users of your applications. First, the message is not informative to an end user. Second, allowing the user to ignore an unhandled error could leave the system in an unstable state, resulting in even more errors.

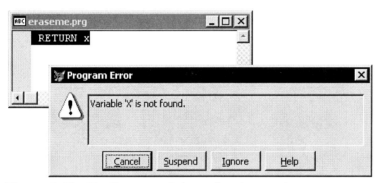

Figure 1. The FoxPro error dialog—development.

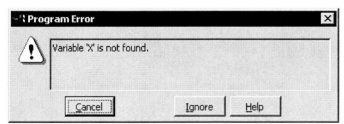

Figure 2. The FoxPro error dialog—run time.

Devising an error handling strategy

Your approach to error handling is largely a matter of personal style. A simplistic approach to error handling may involve only a few lines of code. The following example routes all errors to a custom function, CloseAppOnError(), which informs the user about the state of the application, and then closes it.

```
*--In the startup routine
ON ERROR DO CloseAppOnError()

*--Then in a procedure file
FUNCTION CloseAppOnError()
     =Messagebox("You are hosed!")
     CLEAR EVENTS
ENDFUNC
```

This chapter illustrates a more complex approach to error handling. In the previous example, you could not customize the message or differentiate between errors and take measures to correct the problem or problems. Additionally, use of the MessageBox() function does not accommodate non-visual applications.

Also missing from the simple example is an illustration of how to tap into the power of FoxPro's object model and how you can customize an error handler to meet some additional needs during development and testing.

Handling errors close to their source

Trap and handle errors as close to the source of the error as possible. The following two examples illustrate this point.

For the first example, think of all the things that could go wrong when you access a computer file. The file could be deleted, corrupt, in the wrong format, hidden, or locked at the operating system level. Assume you have a program that imports data from a table. A missing or corrupt file might indicate that the user had not completed a previous step in the import process. For this example, displaying a message to the end user that he or she had not completed the previous step would satisfy the problem.

For another example, assume that you have a data entry screen responsible for updating a table. In this case, a corrupt or missing file would be catastrophic and you most likely would notify the user that a table is missing and shut the application down.

Each of these examples illustrates how a similar error might be handled differently, depending on the circumstances surrounding the error. By handling errors close to their source, you leave your developers in a better position to more appropriately respond to errors, take preventative action, and more accurately inform the user of what is occurring in the application.

Centralized error handling

It is not feasible to trap every error at its source. You cannot foresee all the errors that could occur; even if you could, you can't recover from every error. The term "centralized error handling" conveys the concept that regardless of where an unhandled error occurs, it is forwarded to, and handled by, the same class.

Building on the concept from a previous section, this default error handler is as far from the source of the error as you can get. When an error occurs in a default error handler, you cannot make assumptions about what went wrong and why. For example, a default error handler must assume the worst and, in the case of a missing file, close the application.

A centralized error handling routine should also handle the common aspects of error handling, such as logging the error.

Error handling and containership

Consider the form shown in **Figure 3**, illustrating how controls might be contained in a form.

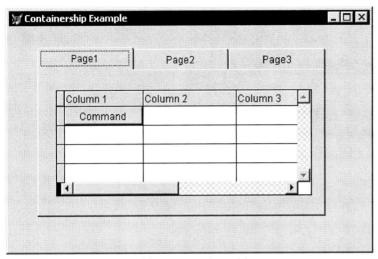

Figure 3. *An example of form containership.*

Figure 3 shows a form and some form controls. An error could occur in any of the controls on the form. Assume an error occurred in the command button's Click() method. Handling the error as close to the source of the error as possible means moving up the containership hierarchy in search of an error handling routine. When the top of the containership is reached (in this case, the form), the error must be passed to the default error handler.

For example, if an error occurs in the button, rather than going to the default error handler directly, the grid column should have a chance to trap for the error after the button's Error() method has attempted, but failed to trap, the error. If the error remains unhandled, the grid should have an opportunity to resolve the problem. If the grid does not resolve the error, the page, page frame, and form should have an opportunity to solve the problem.

This "bubbling up" approach allows the developer to trap for errors at varying levels in the containership hierarchy. Traversing the containership hierarchy offers a few key benefits. First, in situations where controls are dynamically added to a form, you may not have the appropriate error handling set up in the controls themselves. Instead, you could place the error checking at the form level and know that it will be called if an error occurs. A second benefit is that, by changing the default error handling capabilities for the form, you have effectively changed the default error handling capability for each control on the form.

To test if a control's parent contains an error routine, you must check that the parent exists and that it contains code. The following code returns True if the parent of a control contains code in its Error() method:

```
LlParentHasErrorHandler =
        TYPE('this.parent')='O' AND ;
        ! ISNULL(THIS.PARENT) AND ;
        PEMSTATUS(THIS.PARENT,'Error',0)
```

Notice that the last test passes a value of zero (0) to PEMSTATUS. The FoxPro Help states the following about using zero (0) as a parameter: "Changed (properties only). A logical true (.T.) is returned if the property value has changed from its original, default value; otherwise a logical false (.F.) is returned."

In my tests, however, passing 0 as the third parameter works for methods as well as properties. This is true for versions 6.0, 7.0, and 8.0. I have not tested earlier versions. One additional note is that PEMSTATUS returns a logical True if the object contains code in the instance of a class or in the class definition, or if the code is inherited from another class.

Handling procedural errors

An error that occurs in procedural code, unless trapped in a TRY/CATCH block, is immediately passed to the default error handler.

Error handling during development

In the next section, I'll explain an approach for handling errors at run time and design time that emulates FoxPro's debugger and offers the ability to record information about the error. I find logging errors during development especially helpful during testing, where I may prefer to continue testing rather than fix the problem immediately.

Developing an error handler

The responsibility for error handling in MyFrame is divided. All errors are routed to a centralized error handler. Errors that occur in procedural code are directed to the error handler directly by the ON ERROR command. Errors originating in object code, however, are first passed through the containership hierarchy of the object. If the error is unhandled by any of the objects, it is then forwarded to the error handling class.

The error handling class in MyFrame is MyErrorHandler. **Figure 4** shows MyErrorHandler in the class browser. It is built using components developed in earlier chapters. Before reading this section you should be familiar with the following classes:

- aApplication—Chapter 5

- MyCollection—Chapter 8

- MyCursor—Chapter 9

- MyDataEnvironment—Chapter 10

- MyMessages—Chapter 11

- aDialogFrm—Chapter 12

- MyDataEntryForm—Chapter 13

- MyDialogBox—Chapter 12

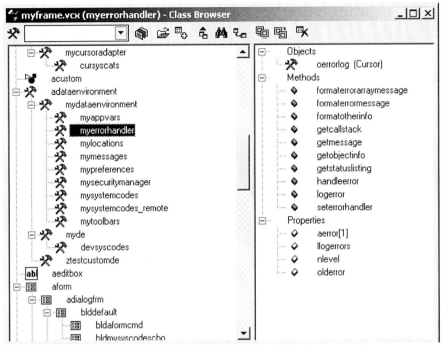

Figure 4. The error handling class, MyErrorHandler.

As Figure 4 illustrates, MyErrorHandler inherits from MyDataEnvironment, as do other framework services. Information about each error is stored in a table, ErrorLog.dbf. MyErrorHandler uses an instance of MyCursor, named oErrorLog, to access the ErrorLog table.

Handling an error

A method of MyErrorHandler, HandleError(), is responsible for processing each error. It accepts the following parameters:

- nError—The error number.

- cMethod—When the HandleError() method is called from an object, cMethod contains the name of the method in which the error occurred. When an error occurs in procedural code, cMethod is the name of the program executing when the error occurred. (This is defined by the Program() function.)

- nLine—The line number in which the error occurred.

- toObject—The object in which the error occurred. The toObject parameter will contain a value only when called from a framework class.

In MyFrame, only unhandled errors make it to the default error handler. In a running application, the error handler notifies the user that an error has occurred and closes the application. During development, the error handler is responsible for notifying the developer that an unhandled error has occurred, and allows him or her to take an appropriate action.

The pseudo code for HandleError() is shown here.

```
IF Development
    Format Error Message
    Notify Developer
    Record Error Information
    Return, Resume, Debug or Cancel
IF InAnApplication
    Record Error Information
    Attempt to solve not fatal errors (Such as "Printer out of paper")
    If the attempt fails
        Display Fatal Error Message
        Close the Application
```

Where to handle

The HandleError() method accepts the following parameters:

```
LPARAMETERS nError, cMethod, nLine, toObject
```

I mentioned earlier in the chapter that MyFrame implements a "bubble up" approach to error handling, where unhandled errors are passed up the containership hierarchy in search of a solution. If the outermost container is reached (usually, but not always a form), the error information is passed to the HandleError() method.

In the cascading form of error handling, the error may be passed along for a while, but ultimately has to be handled somewhere. The toObject parameter is a reference to the object in which the error occurred. If toObject is not an object reference, the error is handled in the HandleError() method. Otherwise, the value is passed back to the object in which the error occurred.

However, not all errors that occur in an application are non-recoverable. For example, error 125, "Printer Not Ready," could be solved by prompting the user to place the printer online and issuing a RETRY after they have confirmed the situation has been fixed. You will notice in the following code that the CanHandleError() method exists as a last chance to resolve errors before notifying the developer or user that an error occurred.

Also, notice that the "debug" option issues a KEYBOARD '{F8}' which is equivalent to issuing STEP INTO, and forces the debugger to step forward one line. This action leaves the developer on the line that caused the error, rather than on the line immediately following SET STEP ON, which is RETRY.

```
*--MyErrorHandler.HandleError() {Partial Code}
*--Attempt to resolve the error
IF THIS.CanHandleError( nError, cMethod, nLine, toObject)

    *--Exit early and resume execution, the error is handled.
    RETURN "Retry"
ELSE
    lcReturn = "Cancel"
ENDIF

llHandleHere = IIF(VARTYPE(toObject)='O',.F.,.T.)
llDevMode=IIF(TYPE('goApp')='O' AND ! ISNULL(goApp),goApp.lDevMode,.T.)
```

```
IF lDevMode
     *--Handle Developer error
ELSE
     *--Hanlde Run Time Error
ENDIF

IF llHandleHere
  DO CASE
     CASE lcReturn='Retry'
        RETRY
     CASE lcReturn='Cancel'
        CANCEL
     CASE lcReturn='Debug'
        lcReturn='Retry'
        KEYBOARD '{F8}'
        SET STEP ON
        RETRY
     CASE lcReturn='Resume'
        RETURN
  ENDCASE
ELSE
  RETURN PROPER(ALLTRIM(lcReturn))
ENDIF
```

Handling the error during development

During development, the application developer expects to have full control of how an error is handled. The MyErrorMsg_Developer dialog shown in **Figure 5** allows the developer to select whether he wants to Debug, Cancel, Retry, or Resume. Additionally, the developer can log information about the error if he so chooses.

 The dialog in Figure 5 appears, by default, only when working in the development environment. You can, however, make it appear in a compiled APP or EXE by changing the lDevMode property of aApplication from False to True. The aApplication class was explained in Chapter 5, "Beginning Development."

The HandleError() method displays the dialog in Figure 5 and, optionally, logs the error. Notice that the HandleError() method checks MyErrorHandler.lShowMessage before displaying a message. This is useful when creating server applications or DLLs. Also notice that suppression of the dialog does not prevent MyErrorHandler from logging the error.

```
*--MyErrorHandler.HandleError() - Development Mode
IF llDevMode

    *--Since the error occurred in an object,
    *      we'll let the object handle it.
    llHandleHere = IIF(VARTYPE(toObject)='O',.F.,.T.)

    IF THIS.lShowMessage
       *--Notify the developer
       lcMessage = THIS.FormatErrorMessage( nError, cMethod, nLine, toObject)
       loErrMsg  = CREATEOBJECT("myErrormsg_Developer")
       loErrMsg.SetMessage( lcMessage )
       loErrMsg.SHOW(1)
       lcReturn  = loErrMsg.GetSelection()
```

```
        lcText = loErrMsg.cDevNote
        THIS.lLogErrors = loErrMsg.chkLogError.VALUE = 1
    ENDIF

    THIS.LOGERROR(nError, cMethod, nLine, toObject, lcText )
    loErrMsg.CLOSE(.T.)

ELSE
*--Handle Run Time Error

ENDIF
```

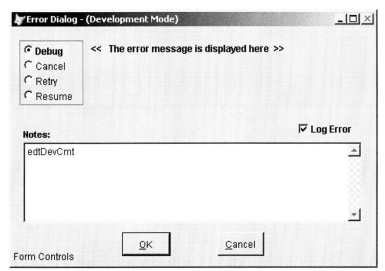

Figure 5. *The MyErrorMsg_Dialog class.*

Handling an error at run time
When an unhandled error occurs in an application, there is little more that the framework can do than log the error, notify the user that the application is experiencing operating difficulties, and then shut down.

```
THIS.LOGERROR(nError, cMethod, nLine, toObject )

IF THIS.lShowMessage
    loErrMsg = CREATEOBJECT("MyErrorMsg_User")
    loErrMsg.SHOW(1)
    loErrMsg.CLOSE(.T.)
ENDIF
goApp.CloseAllForms(.T.)

QUIT
```

Recording error information
Generally, the "I didn't do anything … it just blew up" comment that most users provide is not enough to identify exactly what went wrong. When an error occurs, you want to know as much as possible about what went wrong.

When an error occurs, MyErrorHandler writes information about the error to a table, ErrorLog.dbf. The information stored in ErrorLog.dbf will help you identify the nature and cause of the error. **Table 1** shows the structure of ErrorLog.dbf.

***Table 1**. The structure of ErrorLog.dbf.*

Field	Description
ErrorID	Surrogate Primary Key
ErrDateIn	The date and time of the error
ErrUserID	The user who witnessed the disturbance
ErrNo	The FoxPro error number
ErrMsg	The FoxPro error message
ErrLine	The line number
ErrMethod	The method or program in which the error occurred
ErrObj	The property values of the object in which the error occurred
ErrArray	The contents returned by aError ()
ErrStack	The call stack in effect when the error occurred
ErrStatus	The system status returned by DISPLAY STATUS
ErrResolved	Provided for developers to log whether a change was made to correct a problem
ErrNotes	Notes about the error. The developer can enter information about this error when the error occurs or at a later time.

Information is added to ErrorLog.dbf in the LogError() method of MyErrorHandler. The LogError() method is little more than a series of REPLACE statements. Most of the information is generated in custom methods, which I'll explain after the LogError() method shown here.

```
*--MyErrorHandler.LogError()
LPARAMETERS tnError, tcMethod, tnLine, toObject, tcDevNote
LOCAL lcMessage, lnErrors, lcText, lnError, lnSelect

*--Collect the error
lnErrors = AERROR(THIS.AERROR)
lcText = IIF(lnErrors>0,THIS.AERROR[2],"")
lnError = IIF(EMPTY(tnError),THIS.AERROR[1],tnError)

IF THIS.lLogErrors
    lnSelect=SELECT()
    THIS.oErrorLog.SELECT()
    THIS.oErrorLog.New()

    REPLACE Errorlog.errdatein        WITH DATETIME()
    IF VARTYPE(goApp) = "O" AND PemStatus(goApp,'GetUserID',5)
        REPLACE Errorlog.erruserid WITH goApp.GetUserID()
    ENDIF
```

```
REPLACE Errorlog.errno      WITH lnError, ;
        Errorlog.ErrText      WITH lcText, ;
        Errorlog.errline      WITH tnLine,;
        Errorlog.errmethod    WITH tcMethod,;
        Errorlog.errmsg       WITH THIS.GetMessage()

    IF VARTYPE(toObject) = "O"
        REPLACE Errorlog.errobj    WITH THIS.GetObjectInfo(toObject)
    ENDIF

    REPLACE Errorlog.errArray WITH THIS.FormatErrorArrayMessage(),;
        Errorlog.errstack WITH THIS.Getcallstack(),,;
        Errorlog.errStatus WITH THIS.GetStatusListing()

    IF ! EMPTY(tcDevNote)
        REPLACE Errorlog.ErrNotes WITH tcDevNote
    ENDIF

    SELECT(lnSelect)
ENDIF
THIS.SAVE()
```

As you can see, much of the information stored in the tables is generated in custom methods of the class.

Capturing the line of code

The Message() function returns the text of an error by default. Passing a value of 1 returns one of the following (as listed in FoxPro Help):

- The entire program line if the line is macro substituted.

- A command if the line contains a command without any additional clauses.

- A command followed by three dots (...) if the line contains a command and additional clauses.

The GetMessage() method of MyErrorHandler formats the values returned from the Message() function as follows:

```
*--MyErrorHandler.GetMessage()
Return "Error Description - Message():"   + CHR(10) + ;
        MESSAGE()                          + CHR(10)+ CHR(13) + ;
        " Message(1):"                     + CHR(10) +;
          MESSAGE(1)                       + CHR(10)+ CHR(13)
```

For example, the following code results in an "Operator/operand type mismatch" error.

```
THIS.nCounter = "C"
? THIS.nCounter - 1
```

The GetMessage() method of MyErrorHandler would format the values returned from the Message() function to appear as follows:

```
Error Description - Message():
Operator/operand type mismatch.

Line Of Code - Message(1):
? THIS.nCounter -1
```

Capturing object properties

Sometimes it's not enough to know which error occurred and the line of code in which it
occurred. Consider the previous example in which an "Operator/operand type mismatch" error
occurred. The nCounter property is obviously intended to store numeric data. Knowing the
line of the error does not tell you what value was stored in THIS.nCounter.

GetObjectInfo() collects the name and value for each property that has a non-default
value.

The GetObjectInfo() method of MyErrorHandler accepts an object as a parameter and returns
a list of its properties and their values. GetObjectInfo() uses a combination of aMembers() and
PEMStatus () to loop through and collect the information about each object as follows:

```
LPARAMETERS toObj AS CUSTOM
.
.
.
lcReturn = "The error occurred in "+ SYS(1272,toObj) + ;
    "The relevant properties are listed below"+CHR(10)+CHR(13)

lnCount = loCollection.GetCount()

lnMembers = AMEMBERS(laPems,toObj,1)
#DEFINE NonDefault 0
#DEFINE PropertyExists 5
#DEFINE ProtectedProperty 2

FOR lnI = 1 TO lnMembers
    lcObjectAndPEM  = "toObj."+ALLTRIM(UPPER(laPems[lnI,1]))
    lcPemName = ALLTRIM(UPPER(laPems[lnI,1]))
    lcType = ALLTRIM(UPPER(laPems[lnI,2]))

    IF      PemStatus(toObj,lcPemName ,   NonDefault) AND;
            PemStatus(toObj,lcPemName ,   PropertyExists) AND;
            ! PemStatus(toObj,lcPemName, ProtectedProperty)

        IF lcType == "PROPERTY"
            luValue = &lcObjectAndPEM

            IF VARTYPE(luValue) = "O"
                lcReturn = lcReturn +;
                    " Property "+lcPemName+;
                    " references an object: "+ toObj.NAME
            ELSE
                lcReturn = lcReturn + SPACE(5)+;
                    lcPemName +" = "+TRANSFORM(luValue)+CHR(10)+CHR(13)
            ENDIF
        ENDIF
    ENDIF
ENDFOR
.
.
.
RETURN lcReturn
```

The results of this method are stored in ErrorLog.ErrObj. The sample error illustrated in the previous example might appear as follows:

```
The error occurred in <<ObjectName>>
The relevant properties are listed below

Object: <<ObjectName>>
    NCounter = C
```

Capturing the call stack

Knowing the events that lead up to an error can also be helpful. FoxPro provides a system function, SYS(16), which returns the file name of the current program. SYS(16) also accepts a parameter that indicates how far back in the call stack you want to go. When the number passed to SYS(16) exceeds the number of levels in the call stack, SYS(16) returns an empty string.

Program(), another FoxPro function, behaves similarly to SYS(16). However, Program() returns only the name of the currently running program. I use SYS(16) in favor of Program() because SYS(16) returns the name of the currently executing program file as well as the name of the program.

Using the information returned from SYS(16), it's possible to capture the call stack by calling SYS(16) with successfully increasing values until the level of the call stack is exceeded, as shown here:

```
*--MyErrorHander.GetCallStack()
LOCAL lcReturn, lnI

lcReturn = "Call Stack "            + Chr(10)
lnI = 0

DO WHILE LEN(SYS(16,lnI )) <> 0
    lcReturn = lcReturn +;
        "Level " + ALLTRIM(STR(lnI))+")  "+;
        SYS(16,lnI ) + CHR(10)

    lnI = lnI + 1
ENDDO

RETURN lcReturn
```

A sample of the output returned by GetCallStack() is shown here.

```
Call Stack
Level 0) TRAPERRORS.APAGEFRAME1.CLICK C:\...CHAP15_ERRORHANDLING.SCT
Level 1) TRAPERRORS.APAGEFRAME1.CLICK C:\...CHAP15_ERRORHANDLING.SCT
Level 2) TRAPERRORS.APAGEFRAME1.ERROR C:\...\MYFRAME.VCT
Level 3) TRAPERRORS.ERROR C:\...\MYFRAME.VCT
Level 4) MYERRORHANDLER.HANDLEERROR C:\...\MYFRAME.VCT
Level 5) MYERRORHANDLER.LOGERROR C:\...\MYFRAME.VCT
Level 6) MYERRORHANDLER.GETCALLSTACK C:\...\MYFRAME.VCT
```

Capturing display status

The DISPLAY STATUS command lists information about the FoxPro environment to either the screen or a file. Using a combination of StrToFile() and DISPLAY STATUS, it is possible to capture information about the FoxPro environment.

```
*--MyErrorHanlder.GetStatusListing()
lcFileName =SYS(2015)+".txt"
LIST STATUS TO FILE(lcFileName) NOCONSOLE
lcReturn = FILETOSTR(lcFileName)
ERASE(lcFileName)
RETURN lcReturn
```

Object Error()

Every class in Visual FoxPro has an Error() method. So far in this section, you have seen how the error handler works. The Error() method for each class is the other half of the error handling equation. To understand it better, I've broken the code into four parts: identifying who should handle the error, bubbling, handling the error, and handling the error when the error handler is not available.

Where to handle

FoxPro passes three parameters to an error method. Notice that this method accepts a fourth parameter that is a reference to the object that encountered the error. (Refer back to "Capturing object properties" earlier in the chapter.)

In the object in which the error originates, toObject will never evaluate to an object reference because FoxPro does not pass a fourth parameter. Therefore, the toObject parameter identifies whether the error occurred in this object or if it has been forwarded by another object.

```
LPARAMETERS nError, cMethod, nLine, toObject
IF ! VARTYPE(toObject)='O'
    toObject=THIS
    llHandleHere=.T.
ENDIF
```

Bubbling

The "bubbling effect" described earlier in the chapter occurs when unhandled errors are passed to the parent container. To pass an error to the parent container, the following code checks to see if an object's parent class contains code to handle the error. If it does not, the error method of the form is checked. If the form cannot handle the error, the code is passed directly to the global error handler. The code to pass the error to a control's container is shown here:

```
*--Identify object to pass the error handling to
DO CASE

    CASE TYPE('this.parent')='O'       AND ;
            ! ISNULL(THIS.PARENT)           AND ;
            pemstatus(THIS.PARENT,'Error',0)
```

```
      *--Pass control to the parent
      lcAction=THIS.PARENT.ERROR(nError,cMethod,nLine,toObject)

   CASE TYPE('THISFORM')='O' AND;
         ! ISNULL(THISFORM) AND;
         pemstatus(THISFORM,'Error',0)

      *--Pass control to thisform.
      lcAction=THISFORM.ERROR(nError,cMethod,nLine,toObject)

   CASE TYPE('_SCREEN.goErrorHandler')='O' AND;
         ! ISNULL(_SCREEN.goErrorHandler)

      *--Call the default error handler directly
      lcAction = _SCREEN.goErrorHandler.HandleError(
            nError,cMethod,nLine,toObject)

ENDCASE
```

What? No error handler?

When you are working within MyFrame, the previous code will always result in a value for lcAction. However, if you use framework components outside of the framework, lcAction will be empty and a generic error message (shown in **Figure 6**) is prepared as follows:

```
IF EMPTY(lcAction)
      =MESSAGEBOX("Error: " +ALLTRIM(STR(nError))+ ;
         ": "+ MESSAGE()+ CHR(10)+CHR(13)+;
         "Line "+ALLTRIM(STR(nLine))+;
         " of "+toObject.NAME+"."+ cMethod+ CHR(10)+CHR(13)+;
         SYS(1272,toObject)+ CHR(10)+CHR(13)+;
         "Reported by "+THIS.NAME)

      lcAction='Cancel'
ENDIF
```

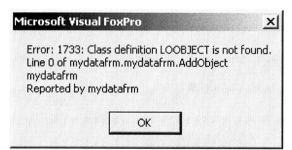

Figure 6. A makeshift error message.

Handling the error

Handling the error here means telling FoxPro what to do. Depending on the value of lcAction, you can retry the line that caused the error, or you can cancel, debug, or resume the program.

```
IF llHandleHere
    DO CASE
        CASE lcAction='Retry'
            RETRY
        CASE lcAction='Cancel'
            CANCEL
        CASE lcAction='Debug'
            Keyboard '{F8}'
            SET STEP ON
            RETRY
        CASE lcAction='Resume'
            RETURN 'Resume'
    ENDCASE
ELSE
    RETURN lcAction
ENDIF
```

Trapping for errors in classes

To this point, you have seen how all errors are routed to the framework error handler and that you can solve some errors in the error handler's CanHandleError() method. However, as discussed earlier, it is preferable to handle the error as close as possible to the source of the error. For classes, this means inserting your own code into the class' error method.

Using a CASE statement, for example, you can trap for a specific error and take an appropriate action. If the action remains unhandled by the CASE statement, you then invoke the framework's error handler by calling DODEFAULT(). An example of how this code might appear is shown here:

```
LPARAMETERS nError, cMethod, nLine, toObject

DO CASE

CASE nError = 12
      *--Take Some Action
OTHERWISE
        *--Find another object to handle
  RETURN DODEFAULT(nError, cMethod, nLinem toObject)

ENDCASE
```

Viewing the error log

MyFrame contains a form, MyErrorLog (see **Figure 7**), which makes it easy for you to identify and learn about the latest errors in your applications. You can access the form in the sample framework by selecting Error Log from the framework menu pad.

The examples for this chapter illustrate various types of errors. Take a moment to run the examples and view the information generated by the MyFrame error handler.

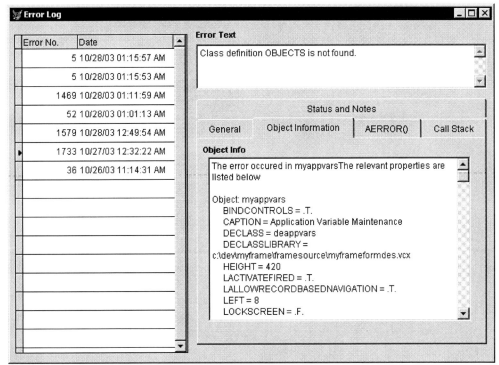

Figure 7*. Accessing error information in MyFrame.*

Summary

In this chapter, you have learned a comprehensive error handling strategy that allows developers to easily trap for errors in the object containership hierarchy. You've also learned how to record vital information about each error and how to incorporate the new TRY/CATCH error handling into your overall error handling strategy.

Updates and corrections to this chapter can be found on Hentzenwerke's Web site, **www.hentzenwerke.com**. Click "Catalog" and navigate to the page for this book.

Chapter 16
Security

Applications require differing levels of security, including none at all. In this chapter, you will review an approach for implementing security and have a better understanding of how to incorporate security into your framework.

A variety of techniques exist to make your applications secure. Externally, security can be implemented by restricting access to network folders, requiring network login, or, if you use a database server such as SQL Server, by requiring a login to access the data. Each of these tools restricts unauthorized users from accessing your application.

Once a user has entered your system, external security measures offer little help for restricting access within your system. In this chapter, you will create a login screen that acts as a barrier into your system, and you'll implement a security system that restricts user access within your applications once they have logged in.

When users log in to an application, they can be restricted from accessing portions of the application or from performing specific tasks once they are in a portion of the system. For example, in MyFrame you can restrict access to menu options, restrict the visibility of forms or fields, and control whether users can add or modify data.

Developers and system administrators will appreciate the ability to manage security for individuals as well as groups of individuals. Applying security to individuals is the most flexible approach you can offer. However, maintaining large numbers of people can be time consuming and somewhat of a maintenance headache.

Adding the ability to manage groups of users means that when you assign security to a group, all users belonging to that group "inherit" the same security settings. However, working with groups offers a few challenges. The main challenge is that you must allow an individual's security settings to override any group settings they may have. In this chapter, I present a way to add both user and group security to your application.

In this chapter you will also see how the pieces of the security module are constructed, understand the communication between components, and learn how to work with (apply) security in MyFrame. You will also see an overview of the screens used to administer the security module.

When you have completed this chapter, you will be familiar with the security system in MyFrame and will be able to design a security module for your framework.

Before reading this chapter, you should be familiar with the FoxPro Menu Designer as well as the following framework classes:

- myCollection—Chapter 8

- myCursor—Chapter 9

- myDataEnvironment—Chapter 10

- SysCodes Framework Service—Chapter 11

- aForm—Chapter 12

Security overview

The security module in MyFrame behaves like a "security server." Non-object controls, such as menus and report controls, call a method, IsAuthorized(), on the security server that returns a logical value. Calling IsAuthorized() from a menu's SKIP clause results in menu pads that are either enabled or disabled. Similarly, calling IsAuthorized() from a report control's PRINT WHEN command results in controls that are either visible or not visible. You can also conditionally execute code depending on a user's authorization level.

Security is applied to objects by passing the object to the Security Manager's SetSecurity() method. In Chapter 12, "Forms," I illustrated that each form has a framework Form Controls collection that stores a reference to each control on the form. The form class passes control references to the server for each control on the form. The security server accepts the request and sets the control's Visible, ReadOnly, and Enabled properties as appropriate.

Figure 1 shows the relationship between the security module and other elements in the framework. The double-headed arrows indicate that the security module returns a value to the calling program, while the single-headed arrows indicate that the security module makes the setting directly.

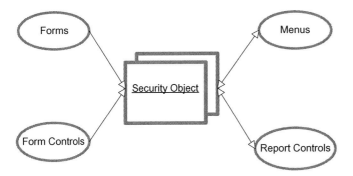

Figure 1. How objects communicate with the security module.

A robust security system allows you to implement security in a number of ways. By implementing security in your system menu, you can restrict access to entire portions of your application. For example, imagine you have just completed a new system and one menu is labeled "Administration." From this menu, you might offer the ability to pack databases, rebuild indexes, or access the security maintenance forms. Depending on your requirements, you may choose to not display the menu or disable it—leaving it visible but unavailable to an unauthorized user.

You can achieve a finer degree of control by limiting access to individual menu options, controlling access to forms, or even controlling access to the individual controls within a form. Consider a form for administering employee benefits. You may want to limit the display of salary information to certain individuals and medical history to other individuals.

Using a combination of approaches, you can devise a comprehensive security system that will accommodate almost any situation.

Setting up security in an existing system can be time consuming. Default values ease this burden. For example, payroll information is most likely restricted to a few users of a system.

Restricting access to a control by default means that you only have to grant access to the few individuals who should see the information, rather than the majority of users who should not.

The security module works by defining users, groups of users, and a list of security items. Each security item represents a logical partition in your application. For example, you might create a "Payroll" security item for payroll-sensitive information, and "Financial" for financial information. To administer security, you assign rights to an individual who has the ability to access the financial or payroll information.

Each object in the MyFrame framework has a cSecuritySetting property that references a security item. When the object is passed to the security server, the value in the cSecuritySetting property determines how the security server responds to that control. Alternately, the IsAuthorized() method of the security server accepts a security item as a parameter and returns a logical value.

Form controls, however, are not limited to an "on" or "off" choice. Form controls may be set as read-only, read-write, or made invisible. **Table 1** shows the default security settings, the property settings affected when an object is passed to the security server, and the logical return value returned from the IsAuthorized() method. Notice that the fourth option, Inherit From Form, has "Not Applicable" (NA) in the Properties and Logical columns. When a control's security setting is "Form," the form's security setting is substituted as the setting for the control. (That is, a value of "RW," "RO," "HIDE," or "NONE" is passed instead of "FORM.") This allows you to set security once, at the form level, rather than requiring you to identify a security setting for each control on the form.

Table 1. Default security code values.

Setting	Abbreviation	Level	Properties	Logical
Read Write	RW	10	Enabled = .T. Visible = .T.	.T.
Read Only	RO	20	Enabled = .F. Visible = .T.	.F.
Hidden	HIDE	30	Visible = .F.	.F.
Inherit From Form	FORM	40	NA	NA
None	NONE	50	(None)	.T.

The security module

The security module is a subclass of MyDataEnvironment, developed in Chapter 10, "Business Objects." Before reading this section, you should be familiar with the classes MyCursor and MyDataEnvironment.

Table structure

To gain an understanding of the security in MyFrame, it will be best to start with the data. **Figure 2** shows the tables, fields, and relations for the security module.

The security module consists of the following tables:

- Users—A list of users that can access the system.

- Groups—A list of user groups.

- UsrGrps—A linking table between users and groups.

- SecItems—A list of security settings (Read Only, Read Write, and so on).

- Security—The security settings for users and groups.

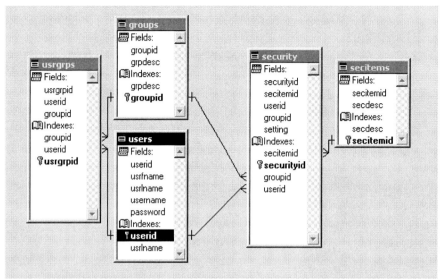

Figure 2*. The security module data structure.*

The relationship between users and groups is a many-to-many relationship because one user can belong to zero or more groups and a group can contain zero or more users. A many-to-many relationship in a relational database is modeled by creating a third table that holds the relationship between the other two. In this case, the table UsrGrps is used to hold the reference between users and groups.

The Security table holds references between security items, users, and groups. It also contains the settings (Read Write, Read Only, and so on) for a user or group.

The Security class

The Security class accesses and retrieves values from the security tables. **Figure 3** shows the Security Manager as displayed in the class browser.

Applying security

Applying security is a collaborative effort between the Security Manager and the other elements of the framework. Each framework control has two properties that store the security settings for the control: SecurityID and cSecuritySetting. During the Init() method of a form, each control is passed to the Security Manager's SetSecurity() method. The SetSecurity() method reads the properties and makes the appropriate security settings. In this section, you will see how the various components communicate.

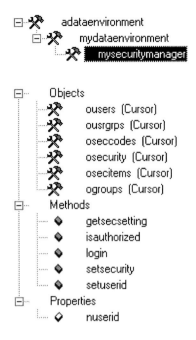

Figure 3. *The Security Manager.*

Control properties

Each control has a cSecuritySetting property and a SecurityID property. The SecurityID property contains a value from the SecItems table. Values in the Security Items table for an accounting application might include values such as "Financial," "Payroll," or "Clerical." The cSecuritySetting property stores the default value for the control. Values in the sample framework are "Read Only," "Read Write," "Hidden," and "None." The framework has a default builder (see **Figure 4**) that makes it easy to set these properties.

Setting security—form and form controls

Security is set when the form is created. To accomplish this, the SetSecurity() method of the aForm class loops through the oFormControls collection and passes each control to the security module, excluding labels.

The form's security setting is assigned to the control when a control does not have a security setting or the control has a security setting of "FORM." This allows the developer to set security at the form level, rather than for each control. In a form that has many controls, it can be tedious, and annoying, to apply security to each individual control. Here's the code for the SetSecurity() method of the aForm class:

```
*--aForm.SetSecurity()
LOCAL lnControlCount, lnI, loControl
THIS.oFormControlsCollection.GOFIRST()
lnControlCount = THIS.oFormControlsCollection.GetCount()
```

```
FOR lnI = 1 TO lnControlCount
    loControl = THISFORM.oFormControlsCollection.ADATA[lnI,1]
    IF ! IsContainer(loControl) AND PEMSTATUS(loControl,"SecurityID",5)
        IF EMPTY(loControl.cSecuritySetting) OR ;
                ALLTRIM(UPPER( loControl.cSecuritySetting)) == "FORM"

            loControl.cSecuritySetting= THIS.cSecuritySetting
        ENDIF

        _SCREEN.goSecurity.SetSecurity(loControl)

    ENDIF
ENDFOR
```

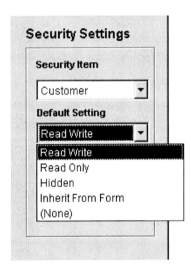

Figure 4. Setting security properties with the framework builder.

MySecurityManager
The SetSecurity() method of the Security Manager applies security settings to controls. Security is applied to objects by setting the object's Visible and/or Enabled properties. For example, the ReadOnly setting sets the Visible property to True (.T.) and the Enabled property to False (.F.), allowing the user to see the control but not make changes to it.

The security module makes the appropriate settings based on the information supplied in the object's SecurityID and cSecuritySetting properties. However, the developer does not have to assign a security setting to cSecuritySetting. Instead, the SetSecurity() method (see following code) first obtains the default setting for a security item. If the developer has not provided a value, the default value is used instead. For example, controls designated as Financial (by placing "Financial" in the control's cSecurityID property) may have a default value of Read Only. This means that unless a user is specifically authorized for Read Write access (by placing "Read Write" in the control's cSecuritySetting property), the control will be disabled by default.

After evaluating the security setting, a CASE statement is used to determine which settings to make, as shown here:

```
*--MySecurityManager.SetSecurity()
LPARAMETERS toObject
LOCAL llSetSecurity, lnSecID, lcSetting, llVisible, llEnabled, llSecControlled
llSetSecurity = .T.

IF PemStatus(toObject,'SecurityID',5)

    lnSecID = toObject.SecurityId
    IF VARTYPE(lnSecID) = 'N'
        lcName = toObject.NAME
        SET STEP ON
    ENDIF

    lcSetting = THIS.GetSecSetting(lnSecID)

    *--If there is no security setting for this user,
    *) use the default value assigned to the control
    IF EMPTY(lcSetting) OR ISNULL(lcSetting)
        *--Pull the default value from the control
        lcSetting = toObject.cSecuritySetting
    ENDIF

    DO CASE
        CASE lcSetting = 'RO'
            llVisible = .T.
            llEnabled = .F.
            llSecControlled  = .T.

        CASE lcSetting = 'RW'
            llVisible = .T.
            llEnabled = .T.

        CASE lcSetting = 'HIDE'
            llVisible = .F.

        OTHERWISE
            llSetSecurity = .F.
    ENDCASE

    IF llSetSecurity
        IF PemStatus(toObject,'lSecurityControlled',5)
            toObject.lSecurityControlled = llSecControlled   && Turn off the refresh
        ENDIF
        IF PemStatus(toObject,'visible',5)
            toObject.VISIBLE = llVisible
        ENDIF
        IF PemStatus(toObject,'enabled',5)
            toObject.ENABLED = llEnabled
        ENDIF
    ENDIF
ELSE
    *--Framework security not on this object, quick exit
ENDIF
```

Incorporating refresh code with security code

The code for each control's refresh has the potential to enable a control that was disabled for security reasons. To prevent a conflict, the refresh code includes a check to see if the lSecurityEnabled setting has been set. The relevant line of code is underlined.

```
*--The Refresh() code for all controls
IF   TYPE('_screen.activeform')='O'    AND ;
        ! ISNULL(_SCREEN.ACTIVEFORM) and;
        pemstatus(this,'ENABLED',5) and;
        ! this.lSecurityControlled

    IF _SCREEN.ACTIVEFORM.lAlwaysEdit
        THIS.ENABLED = .T.
    ELSE
        THIS.ENABLED = THIS.lEnabledInEditMode= _SCREEN.ACTIVEFORM.lEditMode
    ENDIF
    *--Else Leave it to the developer
ENDIF
```

Securing non-objects

Non-object-oriented controls, such as menu and report controls, do not have Enabled or Visible properties that control how they are displayed. Instead, menus have a SKIP FOR clause and report controls have a PRINT WHEN clause.

Each of these conditions requires that a logical value be returned. The Security Manager class has an IsAuthorized() method that returns a logical value. The IsAuthorized() method is similar to the SetSecurity() method illustrated earlier, so the code is not repeated. IsAuthorized() accepts two parameters: the SecurityID and a default logical value. For example, the payroll module may be secured by default and users would be excluded from accessing it unless specifically authorized. The SKIP FOR option of the payroll menu, for example, would then read as follows:

```
_Screen.goSecurity.IsAuthorized("PayRoll",.F.)
```

Logging in

A user's name and password are validated using a login screen and the Security Manager. The following section explains each class and how the startup routine accommodates the login process.

Login screen

The login screen is a subclass of MyDialogFrm. It is responsible for collecting the login information from the user and passing the information to the Security Manager. If the Security Manager finds that the user name and password are valid, the application continues to load. The login screen is shown in **Figure 5**.

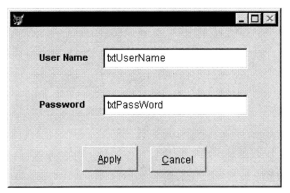

Figure 5. *The framework login screen.*

Validating a login

The Security Manager validates a user's login information by querying the Users table. If the user name and login are found, the UserID is returned; if they are not, a null value is returned. Notice the DOWHILE loop. You can control the number of attempts allowed before closing the application by adjusting the Security Manager's nMaxLoginAttempts property. The default setting is 3. The code to validate a user's login is shown here:

```
*--MySecurityManager.Login()
LOCAL lologin AS MyLoginForm, lnUserID
lnUserID = .NULL.


*_SCREEN.VISIBLE=.T.
lologin = CREATEOBJECT("MyLoginForm")
lologin.SHOW(1)

*--Code is suspended while form is in "Modal State"

*--If the user pressed OK or cancel, grab the User ID and
*) return it.
IF lologin.lReturnValueFromForm
    lcUsername = ALLTRIM(UPPER(lologin.txtUserName.VALUE))
    lcPassword = ALLTRIM(UPPER(lologin.txtPassword.VALUE))
    _TALLY = 0

    SELECT  USERID;
        FROM USERS ;
        WHERE ALLTRIM(UPPER(UserName)) = lcUsername AND ;
        ALLTRIM(UPPER(PASSWORD)) = lcPassword ;
        INTO ARRAY laUser

    IF _TALLY>0
        lnUserID = laUser[1]
        lologin.CLOSE(.T.)
    ENDIF
ENDIF
RETURN lnUserID
```

Adding user logins to the main startup routine

In Chapter 5, "Beginning Development," I presented an application object that controls the startup and shutdown of each application. Developers can control whether a user is required to log in to an application by setting the lLoginRequired property of the aApplicaton class to True. Part of the application startup sequence is to call the OnLoadSecurity() method. Returning a value of False from OnLoadSecurity()—in other words, the user failed to properly log in—causes the application to shut down. Here's the code:

```
PROTECTED FUNCTION OnLoadSecurity()

    IF THIS.lLoginRequired
        lnUserID = _SCREEN.goSecurity.Login()
        IF ISNULL(lnUserID)
            RETURN .F.
        ELSE
            THIS.nUserID = lnUserID
            RETURN .T.
        ENDIF
    ENDIF
ENDFUNC
```

Summary

In this chapter, you have learned a comprehensive approach for applying security in your applications.

Updates and corrections to this chapter can be found on Hentzenwerke's Web site, **www.hentzenwerke.com**. Click "Catalog" and navigate to the page for this book.

Chapter 17
Developer Tools

Developer tools are an integral part of any framework. In this chapter, you will see tools that help you develop your framework as well as tools that assist developers as they build their applications.

Visual FoxPro 8.0 ships with 43 base classes. Whoa! That's a lot of classes. Subclassing each of these to create your framework base classes can take a lot of time. This chapter begins by introducing a tool you can use to programmatically create your framework base classes.

As you have seen throughout this book, the framework base classes have several properties and methods in common. The Base Class Configurator tool illustrates how to programmatically add properties and methods to each of your base classes.

Builders are an invaluable feature that developers using your framework will come to rely on while they are learning to use your framework and during the development cycle. This chapter illustrates one way to create builders without affecting the Builders table that ships with Visual FoxPro.

Creating your base classes

One of the first development tasks you will undertake when creating your framework is to create your framework base classes. You create your base classes by subclassing each of the FoxPro base classes. You can create subclasses programmatically by using the CREATE CLASS command or by instantiating each class and using the SaveAsClass() method. I prefer the SaveAsClass() method over the CREATE CLASS command because SaveAsClass() allows you to enter a description of the class.

You can create your base classes by running zBaseClassCreator.prg. The code samples presented in this section are excerpts from .\tools\zBaseClassCreator.prg included with the accompanying source code.

First, we define variables to store the relative path and file names for the visual and non-visual classes.

```
lcVCX = '..\..\myframe\framesource\myframe.vcx'
lcPRG = '..\..\myframe\framesource\myframe.prg'
```

Next, we must differentiate between visual and non-visual classes. Because there are far fewer non-visual classes, I find it easier to identify the non-visual ones and assume the remaining classes are visual. In the following code, you will see that a list of non-visual classes is stored to a variable, lcNonVisual.

Another thing I like to do is limit the number of controls that are created. For example, the OLECONTROL cannot be subclassed without defining which ActiveX control it will bind to. If you prefer, you could extend the omitted list to include some controls that you may choose not to include in your class library.

```
DO CASE
   CASE VERSION(5) = 800
       lcOmitted    = "OLECONTROL"
       lcNonVisual = "COLUMN,EMPTY,EXCEPTION,HEADER,SESSION"
   CASE VERSION(5) = 700
       lcOmitted    = "OLECONTROL"
       lcNonVisual = "COLUMN, CURSOR, DATAENVIRONMENT, "+;
                       HEADER, OLECONTROL, PAGE, RELATION, SESSION"
ENDCASE
```

You can use the aLanguage() function to generate the list of classes that are to be subclassed. The aLanguage() function, new in FoxPro 7.0, populates an array with a list of language elements. Passing a value of 1 – 4 indicates the type of information placed into the array. Here's the list of parameters and their return types:

- 1—Commands

- 2—Functions

- 3—Base Classes

- 4—DBC Events

The aLanguage() function returns the number of elements, in this case classes, placed into the array, and can be used to create an array of the FoxPro base classes as follows:

```
lnClassCount  = ALANGUAGE(laClasses,3)
FOR lnI = 1 TO lnClassCount
     * <<Code to create classes goes here>>
ENDFOR
```

To create each class, you need to know the base class, the new name for the class, and a description for the class. Following the naming conventions from Chapter 2, "Project Planning," each class is an "abstract" class and will have a name that begins with the letter "a." Pulling the information from the array, you can define the necessary information as follows:

```
lcBaseClass = UPPER(laClasses[lnI])
lcClassName = 'a'+ PROPER(lcBaseClass)
lcClassDesc = 'Base '+ lcBaseClass + ' class in MyFrame'
```

The way you create a class differs based on whether it's visual or non-visual. For non-visual classes, you are scripting a class definition. For example, your base EXCEPTION class is defined as follows:

```
*--Base EXCEPTION class in MyFrame
DEFINE CLASS aException AS EXCEPTION
ENDDEFINE
```

Visual classes are easily created by instantiating the object using CreateObject() and then saving the object using the object's SaveAsClass() method. One wrinkle for visual controls is the OLEBOUNDCONTROL class. OLEBOUNDCONTROLs cannot be instantiated outside of a form. To accommodate this, you will see that the sample program actually creates a form, and uses AddObject() to create the OLEBOUNDCONTROL class. Once the object is added to the form, the object's SaveAsClass() method is called. Here is the code for creating your base classes:

```
lcPRGClassDefinition = ""

FOR lnI = 1 TO lnClassCount

    lcBaseClass = UPPER(laClasses[lnI])
    lcClassName = 'a'+ PROPER(lcBaseClass)
    lcClassDesc = 'Base '+ lcBaseClass + ' class in MyFrame'

    DO CASE
        CASE lcBaseClass $lcOmitted
            *--Do nothing, the class is omitted

        CASE lcBaseClass $ lcNonVisual
            *--Script non-visual class definitions
            lcPRGClassDefinition = lcPRGClassDefinition + ;
                "*--" + lcClassDesc + CR +;
                "DEFINE CLASS "+ lcClassName + " as " + lcBaseClass + CR + ;
                "ENDDEFINE" + CR_LF

        CASE lcBaseClass = 'OLEBOUNDCONTROL'
                loForm = CREATEOBJECT("Form")
            loForm.ADDOBJECT("oClassToCreate",lcBaseClass)
            loForm.oClassToCreate.SAVEASCLASS(lcVCX,lcClassName,lcClassDesc)
            loForm.REMOVEOBJECT("oClassToCreate")

        OTHERWISE
            LOCAL loClass AS CUSTOM
            loClass = CREATEOBJECT(lcBaseClass)
            loClass.SAVEASCLASS(lcVCX,lcClassName,lcClassDesc)

    ENDCASE

ENDFOR
```

With the loop completed, the lcPRGClassDefinition variable contains the scripted code for your non-visual base classes. The final lines of the program write it to a file as follows:

```
IF ! EMPTY(lcPRGClassDefinition)
    =STRTOFILE(lcPRGClassDefinition,lcPRG,.F.)
ENDIF
```

Adding common behavior

There are 37 visual base classes in the MyFrame framework. Unfortunately, the creators of FoxPro did not provide one "super class" that serves as the parent for all classes. This means that if you want to add a property, such as cBuilderClass, or a method, such as zReadMe(), to each of your base classes, you must add the properties and methods 37 times. Consider the changes required to implement security or error handling. Ouch! In addition to the time required to add properties and methods to each base class, having the same code in many different classes can be a maintenance nightmare.

The source code that accompanies this book includes a tool that programmatically adds or modifies properties and methods for each of your base classes. The name of the program is zVisualBaseClassConfigurator.prg. You can access it by selecting DevTools | Configure Visual Base Classes from the framework system menu. The source code can be found in the .\Tools\ folder, while the relevant portions are presented in the next section.

zVisualBaseClassConfigurator.prg

FoxPro provides two methods to programmatically read and write method code at design time: ReadMethod() and WriteMethod(). New to FoxPro 8.0 are the AddProperty() and RemoveProperty() functions that allow you to add and remove properties at design time and at run time.

The zVisualBaseClassConfigurator program (also known as the PEM Adder tool) uses these methods and functions to programmatically add and remove properties and methods to your base classes. The property and method information is stored in a table, FramePems.dbf. Its structure is shown in **Figure 1**.

The sample framework includes an entry screen (see **Figure 2**) that allows you to edit the information in the FramePems table. You can access this by selecting MyFrame | FramePems from the system menu.

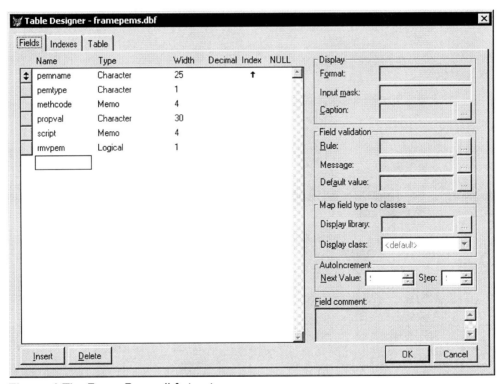

*Figure 1.*The FramePems.dbf structure.

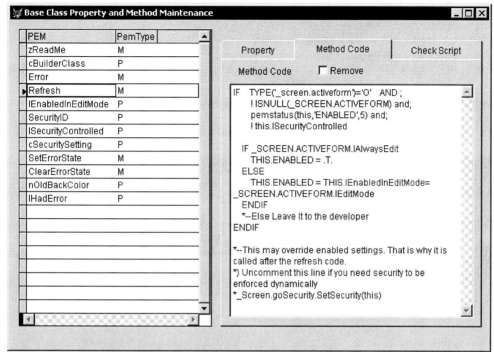

Figure 2. *The FramePems entry screen.*

The management screen allows you to define whether an entry is a property or method; record its name; assign a default value for properties or code for methods; and select a check box to indicate whether you want to add or remove the property or method.

The Check Script tab allows you to conditionally add properties or methods based on some test performed on the class. For example, you may choose to add properties only to container objects.

To understand the design of the PEM Adder tool, let's review what happens when you modify a class.

When you modify a class, the class is opened in the Class Designer. Also opened are any code windows that were open when you last closed the class. I have found the most consistent way to modify a class, make changes, and close all open windows associated with the class, is to divide these responsibilities between two classes.

The first class, PemAdder, is responsible for creating a list of classes in a class library file (VCX) and issuing a MODIFY CLASS command on the framework base classes. The second class, tmrPemAdder, reads the FramePems table and either adds or removes the properties and methods from the object being modified.

In zVisualBaseclassConfigurator.prg, you will find the two classes, PemAdder and tmrPemAdder. The remainder of this section describes their construction.

Class definition for PemAdder

The PemAdder class is responsible for identifying each class in a class library file (VCX). It then tests each class to determine whether it is a framework base class. If it is, it instantiates the tmrPemAdder class and modifies the class. That's all this class is responsible for.

The class definition contains three properties: cClassLib is the class library to modify, cFramePems is the table that holds the properties and methods that are added to each base class, and aClassList is an array property that stores the name of each class in the library. Following is the class definition.

Only the method definitions are shown. The code for each method is explained in detail in the sections following this section.

```
DEFINE CLASS PemAdder AS CUSTOM
    cClassLib = "..\FRAMESOURCE\MYFRAME.VCX"
    cFramePems = "FRAMEPEMS.DBF"
    DIMENSION aClassList[1,1]

    FUNCTION AddPems()
    ENDFUNC

    FUNCTION CreateClassList()
    ENDFUNC

    FUNCTION ModiClasses()
    ENDFUNC

    FUNCTION IsBaseClass(tcParentClassName)
    ENDFUNC

ENDDEFINE
```

Identifying classes in a VCX file

The CreateClassList() method uses the AVCXClasses() function to obtain a list of classes in a class library, and stores the list to the aClassList property array.

```
    FUNCTION CreateClassList()
        AVCXCLASSES(THIS.aClassList,THIS.cClassLib)
    ENDFUNC
```

Testing for a base class

You have seen the aLanguage() function used earlier in the chapter to create the base classes for your framework. You can also use the aLanguage() function to test whether a class is one of your framework base classes. The IsBaseClass() function accepts a class as a parameter and returns a logical True (.T.) if the class is contained in the list of FoxPro base classes.

Here's the code to test whether a class is one of FoxPro's base classes.

```
*--Testing for Base Class
    FUNCTION IsBaseClass(tcParentClassName)
        LOCAL laBaseClasses[1]
        ALANGUAGE(laBaseClasses,3)
        RETURN  ASCAN(laBaseClasses,tcParentClassName,-1,-1,1,15)>0
    ENDFUNC
```

Modifying base classes

When adding properties and methods to every class in your framework, you only want to add them to your framework base classes. Inheritance will propagate the changes to every class built from your base classes.

The aClassList[] array contains a list of each class in a class library. The third column contains the parent class. You can use the IsBaseClass() function outlined in the previous section to test whether a class is one of your framework base classes. To review, your framework base classes are direct subclasses of FoxPro's classes. By definition, then, your framework base classes will have a FoxPro base class as their parent class.

Notice that the following code creates the tmrPemAdder class just before modifying the class. The MODIFY CLASS command is then issued without using the NOWAIT clause, suspending program execution until the class being modified is closed. However, the tmrPemAdder class is based on the Timer class, and its code fires even though all other code is suspended. When the tmrPemAdder has finished its work, it will close the Class Designer; then the ModiClasses() method resumes execution.

```
*--Modi Classes
   FUNCTION ModiClasses()
      LOCAL lnI, loTimer, lcClass
      WITH THIS
         FOR lnI = 1 TO ALEN(THIS.aClassList,1)

            IF THIS.IsBaseClass(.aClassList[lnI,PARENT_CLASS])
               loTimer = CREATEOBJECT("tmrPemAdder")
               lcClass = ALLTRIM(.aClassList[lnI,CLASS_NAME])
               MODIFY CLASS (lcClass ) OF (.cClassLib)
            ENDIF

         ENDFOR
      ENDWITH
   ENDFUNC
```

The Timer class

The timer control, tmrPemAdder, takes over once the class is modified. The first thing the timer does is set its interval property to 0, preventing subsequent firings of the Timer event. Next, a reference to the class being modified is obtained using the ASelObj() function. If ASelObj () returns a reference to an object, you run a custom script to determine if the class is "OKToModify()", then SCAN through the FramePems table. Depending on the value in the FramePems.PemType field, a call is made to add or remove a property or method.

Once all the records in the FramePems table are scanned, the changes are saved and the Class Designer is closed. This returns control to the PemAdder class presented earlier.

Here's the class definition and the Timer() method. I'll explain the remaining methods next.

```
DEFINE CLASS tmrPemAdder AS TIMER
   lSafeMode     = .F.
   cPemFile      = "FramePems"
   oClassToModify = .NULL.
```

```
INTERVAL        = 100

FUNCTION TIMER()
    THIS.INTERVAL = 0

    *--If an object is selected
    IF ASELOBJ(aSelectedObject,1)>0 AND VARTYPE(aSelectedObject[1])='O'

        THIS.oClassToModify = aSelectedObject[1]

        *--scan through the pems table
        SELECT (THIS.cPemFile)
        SCAN

            IF THIS.OKToModify()

                IF UPPER(FramePems.pemtype) = 'M'
                    THIS.AddMethods()
                ELSE
                    THIS.AddProps()
                ENDIF
            ENDIF

        ENDSCAN

        THIS.CloseWindow()

    ENDIF
ENDFUNC
```

Conditional formatting

You may not want every class to receive every property or method that is in the FramePems table. For example, each class has a SetErrorState() and ClearErrorState() method. However, code that sets the BackColor property of a control is not appropriate because not every control has this property. A custom check allows you to prevent the tmrPemAdder from overwriting the code that exists in the class definition.

The IsOKToModify() method reads the conditional code from the FramePems table and runs it using FoxPro's ExecScript() function. Notice that the control to modify is passed as a parameter to the called script.

```
FUNCTION OKToModify()

    IF ! EMPTY(FramePems.Script)
        llOK = EXECSCRIPT( FramePems.Script,THIS.oClassToModify )
        RETURN llOK
    ENDIF

ENDFUNC
```

Following is an example of the code that might be included in the Script field. In this example, a test ensures that changes are not made to classes with a base class of Form, Toolbar, CommandButton, PageFrame, or DataEnvironment.

```
*--Sample Contents for FramePems.Script
LPARAMETERS toObject
LOCAL llOK

DO CASE
    CASE UPPER(ALLTRIM(toObject.BASECLASS))  ="FORM"
    CASE UPPER(ALLTRIM(toObject.BASECLASS))  ="TOOLBAR"
    CASE UPPER(ALLTRIM(toObject.BASECLASS))  ="COMMANDBUTTON"
    CASE UPPER(ALLTRIM(toObject.BASECLASS))  ="PAGEFRAME"
    CASE UPPER(ALLTRIM(toObject.BASECLASS))  ="DATAENVIRONMENT"



    OTHERWISE
        llOK = .T.
ENDCASE

RETURN llOK
```

Adding and removing properties

New to FoxPro 8.0 are the AddProperty() and RemoveProperty() functions. As their names
suggest, these methods will either add or remove a property from an object. Classes also have
an AddProperty() method. Calling a method of a class is preferable to calling a function
because you can take actions to amend the behavior within the class.

The code for the AddProps() method either adds a property using the AddProperty()
method of the class or removes the property using the RemoveProperty() function.

```
FUNCTION AddProps()

    IF FramePems.rmvpem
        REMOVEPROPERTY(THIS.oClassToModify, ALLTRIM(FramePems.pemname))
    ELSE
        THIS.oClassToModify.ADDPROPERTY(ALLTRIM(FramePems.pemname),propval)
    ENDIF

ENDFUNC
```

Writing method code

The AddMethods() method either adds a method to a class or removes the method code for the
class. The tmrPemAdder class has a property, lSafetyMode, that indicates whether existing
method code is replaced or commented before adding the latest code. You cannot remove a
method from a class as you can with RemoveProperty(). So, when the FramePems.RemPem
field is set to .T., the code is removed from the class, but the method declaration remains.

Here's the code.

```
FUNCTION AddMethods()
    LOCAL lcOldUnformattedMethodCode,lcNewPem
    LOCAL lcOldMethod, llHasMethod

    lcOldUnformattedMethodCode = ''
    llHasMethod = .F.
```

```
    IF PEMSTATUS(THIS.oClassToModify, ALLTRIM(FramePems.pemname),5)

        lcOldMethod =
THIS.oClassToModify.READMETHOD(ALLTRIM(FramePems.pemname))
        lcOldUnformattedMethodCode = THIS.CommentOldCode(lcOldMethod)
        llHasMethod = .T.

    ENDIF

    IF !( UPPER(THIS.oClassToModify.BASECLASS) = 'OLECONTROL' AND ;
          llHasMethod = .F.) AND ;
          ! UPPER(THIS.oClassToModify.BASECLASS) = 'FORMSET'
        *) Note: there is a problem using WRITEMETHOD() with
        *) OLEControls.
        *) An error is generated when using WRITEMETHOD()
        *) if the class does not already have the method defined.
        *) You must manually add the method to OLEControl Objects.

        IF FramePems.rmvpem
            THIS.oClassToModify.WRITEMETHOD(ALLTRIM(FramePems.pemname),"",.T.)
        ELSE
            THIS.oClassToModify.WRITEMETHOD(ALLTRIM(FramePems.pemname),
                FramePems.MethCode+lcOldUnformattedMethodCode ,.T.)
        ENDIF
    ENDIF

ENDFUNC
```

Saving the class

To save the class and close the Class Designer, issue the KEYBOARD command with '{CTRL+E}'.

```
FUNCTION CloseWindow()
    KEYBOARD '{CTRL +E}'
ENDFUNC
```

Creating your own builders

Builders are a key of framework development. In addition to the time savings they provide, builders allow you to reinforce key framework design decisions.

While you can add builders to the FoxPro builder table, Builders.dbf, the change is unconditionally added to the developer's machine. While that may be desirable for developers who always develop using a specific framework, it is not an acceptable solution for a sample framework.

The approach for builders in MyFrame is to intercept a call to the builder and, optionally, redirect it to a builder within the framework. In this way, the builders work while the framework is in use, but do not impact the user's machine when the framework is not in use.

Redirecting FoxPro's builder

The _Builder variable points to the application called when you select Builder from the context-sensitive menu that appears as you right-click on a control in design mode. FoxPro passes the following variables to the builder:

```
parameters wbopCtrl, wbcpOrigin, wbcpClass, wbcpName, wbcpOptions, wbcpP1,
wbcpP2, wbcpP3, wbcpP4, wbcpP5, wbcpP6, wbcpP7, wbcpP8, wbcpP9
```

Accordingly, your solution must be able to accommodate these parameters.

The framework has a class, MyBuilder, which saves the value in the _Builder variable and changes it to point to the framework builder. When the class is released, it restores the _Builder variable to its original value. Here's the class definition and the Init() code:

```
*--MyBuilder class definition and Init() method
DEFINE CLASS MyBuilder AS CUSTOM
    cOldBuilder = _BUILDER

    FUNCTION INIT(tcFileLocation)
        THIS.cOldBuilder = _BUILDER
        _BUILDER = tcFileLocation
    ENDFUNC

ENDDEFINE
```

This class definition exists in MyBuilder.prg. The program has a little stub that runs when you call it. This little bit of code accepts the default variables that FoxPro passes to a builder. If the custom builder is not created, the object is first created. Every call is then forwarded to the builder.

```
*--MyBuilder.Prg - Code
LPARAMETERS toObjectToBuild,
 tcSource, wbcpClass, wbcpName,
 wbcpOptions, wbcpP1, wbcpP2,
 wbcpP3, wbcpP4, wbcpP5, wbcpP6,
 wbcpP7, wbcpP8, wbcpP9

IF ! VARTYPE(goBuilder) = 'O'
    RELEASE goBuilder
    PUBLIC goBuilder
    goBuilder = CREATEOBJECT("MyBuilder",SYS(16))
ENDIF

goBuilder.DoBuilder(toObjectToBuild,
 tcSource, wbcpClass, wbcpName,
 wbcpOptions, wbcpP1, wbcpP2,
 wbcpP3, wbcpP4, wbcpP5, wbcpP6,
 wbcpP7, wbcpP8, wbcpP9)
```

To invoke a custom builder, each class has a property, cBuilderClass, that contains the class name of the custom builder for this object. If the value of the cBuilderClass is empty, the FoxPro builder is called directly. However, if cBuilderClass has a value, I display a context-sensitive menu so that you can select which builder should be presented—your own or FoxPro's.

```
      FUNCTION DoBuilder(toObjectToBuild, tcSource, wbcpClass, wbcpName,
wbcpOptions, wbcpP1, wbcpP2, wbcpP3, wbcpP4, wbcpP5, wbcpP6, wbcpP7, wbcpP8,
wbcpP9)

      LOCAL lnSelection
      lnSelection = 0

      IF VARTYPE(toObjectToBuild) = 'O'
        IF PEMSTATUS(toObjectToBuild,'cBuilderClass',5)
          IF ! EMPTY(toObjectToBuild.cBuilderClass)

              *--Select a builder - MyFrame or Fox

              DEFINE POPUP shortcut RELATIVE FROM MROW()-1,MCOL()-3
                DEFINE BAR 1 OF shortcut PROMPT "MyFrame Builder"
                DEFINE BAR 2 OF shortcut PROMPT "FoxPro Builder"
                ON SELECTION BAR 1 OF shortcut lnSelection  = 1
                ON SELECTION BAR 2 OF shortcut lnSelection  = 2
                ACTIVATE POPUP shortcut
                RELEASE POPUP shortcut

          ENDIF
        ENDIF
      ENDIF
```

Depending on the object for which you are writing the builder, you may need to reference the object itself, its container, the form on which it resides, and a reference to its data environment. You can get these references as follows:

```
      LOCAL lnContainers, loContainer,
      LOCAL lnEnvironments, loEnvironment, loForm

      lnContainers = ASELOBJ(laContainer,1)
      loContainer = IIF(lnContainers=1,laContainer[1],.NULL.)
      lnEnvironments = ASELOBJ(laDataEnvironment,2)
      loEnvironment = IIF(lnEnvironments = 1,laDataEnvironment[1],.NULL.)
      loForm = GetForm(toObjectToBuild)
```

Note that GetForm() is a custom method that returns a reference to the form on which a control resides. It is shown following the completion of this method.

Now that you have a reference to all the major builder elements, you can call the custom builder as follows:

```
      DO CASE
      CASE lnSelection = 1
        lo = CREATEOBJECT(ALLTRIM(toObjectToBuild.cBuilderClass),
              toObjectToBuild,tcSource, loForm,
                loContainer ,loEnvironment )
        lo.SHOW(1)
      CASE lnSelection = 2
        DO (THIS.cOldBuilder)  WITH toObjectToBuild,
                  tcSource, wbcpClass, wbcpName,
                  wbcpOptions, wbcpP1, wbcpP2,
                  wbcpP3, wbcpP4, wbcpP5, wbcpP6,
                  wbcpP7, wbcpP8

      ENDCASE
      ENDFUNC
```

The GetForm() function is in GenProc.prg. It returns the form on which a control resides, and works at design time or run time. The reason it is a separate function, rather than a method of the class, is that it may be useful elsewhere.

The GetForm() function accepts an object reference and uses recursion to search each parent until it finds a form.

```
FUNCTION GETFORM(toObject)
    DO CASE
        CASE UPPER(toObject.BASECLASS) = "FORM"
            RETURN toObject
        CASE VARTYPE(toO bject.PARENT)<> 'O'
            RETURN .NULL.
        OTHERWISE
            RETURN GETFORM(toObject.PARENT)
    ENDCASE
ENDFUNC
```

aBuilderForm

The builder form class is the heart of building custom builders in MyFrame. Each of the objects passed by the calling builder program—Form, Data Environment, Container, and the object itself—is stored as a property of the form. **Figure 3** shows the default builder class.

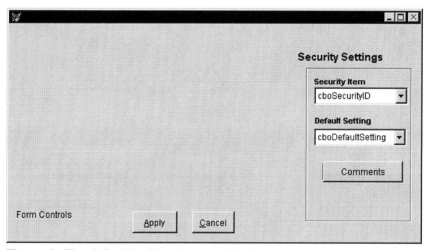

Figure 3. The default builder class: bldDefault.

Every class in MyFrame contains a zReadMe() method that you can use to store development notes. Clicking the Comments button opens an edit box that reads and writes information to the zReadMe() method.

The cboSecurityID and cboDefaultSetting combo boxes allow the developer to make security settings. Each class is security enabled and has SecurityID and cSecuritySetting properties. (For more information, see Chapter 16, "Security.")

To understand how this works, here's the Init() code that accepts the parameters passed on creation:

```
*--aBuilderFrm.Init()
LPARAMETERS toObject,tcSource, toForm, toContainer, toDataEnvironment

WITH THIS

    .oObjectToBuild = toObject
    .cSource = tcSource
    .oForm = toForm
    .oContainer = toContainer
    .oDataenvrionment = toDataEnvironment

    .ReadProperties()

ENDWITH
```

For every class, you can add comments to the zReadMe() method and make default security settings. The following code, which is located in the ReadProperties() method, handles the task of reading and writing text in zReadMe() and applies the security settings to each object. Once the standard settings have been read, the code then calls the OnReadProperties() method, which is where the application developer places his or her code to extend the builder.

Text placed in the zReadMe() method is meant to be a comment, not actually code. To ensure there are no compilation errors, all text in the zReadMe() method is surrounded with #IF and #ENDIF. The StrTran() is used to strip these commands before displaying the code in an edit box.

```
*--Read the framework settings
*) - Security
THISFORM.cboDefaultSetting.DISPLAYVALUE= THIS.oObjectToBuild.cSecuritySetting
THISFORM.cboSecurityID.DISPLAYVALUE = THIS.oObjectToBuild.SecurityID

*-- Comments - Stored in zReadMe()
LOCAL lcComments
lcComments = THIS.oObjectToBuild.READMETHOD("zReadMe")

*--Remove #if/endif
lcComments = STRTRAN(lcComments,"#IF .F."+CHR(10)+CHR(13),"")
lcComments = STRTRAN(lcComments,"#ENDIF","")
THIS.edtComments.VALUE = lcComments

THIS.onReadProperties()
```

The opposite code is called to write the values of the properties back to the controls.

```
*--aBuilderFrm.OnApply()
THIS.oObjectToBuild.cSecuritySetting = THISFORM.cboDefaultSetting.DISPLAYVALUE
THIS.oObjectToBuild.SecurityID = THISFORM.cboSecurityID.DISPLAYVALUE

LOCAL lcComments
lcComments =THIS.edtComments.VALUE
lcComments = ;
    "#IF .F." + ;
    CHR(10)+CHR(13) + ;
    lcComments + ;
    CHR(10)+CHR(13) + ;
    "#ENDIF"
```

```
THIS.oObjectToBuild.WRITEMETHOD("zReadMe",lcComments )

THIS.OnWriteProperties()
```

Finally, as the form is closed, you must make sure to remove all object references so the form closes properly.

```
*--aBuilderForm.Close()
this.oObjecttobuild = .null.
this.oDataenvrionment = .null.
this.oForm = .null.

DoDefault()
```

Creating your own builder form

The class aBuilderFrm is a subclass of aDialogFrm. To create your own builders, you must first subclass aBuilderFrm. As a matter of housekeeping, each of the framework builder forms is kept in a class library called MyBuilderForms, located in the FrameSource directory. If you develop multiple applications, you may prefer to store builders in an application directory instead.

More than 10 builders are included with the sample framework. To illustrate how to create your own builder, I'll show you the builder for the cursor class. The name of the class is bldMyCursor and is shown in **Figure 4**.

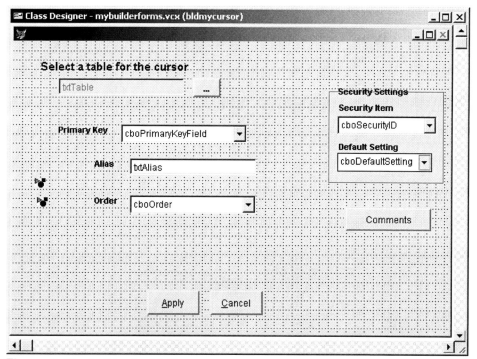

Figure 4. The builder for MyCursor.

In Chapter 9, "Cursor and CursorAdapter," I identified four key properties for each cursor: the name of the table, the primary key, an alias for the table, and the order in which the records are to be displayed. The class bldMyCursor assists you in setting these properties.

Here's the code in the OnReadProperties() and OnWriteProperties() methods.

```
*--bldMYCursor.OnReadProperties()
WITH THIS.oObjectToBuild
    THIS.ADDTABLE( .cTable )

    IF EMPTY(.cPrimaryKey)
            THIS.cboPrimaryKeyField.DISPLAYVALUE= GetPrimaryKey()
    ELSE
              THIS.cboPrimaryKeyField.DISPLAYVALUE= .cPrimaryKey
    ENDIF
    THIS.cboOrder.DISPLAYVALUE = .cOrder
    IF ! EMPTY( .cAlias )
        THIS.txtAlias.VALUE = .cAlias
    ENDIF
ENDWITH
```

And the code for OnWriteProperties():

```
*--bldMyCursor.OnWriteProperties()
WITH THIS.oObjectToBuild

    .cTable = ALLTRIM(THIS.txtTable.VALUE)
    .cPrimaryKey = ALLTRIM(THIS.cboPrimaryKeyField.VALUE)
    .cOrder = ALLTRIM(THIS.cboOrder.DISPLAYVALUE)
    .cAlias = ALLTRIM(THIS.txtAlias.Text)

ENDWITH
```

To review, to create a custom builder we added the appropriate controls and custom code to the OnReadProperties() and OnWriteProperties() methods. That's all that's required to create your custom builder form. Once you've created the builder form, modify the class definition by changing the cBuilderForm property to contain the name of the class you've just created.

 To quickly see which properties a builder changes, set the property sheet to display non-default values only. Run the builder, making the appropriate selections, and voila! You will see exactly which properties a builder changes.

Change parent

FoxPro provides the class browser to simplify many aspects of class library development. While many of the functions performed by the class browser can be accomplished directly in the FoxPro language, changing the parent of a class is not one of them.

The class browser makes it easy to redefine a class to inherit from another class. However, manually using the class browser can be a little time consuming if you have large numbers of classes to change. The following code opens the class browser and loads the MyFrame class library. If a class with the name of NewClass exists in the library, it will have its parent class changed to MyDataEnvironment.

```
*--Sample code to change a class' parent using the class browser
DO (_BROWSER) WITH "MyFrame.vcx"
IF VARTYPE(_OBrowser)= "O"

    IF _OBrowser.seekclass("NewClass")
        _OBrowser.redefineclass("MyDataEnvironment","MyFrame.vcx")
    ENDIF
ENDIF
```

Summary

In this chapter, you have learned how to programmatically create your base classes and add custom properties and methods. You have also seen one way to add a custom builder and an example of how to use the class browser to automate some class-library-maintenance activities.

> Updates and corrections to this chapter can be found on Hentzenwerke's Web site, **www.hentzenwerke.com**. Click "Catalog" and navigate to the page for this book.

Chapter 18
Starting New Projects

Starting a new project is always an exciting time. But the enthusiasm can quickly fade when you think of the many steps required to set up a new project. In this chapter, you will see examples of how to start a new development effort while using a framework.

The start of each new development effort is likely to involve some or all of the following:

- Create a fresh set of folders

- Copy existing code

- Create an application database and tables

- Create a project

- Create a main program

Starting a framework project is similar to starting a non-framework project. However, there are some differences. For example, the framework classes must be subclassed at the start of each project. Another difference is that the "Copy existing code" step is extended to include the framework databases and tables.

In this chapter, you will see examples of how to automate the creation of a new project. Major benefits to automation include the reduced time required to set up each new project, the ability to tailor the process to your particular preferences, and of course, automation eliminates the possibility that you may make mistakes during the setup process.

One of the new tools for FoxPro 8.0 is the Task Pane—a customizable tool that you can modify to meet your development needs. At the end of the chapter, you will see how to add your custom New Project program to the Task Pane.

Before reading this chapter, you should be familiar with Chapters 5 and 6, "Beginning Development" and "Creating a Class Library." The folder structure and most of the files addressed in this chapter were presented in Chapter 5, while several approaches for distributing your class libraries were presented in Chapter 6.

Creating a new project

The first step in creating a new project is to collect information. **Figure 1** shows the form MyProjectInfo.scx, which captures information about the new project.

The remainder of this chapter presents the more important aspects of creating a framework project. All the code for creating the project can be found in the CreateProject() method of MyProjectInfo.scx.

Create a fresh set of folders

Chapter 5, "Beginning Development," identified the folder structure for the framework and applications based on the framework. As a reminder, framework files are stored under the MyFrame folder while project files are stored in application-specific folders. The SampleApp folder represents the root folder of the application. The file structure is shown again in **Figure 2** for your convenience.

Project Details		
Project Name		A 30 character description for the project
Project Folder		The root folder for the project
Project File		The file name of the project manager created for this project
Create Application Database	☐	Check this box to create a separate database for the application and if applicable, the name of the database.
Database Name		
Class Prefix		The default prefix assigned to subclasses. You may specify class specific values in the class copy screen.
Show Splash Screen	☐	Check this box if you would like to display a splash screen at the start of the application.
Enable Security	☐	Check this box if security is to be enabled in your applications.
	Continue	Cancel

Figure 1. Collecting information about a new project.

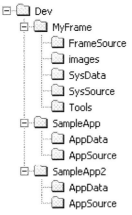

- Dev
  - MyFrame
    - FrameSource
    - images
    - SysData
    - SysSource
    - Tools
  - SampleApp
    - AppData
    - AppSource
  - SampleApp2
    - AppData
    - AppSource

Figure 2. The framework folder structure.

The MyProject.scx form is located in the framework's Tools directory. You can obtain the framework's root directory by using the SYS(1271) function and make it the active directory as follows:

```
*--Defining the root directory
lcFrameRoot =  STRTRAN(SYS(1271,THIS),'myframe\tools\myprojectinfo.scx',"")
CD &lcFrameRoot
```

The developer specifies the root directory for the project by filling in the project folder text box on MyProjectInfo. Memory variables hold the names of the project folders and framework paths. The MKDIR command is issued to create the application folders. Although I don't use the frame paths here, the values of these variables are used later in the program.

```
lcAppRoot    = '.\'+ADDBS(ALLTRIM(THIS.txtprojFolder.TEXT))
lcAppSource = lcAppRoot +'AppSource\'
lcAppData   = lcAppRoot +'AppData\'

lcFrameMetaData   = lcFrameRoot + "MyFrame\SysData\*.*"
lcFrameMetaSource = lcFrameRoot + "MyFrame\SysSource\*.*"
lcFrameSource     = lcFrameRoot + "MyFrame\FrameSource\"

IF DIRECTORY(lcAppRoot )
    =MESSAGEBOX("A directory with this name already exists")
    RETURN .F.
ENDIF

*--Create the project folders
MKDIR &lcAppRoot
MKDIR &lcAppSource
MKDIR &lcAppData
```

Create the framework tables

Certain source code and data files are copied to the application folders at the start of each project. For example, a separate copy of the data files used to store framework preferences, system codes, and so on, is moved into the \<AppName>\AppData folder. Similarly, source code files, such as the splash screen, MySplash.scx, are copied to the application source code folder.

Using the COPY FILE command allows you to place any number of files in the source folders. Every file you add to the folder is dutifully copied at the start of the next project.

```
*--Copy Default Data
lcToDir = ADDBS(lcAppData) + "*.*"
COPY FILE &lcFrameMetaData TO &lcToDir

*--Copy Default Source
lcToDir = ADDBS(lcAppSource) + "*.*"
COPY FILE &lcFrameMetaSource TO &lcToDir
```

Creating an application database

The programmer may choose to create an application database by selecting the Create Application Database check box shown in Figure 1 and by providing a name for the database. Using the path information defined earlier and the information supplied by the developer, you can generate the command to create the new database.

Part of adding a new database to a project is that the OPEN DATABASE command must be added to the main program as well. In situations where a database is created, not only is the file created, but so is the command that opens the database. This command will be inserted into the Main.prg file generated later in this chapter.

```
*--Create the database
IF THISFORM.chkCreateAppDatabase.VALUE = 1

    LOCAL lcDataBase, lcDataBaseAndPath
    lcDataBase  =  ALLTRIM(THISFORM.txtDataBaseName.VALUE)
    lcDataBaseAndPath = lcAppData + lcDataBase

    CREATE DATABASE &lcDataBaseAndPath

    lcOpenDatabaseString = "OPEN DATABASE " + lcDataBase + " SHARED"
ELSE
    lcOpenDatabaseString = ""
ENDIF
```

Subclass the framework classes

The framework contains more than 100 classes. However, not every class is intended for use in an application. For example, some of the classes are abstract classes that provide a base for other classes used in the application. Other classes, such as the error handler, are functional as is and you may not need application-specific subclasses.

You can specify which classes are subclassed at the beginning of an application by filling in the ClassCopy.dbf table. This table controls which classes are subclassed and which classes are not.

By default, all classes are copied with the same name and given the prefix supplied in the MyProjectInfo collection form (see Figure 1).

You also have control over which VCX the resulting class is placed in. **Figure 3** shows the Class Copy management screen.

The subclasses are created by using the CREATE CLASS command. CREATE CLASS allows you to specify the name of a class, the file in which it is stored, and the class from which it inherits.

The classes are created by scanning through the ClassCopy table and executing the CREATE CLASS command for each class you want to create. Here's the code:

```
SELECT "classcopy"
lcClassPrefix = THIS.txtClassPrefix.TEXT

SCAN
    IF classcopy.DoCopy
        lcFromClass = ALLTRIM(classcopy.classname)
        lcFromFile = lcFrameSource  +  ALLTRIM(classcopy.fromfile)
        lcPrefixToUse = ALLTRIM(IIF(classcopy.noprefix,"",lcClassPrefix))
        lcToClass = lcPrefixToUse + ALLTRIM(classcopy.toClass)
```

```
lcToFile =  lcAppSource + ALLTRIM(classcopy.tofile)
THIS.tmrClassCloser.INTERVAL=100

    CREATE CLASS &lcToClass OF &lcToFile  AS &lcFromClass  FROM &lcFromFile
ENDIF

ENDSCAN
```

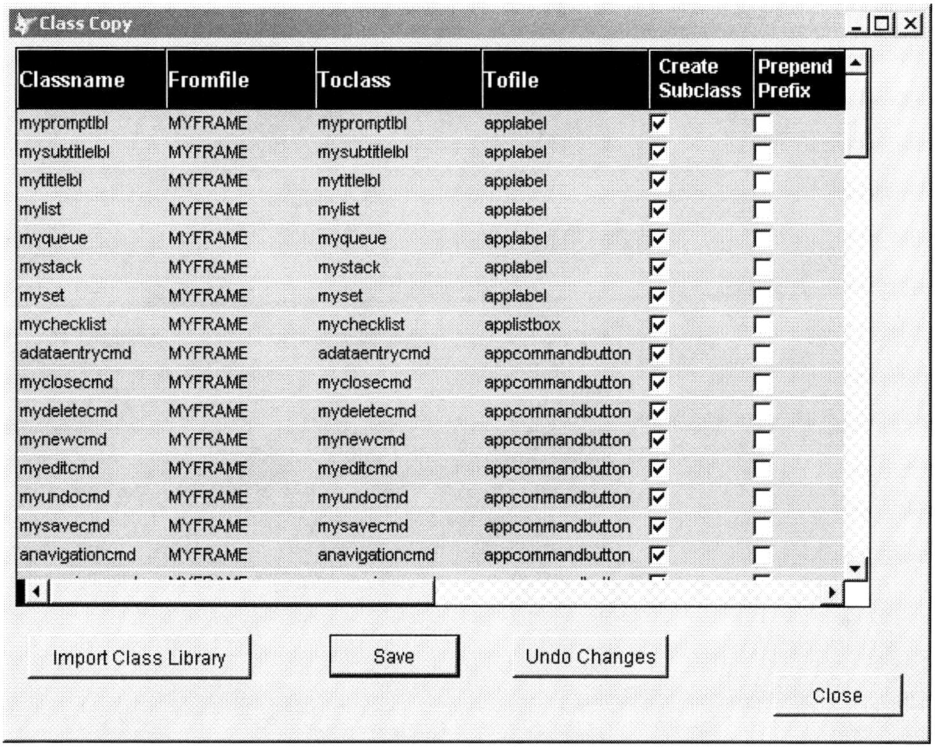

Figure 3. The subclass maintenance screen MyCopyClass.scx.

Adding classes to the subclasser

The form MyClassCopy.scx has an ImportClassLibrary() method that imports class libraries into the table. The ImportClassLibrary() method uses the GetFile() function to prompt for a class to import. Then, a list of classes is obtained from the VCX file using the AVCXClasses() function. After performing a LOCATE to see if the class already exists in the table, the new values are inserted.

```
*--MyClassCopy.scx - ImportClassLibrary()
lcClassLib = GETFILE("vcx")
lcFromFile = JUSTSTEM(lcClassLib)
lnClasses  = AVCXCLASSES(laClassList,lcClassLib)
```

```
FOR lnI = 1 TO lnClasses

    lcFromClass =  laClassList[lni,1]
    lcToClass = lcFromClass
    lcBaseClass = laClassList[lnI,2]
    lcToFile = 'app'+ lcBaseClass

    LOCATE FOR UPPER(ALLTRIM(ClassName) ) == UPPER(ALLTRIM(lcFromClass)) AND;
     UPPER(ALLTRIM(FromFile)) == ALLTRIM(UPPER(lcFromFile))
    IF FOUND()
        IF DELETED('ClassCopy')
           RECALL
        ENDIF
    ELSE
       INSERT INTO  ;
           ClassCopy (ClassName, fromfile, toclass, tofile, docopy, noprefix) ;
           VALUES (lcFromClass, lcFromFile, lcToClass, lcToFile, .T., .F.)
    ENDIF
ENDFOR
```

Creating a main program

The structure of the main program is illustrated in Chapter 5, "Beginning Development." To recap the important aspects, each main program consists of two parts. The first part is a stub program that sets the path and instantiates the application object. The second part is the application class definition.

The application class contains code that opens class libraries, databases, and procedure files. Properties of the application class, such as lShowScreen and lLoginRequired, indicate whether a splash screen is displayed or the user is prompted to log in to the application.

As you might imagine, much of the code in the main program is static and does not change much, or at all, from application to application. The application class definition does not change much between applications, either. However, some of the method code and property settings do differ from one application to the next.

Each new Main.prg file is created from a template file named Main_Template.txt. Tags are placed in the template file to indicate where specific application information is placed. For example, the <CLASS_LIBS> tag indicates the location where the SET CLASSLIB code is placed. A portion of Main_Template.txt is shown here.

```
DEFINE CLASS pApplication AS aApplication OLEPUBLIC
    cSplashScreen       = "MySplash.SCX"
    lShowScreen     = <SHOWS_SPLASH>
    nSplashDelay    = 500
    NAME = "AppEnv"

      cConnectionString = ""

      nUserID = 1 &&Provide a default for development
      lLoginRequired = <SECURITY_ENABLED>

    PROTECTED FUNCTION OnLoadLibraries()
        DODEFAULT()
        *--Load Class Libraries
        <CLASS_LIBS>
    ENDFUNC

FUNCTION OnLoadData()
```

```
        DODEFAULT()
            <APPLICATION_DATABASE>
    ENDFUNC


    PROTECTED FUNCTION OnLoadAppMenu()
            DO AppMenu.mpr
    ENDFUNC

ENDDEFINE
```

Inserting information into the main program template is a two-step process. First, the template file is read into a memory variable using the FileToStr() function. Then, the CreateProject() method inserts information into the template using the StrTran() function as shown here:

```
*--Create Main Program
*--Read the file into memory.
lcMainTemplate = FILETOSTR("..\myframe\tools\maintemplate.txt")

*--Insert
lcMainTemplate = STRTRAN(lcMainTemplate,"<APPLICATION_DATABASE>",
                lcOpenDatabaseString )

lcMainTemplate = STRTRAN(lcMainTemplate,"<SHOWS_SPLASH>",
                    TRANSFORM(THISFORM.chkSplashScreen.VALUE=1))
```

Notice that the information inserted into lcMainTemplate is either generated during the project-creation process, as with <APPLICATION_DATABASE>, or taken directly from the MyProjectInfo form, as is the case with <SHOW_SPLASH>.

Setting classes
Class libraries are loaded into memory by using the SET CLASSLIB command. The framework files are already loaded in Main_Frame.prg, so what you need here is a list of the classes created during the subclass process.

A list of class files to be loaded can be derived from the information provided in ClassCopy.dbf. The following code creates a cursor of class library files identified in the ToFile field of MyCopyClass shown in Figure 3. The appropriate SET CLASSLIB commands are built while scanning through the cursor.

```
*    Create Subclasses
USE ".\myframe\tools\classCopy" IN 0 SHARED

SELECT DISTINCT tofile ;
    FROM classcopy ;
    WHERE ! EMPTY(toClass) AND ;
    DoCopy = .T. ;
    INTO CURSOR "ClassList"

lcSetClassString =''

SCAN
    *--For each class lib, create the class
    lcClass = lcAppSource + ALLTRIM(tofile)
```

```
    cEraseme = ALLTRIM(tofile)
    lcSetClassString = lcSetClassString +
            IIF(EMPTY(lcSetClassString),'',',')+ALLTRIM(tofile)

    CREATE CLASSLIB &lcClass
ENDSCAN
```

And the class library values are inserted into the main program as follows:

```
IF ! EMPTY(lcSetClassString)
    lcSetClassString = "SET CLASSLIB TO " + lcSetClassString+ " ADDITIVE"
    lcMainTemplate = STRTRAN(lcMainTemplate,"<CLASS_LIBS>",lcSetClassString )
ENDIF
STRTOFILE(lcMainTemplate ,"Main.prg")
```

Using techniques like this, you can script your own main programs.

The project file

It's easy to create a project by using the CREATE PROJECT command. However, an empty project does little good. After the project is created, the CreateProject() method grabs a reference to the project using the _VFP.ACTIVEPROJECT variable and adds the main file. Because all of the files an application uses are referenced from the main program (one of the design criteria identified in Chapter 2, "Project Planning"), all that is required to add files to the project is to rebuild the project. You can rebuild the project programmatically by calling the project object's Build() method. The following code adds the main file to the project and rebuilds it:

```
*--Create the project
LOCAL loProj, lcProjectName

lcProjectName = ALLTRIM(PROPER(THIS.txtprojFolder.TEXT))
CREATE PROJECT &lcProjectName NOWAIT

loProj   = _VFP.ACTIVEPROJECT
loProj.FILES.ADD("Main.Prg")

*--Add the database directly
IF ! EMPTY(THISFORM.txtDataBaseName.VALUE)
    lcDB = ".\appData\" + lcDataBase + ".dbc"
    loProj.FILES.ADD(lcDB)
ENDIF

*--...and the splash screen as well.
IF (THISFORM.chkSplashScreen.VALUE=1)
    loProj.FILES.ADD(".\appSource\MySplash.scx")
ENDIF

*--Set the main program
loProj.SETMAIN("Main.prg")
loProj.BUILD(1,.T.)
```

Classes on tap

New to FoxPro 8.0 is the Toolbox, which allows you to quickly access classes from a class library. While this feature is a welcome addition to FoxPro's IDE, it can be time consuming to add and remove large numbers of class libraries. For example, if you are developing more than one application, and each application has its own subclasses, you have to remove the old application class libraries from the Toolbox and add the new ones. Fortunately, the FoxPro team provides the source code for the Toolbox. The workhorse of the Toolbox is the ToolBox engine class located in ToolboxEngine.prg.

To create the Toolbox builder program, I copied the contents of ToolboxEngine.prg and created a new program called zBuildToolbox. You can find it in the source code accompanying this book in the .\Tools\ subdirectory.

The Visual FoxPro Toolbox is data driven and stores the list of classes to display in a table, Toolbox.dbf. The Toolbox table contains an extra field—User—in which you are free to place any information you like. To identify which classes were added by the framework, the zBuildToolbox program inserts MyFrame as the User.

The following code subclasses the Toolbox engine, removes user-defined items from the Toolbox, and adds each class library contained in the application's Source folder. You can access this program by running either DevTools | (Re)Build Toolbox from the system menu or DevTools | ClearToolbox. The first option adds your project classes to the toolbox while the second removes them.

```
LPARAMETERS tlClearFrameClasses

*--Change DEFAULT to the application source code directory
*)  for this project
CD ".\AppSource"

LOCAL loTBEngine AS ToolboxEngine
loTBEngine = CREATEOBJECT("MyToolboxEngine")

*--Remove pre-existing framework entries
*) and add the framework classes for this project
IF CleanTable() AND tlAddFrameworkClasses

    *--Get library list for the project
    lnVCXCount = ADIR(laVCX,"*.vcx")

    FOR lnI = 1 TO lnVCXCount

        lcClassLib = ADDBS(FULLPATH(SET("Default")))+laVCX[lnI,1]
        lnClassCount = AVCXCLASSES(laClasses,lcClassLib)

        IF lnClassCount >0

            loCategory =
loTBEngine.AddCategory(JUSTSTEM(lcClassLib),JUSTSTEM(lcClassLib))
            lcID = loCategory.UniqueID

            loTBEngine.CreateToolsFromVCX(lcID,lcClassLib)

        ENDIF
    ENDFOR
ENDIF
*--Cleanup
```

```
RELEASE loToolbox
USE IN SELECT("ToolboxCursor")
CD ..
```

The custom function CleanTable deletes and packs all entries tagged with "MyFrame" as shown here.

```
FUNCTION CleanTable()
    LOCAL llOK
    TRY
        LOCAL lnSelect
        lnSelect = SELECT()

        USE IN SELECT("ToolBoxCursor")
        USE HOME(7) +"Toolbox.dbf" EXCLUSIVE IN 0
        DELETE FOR USER =='MyFrame'
        PACK
        REINDEX
        USE
        USE HOME(7) +"Toolbox.dbf" SHARED ALIAS ToolBoxCursor
        SELECT(lnSelect)
        llOK = .T.
    CATCH
        =MESSAGEBOX("Cannot find or access Toolbox.dbf")
         llOK = .F.
    ENDTRY
    RETURN llOK

ENDFUNC
```

Creating a new project from the Task Pane

The Task Pane is one of the new utilities added in VFP 8.0 that presents several useful screens (panes) in a Web browser control that make it easy to access a variety of useful resources. The default panes include Start, Community, Environment Manager, Solution Samples, XML Web Services, Filer, and Minesweeper. However, you can add your own custom panes if you prefer.

The Start pane provides links to your most recently used projects and databases, a way to create new projects and databases, as well as links to FoxPro articles and resources. For example, you can read about the Task Pane and how to customize it by clicking the "Inside the Visual FoxPro 8.0 Task Pane Manager" link as shown in **Figure 4**.

One issue with the default Start pane is that the New Project button creates a project based on the Visual FoxPro framework rather than on your framework. This section illustrates a way to add a hyperlink to the Start pane that creates a new MyFrame project.

The steps for creating a new MyFrame project were outlined in the beginning of the chapter in the section titled "Creating a new project." As a reminder, the bulk of the work for starting a new project is contained in the NewProject form. Additionally, I have added a program, zNewProject, to the .\Tools\ subdirectory that clears the environment before calling the NewProject form. The hyperlink created in this section will call the zNewProject program.

One of the many nice features about the Task Pane is that it is customizable. The following steps are all that is required to add a link to a program file, in this case zNewProject.prg.

Figure 4. *The Task Pane Manager with the Start pane displayed.*

First, open the Task Pane by clicking Tools | Task Pane from the system menu. When the Task Pane appears, click the Options button located on the top right of the screen (see Figure 4). In the Task Pane Options dialog, select Customize under the Task Pane Manager branch in the treeview as illustrated in **Figure 5**.

Next, click the Customize Panes button to open the Pane Customization dialog shown in **Figure 6**.

Next, click the Add button located over the second treeview control to add a new entry to the Start pane. **Figure 7** shows the Pane Customization dialog with the new entry.

The next step is to create a link to the zNewProject program. To create that link, you're actually adding HTML code, and not FoxPro code. If you aren't familiar with HTML, the "a" tag defines a hyperlink and the "href" property identifies the target.

However, you cannot link directly to a FoxPro program from an HTML page. Instead, the Task Pane provides several custom handlers that allow you to link to FoxPro code from HTML. Custom handlers begin with a "vfps" prefix. The custom handler used in this example is the "vfps.application" handler. When a hyperlink is clicked, the Task Pane intercepts the request and checks for links with a "vfps" prefix.

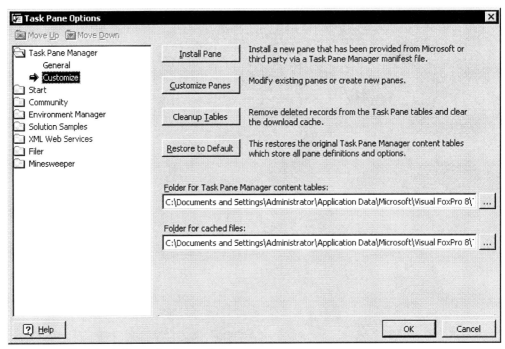

Figure 5. The Task Pane Options dialog.

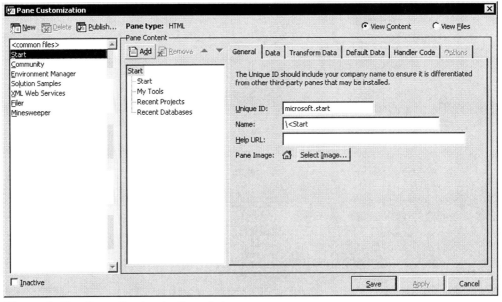

Figure 6. The Pane Customization dialog.

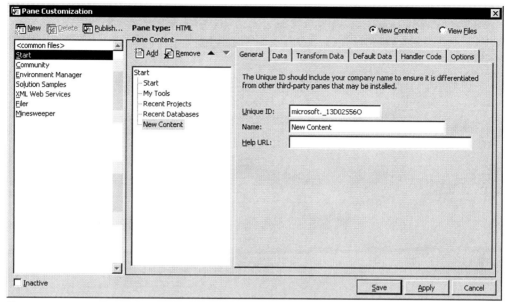

Figure 7. *The Pane Customization dialog with a new entry.*

To add the custom handler, change the Name field to "MyFrame." Next, select the Data tab, select Static Text from the Source combo box, and enter the following in the edit box (see **Figure 8**):

```
<HTML>

   <A href="vfps:doapplication?appname=
      (&quot;C:\Dev\MyFrame\Tools\znewproject.prg&quot;)">
    <b>
      <font color="#cc0000">
          New "MyFrame" Project
      </font>
    </b>
   </A>

</HTML>
```

The path C:\Dev\MyFrame\Tools\zNewProject.prg should reflect the path in which you placed the framework examples.

The final step is to save your changes. This completes the steps necessary to add a link to the program that creates projects based on the MyFrame framework. To see your changes, open the Task Pane. It should appear similar to **Figure 9**. Try clicking on the link to start a new framework project.

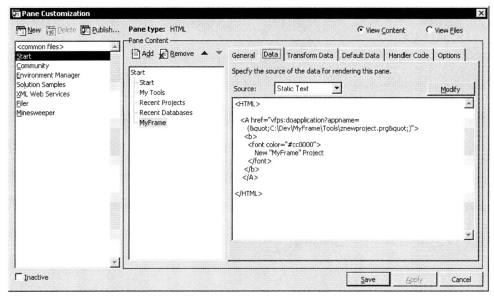

Figure 8. *The completed Task Pane configuration.*

Figure 9. *The Task Pane with a link to create projects using your framework.*

Summary

As you have seen in this chapter, starting a project requires many steps. Most of the steps are required regardless of whether or not you are using a framework. Having read this chapter, you should have some ideas for automating the start of your projects.

> Updates and corrections to this chapter can be found on Hentzenwerke's Web site, **www.hentzenwerke.com**. Click "Catalog" and navigate to the page for this book.

Chapter 19
Sample Application
(Bringin' it All Together)

This chapter brings it all together, illustrating step-by-step how to create an application using the sample framework developed throughout this book.

A framework is a cooperative effort between many, many classes. Earlier chapters illustrated various pieces of the MyFrame framework. In this chapter, you will see how the pieces of the framework fit together, creating a more productive development environment than exists without using a framework.

To illustrate how the framework classes work together, you'll create a simple customer billing application that contains information about customers and invoices. The data structure for the sample application contains a customer table, invoice header and line items tables, and a general ledger table. The sample application also contains forms and business objects that collect, validate, and present this information.

The first step in developing the sample application is to create a new project. Next, you'll begin the development cycle that consists of creating tables, forms, and business objects. This chapter walks you through two cycles, one for customers and one for invoices. After the step-by-step guide through each cycle, I'll review some of the many features built into the framework.

Figure 1 shows the table structure for the sample application, which I'll call "Billing."

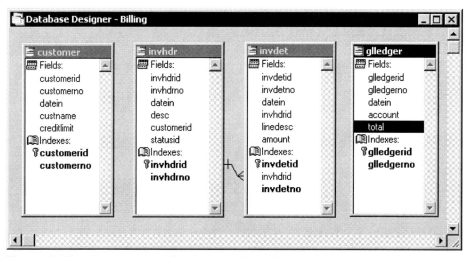

Figure 1. The data structure for the sample Billing application.

Working with the framework

Some developers prefer to compile their source code into APP or EXE files before running them. Others prefer the ability to run and test portions of their applications (forms, programs, functions, reports, and so on) in the design environment without first compiling the entire application. Using the MyFrame framework, either approach is possible.

If you are unfamiliar with executing code in the design environment before compiling applications, a few tips may help you avoid a frustrating experience. To run an application in the design environment, you must load all procedure files and class libraries into memory. For MyFrame projects, this is easily accomplished by running the main program for the project. While you are still able to compile your application while class libraries and procedure files are loaded into memory, you may get errors if the "Recompile All Files" option is selected when you rebuild your application.

Attempting to run a form from the MyFrame framework, without first running the main program, will result in errors, because none of the framework class libraries have been loaded into memory. However, this will not be an issue if you prefer to run your applications only from APP or EXE files (compiled applications).

Working with the framework (and FoxPro in general) interactively—that is, while classes and procedure files are loaded into memory—can be problematic. For example, making a change to a procedure releases all procedures contained in the PRG file from memory. Attempting to run a form that calls any one of the procedures contained in that PRG file will result in an error. With the MyFrame framework, running the main program again reloads the procedure file into memory and will generally fix errors such as "File XXX not found."

Lastly, if you choose to work with the MyFrame framework interactively, the default behavior of the framework is to release all framework files and restore FoxPro to its original state on your first attempt to quit FoxPro. A second attempt to quit FoxPro will be successful, and FoxPro will close. You can change this behavior by locating the following code segment in the OnShutDown() method of aApplication (found in Main_Frame.prg) and then uncommenting the line that says "QUIT."

```
IF THIS.lDevMode
    *--Do nothing
    *) The Framework is released. IF you really want to exit
    *) the program, uncomment the next line
    * QUIT
ELSE
    CLEAR EVENTS
ENDIF
```

Before you start

The sample application developed in this chapter illustrates every aspect covered in the book. Although this chapter walks you through the steps required to create the sample application, a completed version is included in the sample code accompanying this book.

 You will find the completed sample application in the folder named SampleApp.

I encourage you to refer to the prepared sample application while reading this chapter. Although this chapter has many screen shots, there are many, many steps required to complete this walkthrough and it can be quite time consuming to complete. After you have read this chapter, you will have an understanding of how to work with the framework, and you can then reproduce some or all of the steps as you like, or create projects of your own.

 The main program of the sample Billing project contains an ODBC connection string that is used for the remote data examples. If you have placed the framework source code in a directory other than C:\, you will need to alter this connection string for the remote examples to work properly. See the section titled "Remove wizard code" toward the end of this chapter to see an example of the connection string provided in the sample application.

In addition to the sample application, be sure to look in the Examples folder to see additional framework examples not covered in the step-by-step guide. Examples include error handling, object hierarchies, and using the collections classes developed in Chapter 8, "Collections," to name a few.

Creating the Billing project

Creating a new framework project involves many steps, as I explained in detail in Chapter 18, "Starting New Projects." In this section, you'll create the sample Billing application. As part of this process, you'll create a project called "Billing" and place it in a subfolder of your framework folder, also called "Billing." Additionally, you'll subclass the framework classes to create application-specific versions of your classes.

Step by step

There are three ways to create a new framework project. One is to open FoxPro and run the zNewProject program located in the Tools subdirectory of the framework folder. For example, if you have placed the framework folder in your C:\ drive, type the following into the command window:

        do c:\dev\MyFrame\tools\zNewProject.prg

If you have created the button on the start page of the FoxPro task pane (see Chapter 18, "Starting New Projects," in the section titled "Adding your project to the task pane"), a second option is to open the task pane and click the MyFrame: New Project button.

A third option is to select DevTools | New Project from the system menu. This option is available only after you have run the "main_frame" program or the "main" program for one of the framework projects.

Either of these approaches opens the Project Details form, which contains the information to create the sample Billing application (see **Figure 2**).

 All of the framework tables are located in a database named SysData. Although this example creates a database named Billing, it is not necessary to create a separate database for your applications.

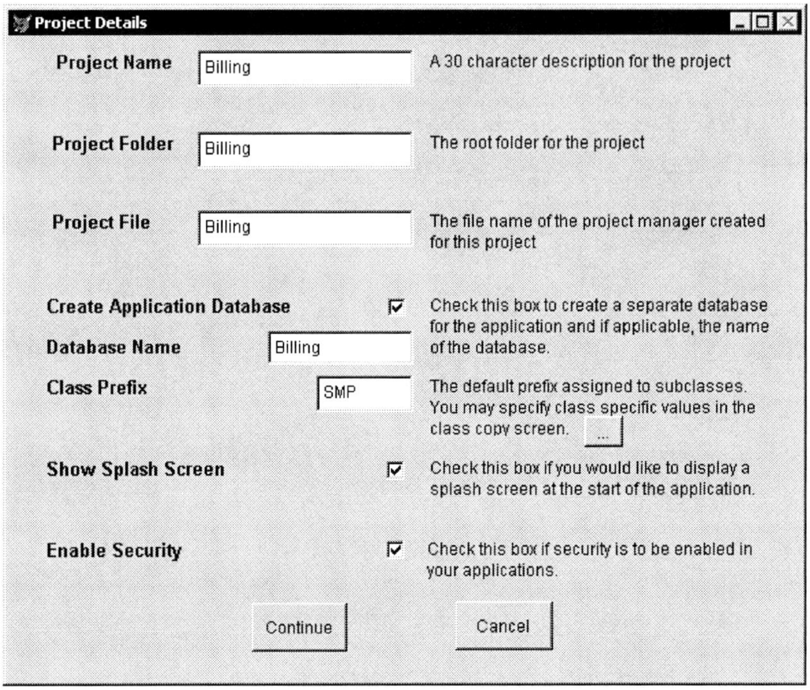

Figure 2. *The Project Details form for the sample Billing application.*

Click the Continue button to create your new project. While the project is being created, you will see a series of windows being opened and closed; one window is created for each of the application subclasses. When the program completes, you will see a new project that contains the necessary framework files to begin developing your application. **Figure 3** illustrates the resulting project.

I've expanded the treeview to show all the project files.

Design review

One of the many tasks performed when starting a new project—that is, when running the zNewProject program—is to create a new folder under the MyFrame folder. For this example, the name of the folder is Billing as shown in **Figure 4**. Notice that the Billing folder also contains two subfolders, AppData and AppSource, that hold the application's data files and source code files, respectively.

The Billing project is located in the Billing folder. Compile the project into an EXE, accepting the default name and location. FoxPro will place the resulting Billing executable in the Billing folder. From Windows Explorer, run the EXE by double-clicking the Billing.exe icon. You will notice that a splash screen appears, as well as a prompt for you to log in to the application. Enter "Joe" for both the user name and password. Admittedly, there's not much exciting to look at after this. What you do have, however, is an application shell that is security-enabled.

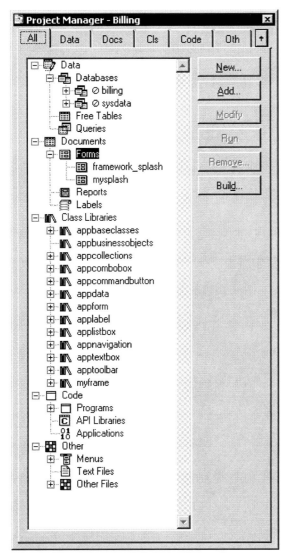

Figure 3. The Billing project (expanded).

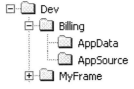

Figure 4. The folder structure for the Billing project.

Try entering an incorrect user name or password and you cannot access the application. Enter the incorrect user name or password more than three times and the application will shut down completely. Once you have entered the application, there is a menu option to close the application.

Throughout the remainder of the chapter, you'll add the functionality required for the sample application.

A simple data entry form (Customers)

In this section, you'll create a data entry form to administer customer information. This customer form is a simple one, in that it involves writing to only one table. However, in the "Design review" section of this chapter, I will review many features of the form that are common to all framework forms, whether they contain data or not.

Step by step

To manage customer information, you need a table to hold the information, a form to present and collect information from the user, and a business object that ensures that information written to the customers table is accurate and complete.

Create the customers table

The sample project contains two databases: the SysData database, which contains all the framework tables; and the Billing database, which is empty and ready for you to begin adding your application tables.

If you haven't already done so, run the main program from the Billing project. This loads the framework classes and the framework menus.

 Many of the forms used in this section are framework forms and not FoxPro forms. Additionally, many of the forms are created using the framework classes and serve as additional examples of how to use the framework.

To create a customers table, select the menu option DevTools | New Table. You are asked to select the database to which the customers table should be added. See **Figure 5**. Select the Billing database.

When prompted for the name of the table, type "Customer" and save it in the AppData directory. Your new customers table is created and presented for you to change as needed.

Notice that the new table already contains a few fields—CustomerID, CustomerNo, and DateIn—as well as two indexes: CustomerID (primary) and CustomerNo (candidate). Add two additional fields in the Table Designer: CustName (character 30) and CreditLimit (currency). Then save your changes and close the Table Designer.

The New Table program will then add framework classes to the DisplayClass and DisplayClassLibrary settings for each field and again open the Class Designer so you can review the changes. **Figure 6** shows the revised table structure.

 Setting the display class in the Table Designer ensures that the proper classes are added to a form when you drag fields from the data environment and drop them on the form.

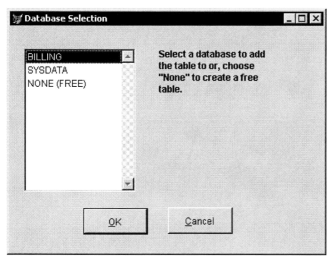

Figure 5. Selecting a database.

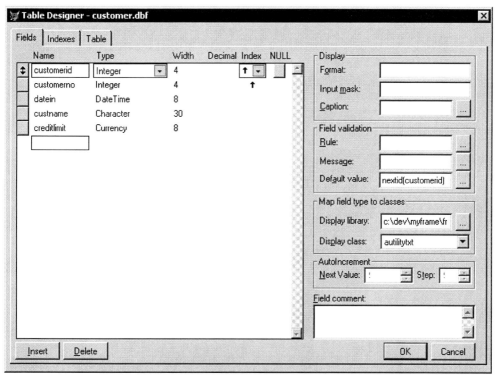

Figure 6. The customers table with the framework display class and display library.

The values for which classes are added to the form are maintained in the AppVars module. An application variable exists for each data type. For example, DisplayClass_C contains the class name added for character data; DisplayClass_I for integers; and so on. You can change the values added for each project by selecting MyFrame | AppVars, and then locating and amending the appropriate DisplayClass and DisplayClassLib variables.

Create customer form

To create a data entry form for the customers table, select DevTools | New Form from the development menu. You are prompted for the name of the form and the folder in which you want to save it. Name the form "Customers" and save it to the AppSource folder. After supplying this information, the form is created and opened in the Form Designer.

Every framework form contains an object named oFormControlsCollection. It inherits from MyCollection (see Chapter 8, "Collections"). You will see it on the form at design time, but it is not visible at run time.

Add the customers table to the data environment by right-clicking the form and selecting DataEnvironment from the context menu. Next, add the fields from the customers table to the Customers form by selecting the Customer cursor and dragging the Fields icon onto the form. Notice that several text boxes are added to the form, each having a name that begins with "txt" and then the field name.

Change the name of the form to frmCustomers and the caption to "Customer Maintenance."

When you drag fields from a form's data environment and drop them onto the form's design surface, a control (and, where appropriate, a label) will be added to the form.

*Unless you change the field mapping, the added label is from the FoxPro base class, and not a label from your framework. To change the default labels to your framework labels, go to Tools | Options and select the Field Mapping tab (see **Figure 7**). While this is not critical for this example, the default FoxPro label does not have properties to accept security settings. This will be explained later in this chapter, in the section titled "Adding security."*

Finally, add a control that enables the user to navigate from one record to another. Select the Classes tab on the Billing project, and then expand the AppNavigation node. Select and drag the smpMyNavLst class onto the form. Right-click the control and select Builder. You are prompted to select either the FoxPro builder or the framework builder. Select the FoxPro builder. You might receive a message stating "The builder registration table is missing. Do you want to locate it, or build a new one?" Then select "Build it." This message may show up if you have a fresh installation of VFP and have never used a builder. Select the fields as shown in **Figure 8**. On the Value tab (details not shown), change the value to CustomerID.

Save and run the form. **Figure 9** shows the form and the toolbars that manipulate the data entry and navigation capabilities of the form. The navigation toolbars may be docked with the main window's toolbars.

Notice that the data entry and navigation toolbars are automatically loaded. This is because the default value of the form's cToolbars property is "MyDataTlb. MyNavTlb."

Try clicking the New toolbar button. You'll see that a new record is appended to the customers table. Enter a name for the customer and click the Save toolbar button. Experiment by adding a few more records. Try closing the form or clicking Undo at various points during the entry process. You'll see that you are prompted to confirm unsaved changes before closing a form when changes are pending, and that the form will close when edits are not pending. Similarly, you are prompted before undoing changes only when edits are pending.

However, you'll also notice that you can save a customer without supplying a customer name. In the next section, you'll create a business object where you can validate the information before making an update.

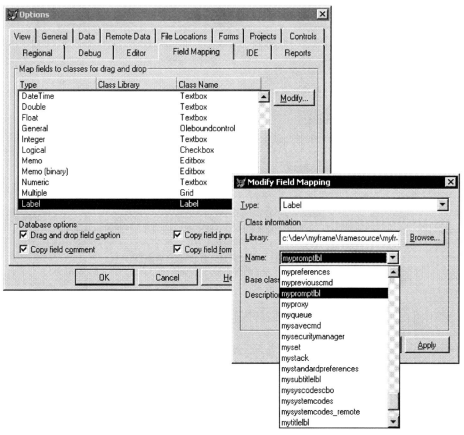

Figure 7. The FoxPro Field Mapping dialog.

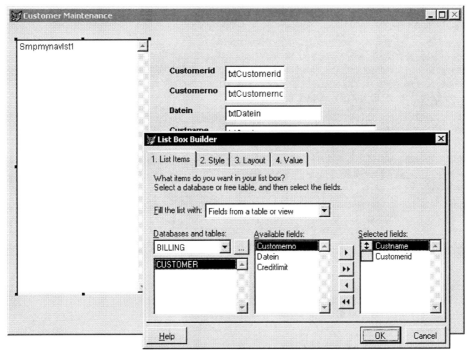

Figure 8. *Using the List Box Builder to configure the list box navigation control.*

Create a customer business object

To create a customer business object, run the form and then select DevTools | Create Business Object. When prompted for the name of a business object, enter "boCustomer." The framework creates the business object and stores it in the appBusinessObjects class library. The framework also modifies the form and appropriately fills in the DEClass and DEClassLibrary properties.

 When either the DEClass or DEClassLibrary properties of a form are changed, all tables manually added to the default data environment are removed.

Run the form again. You'll find that the form behaves exactly as before. Behind the scenes, however, your customer business object opened the customers table and is controlling the reading and writing of data.

Again, while the form is running, select DevTools | Modify Business Object from the development menu to modify the customer business object. Selecting this option closes the form and opens the customer business object in the Class Designer. Notice that the business object contains a cursor class named oCustomer. The oCustomer cursor is responsible for loading the customers table. For more information about cursors, see Chapter 9, "Cursor and CursorAdapter."

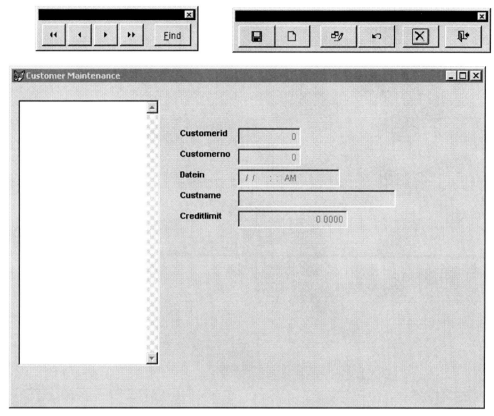

Figure 9. The Customer Maintenance form for the Billing application.

Add validation rules

To ensure that your customer records do not contain blank values in the CustName field, open the IsValid() method of oCustomer and type the following:

```
*--oCustomer.IsValid()
IF EMPTY(Customer.CustName)
    THIS.PARENT.AddError("Customer name  " + ;
        "cannot be empty.","Customer","CustName")
    RETURN .F.
ENDIF
```

The previous code checks whether the CustName field is empty. If it is, it adds an error message to the business object's error collection and returns a value of False. Run the Customer Maintenance form again and try to save a record with an empty customer name. The entry won't be saved, and you'll see a prompt as shown in **Figure 10**.

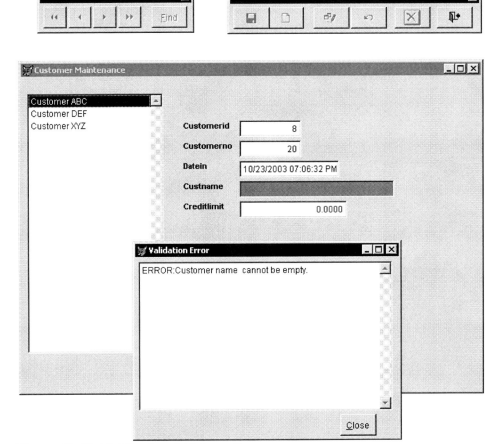

Figure 10*. Highlighting invalid information.*

Add the form to the application menu

To add the form to the application menu, open AppMenu. You can find AppMenu by clicking the Other tab of the Billing project and expanding the Menu node.

Create a new submenu named Forms and add a menu pad named Customers. Enter the following command:

```
Do Form Customers.scx
```

Save and compile the menu. To see your selections, run the main program again. This will force the menu to reload so you can see the latest version.

Adding security

This section walks you through the process of assigning security to a form control. For this example, you'll limit which users are able to see the txtCreditLimit text box.

The data entry illustrated in this section is already established. You do not need to re-key the information in order to complete the example. The steps are illustrated so that you can become familiar with the process of setting up security.

Setting up a user

To add a new user, select MyFrame | Security | User Maintenance. The User Maintenance form appears as shown in **Figure 11**.

A few users have been supplied by default. If you like, you can add a new user by clicking the New button on the toolbar, filling in the appropriate fields, and then clicking the Save button on the toolbar. However, the users supplied are adequate for the remainder of this example.

Creating security groups

In applications with many users, it is often easier to create groups of users and administer security by group, rather than for each individual. **Figure 12** shows the Group Maintenance form, with the default groups supplied.

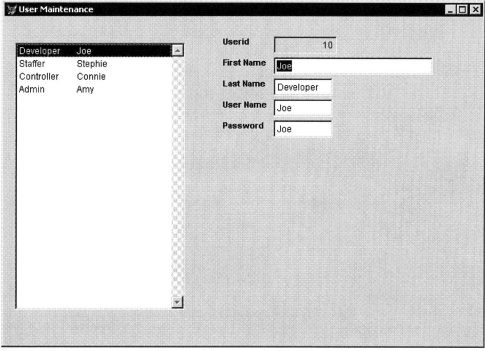

Figure 11. *Adding new users.*

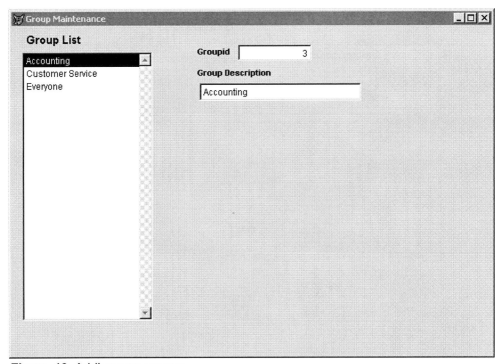

Figure 12*. Adding new groups.*

Assigning users to groups

The User Group Maintenance form, shown in **Figure 13**, allows you to assign each person to one or more groups. You can assign a user to a group by selecting a user in the left pane and placing a checkmark next to the appropriate group or groups. Notice that Connie Controller is assigned to the Accounting group.

Creating security items

You can apply security to every object in the framework. For example, the txtCreditLimit text box (part of the Customer Maintenance form created earlier in the chapter) can be made read-only, hidden, or read-write for individual users or for groups of users.

Security items are really tags that developers can use to identify and categorize controls that logically belong together. For example, this simple application has the following security items: Financial, Invoicing, Customer, and Billing. You can declare that each customer's credit limit belongs to the Financial security item. This is accomplished in the section titled "Applying security to form controls," later in this chapter.

The Security Items Maintenance form is shown in **Figure 14**.

Granting security

So far, you've set up users and groups, assigned users to groups, and created security items. In this step you'll define which groups have access to which security items and at what level. To do this, run the Group Security Manager form by selecting MyFrame | Security | Group.

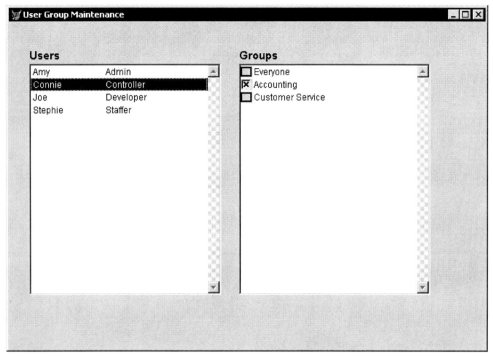

Figure 13. *Adding users to groups.*

The Group Security Manager, shown in **Figure 15**, shows that the Customer Service group has read-write access to Customer security items and read-only access to Financial and Billing security items.

 The User Security Maintenance form is similar to the Group Security Maintenance form. It is not shown here but is included in the source code for the sample framework.

Applying security to form controls

Figure 15 shows that a user belonging to the Customer Service group has read-only access to financial information. Not shown in Figure 15 is that users belonging to the Accounting group have read-write access to financial information. Earlier in the chapter, you created a Customer Maintenance form that has a txtCreditLimit text box. In this section, I'll illustrate how to make this control not visible by default, ensuring that only users belonging to the Customer Service and Accounting groups can view the data, while only Accounting members can modify the data.

To identify the txtCreditLimit control as belonging to the Financial security item, modify the Customer Maintenance form, Customers.scx. Then right-click the txtCreditLimit text box. From the drop-down menu that appears, select Builder and choose the framework builder.

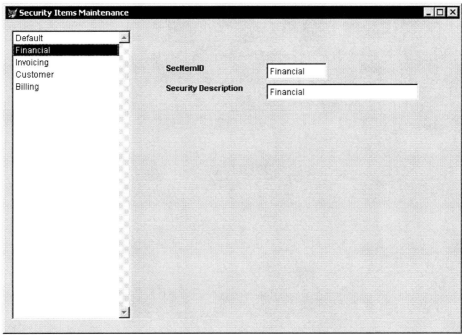

Figure 14. The Security Items Maintenance form.

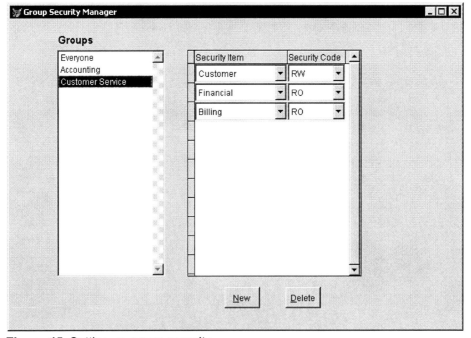

Figure 15. Setting up group security.

The default builder will appear, enabling you to select security settings for the txtCreditLimit text box. Select Financial and Hidden as shown in **Figure 16**. If you have used a framework label to identify the txtCreditLimit text box, you may want to set the security item and default setting to Financial and Hidden for the label as well. This will ensure that the label has the same settings for Visible and Enable as does the txtCreditLimit text box.

That's all that is required to set up and administer security using the MyFrame framework. In the next section you'll compile and run the application to see how your security works in action.

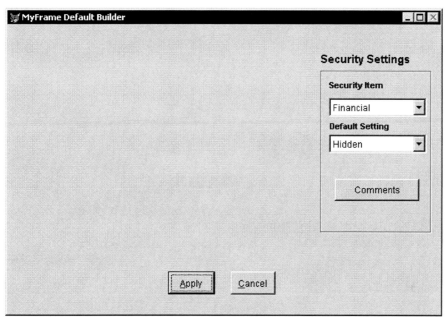

Figure 16. *Applying security using the framework builder.*

Compile and run

Compile and run the executable. First, log in as Connie Controller (User Name: Connie, Password: Connie). Notice that you are able to modify the customer credit limit. Run the executable again, this time logging in as Amy Admin (User Name: Amy, Password: Amy). Notice this time you are able to view the customer credit limit, but cannot edit it. Finally, log in as Stephie Staffer (User Name: Stephie, Password: Stephie). Notice that you cannot see the customer's txtCreditLimit control at all.

Design review

Some of the features provided by the MyFrame framework have been illustrated already. Specifically, a native FoxPro form is not capable of opening toolbars automatically or conditionally writing information to buffered tables. The remainder of this section highlights additional framework features.

Edit style

The default setting for each form is to always allow edits. This means that you can navigate from record to record and change information without first clicking an Edit button. You can change this behavior at design time by changing the form's lAlwaysEdit property to True.

Additionally, each user can optionally change this property by setting a form preference. To see how this works, run the form and select MyFrame | FormPreferences. On the Preferences screen, select Edit First to change the form setting for an individual user.

Data entry (unsaved changes, default values, and so on)

The MyFrame framework ensures that no data is lost without the user specifically directing the framework to discard it. For example, clicking the New toolbar button and then the Undo button results in a prompt that confirms you want to discard the new record. Similarly, this same prompt appears if you have changed information on an existing record. Additionally, this same prompt appears, assuming unsaved changes exist, if you try to close the form, exit FoxPro, navigate to a new record, or add a new record.

 The ability to navigate from one record to another exists only when a form's lAlwaysEdit property is set to True.

Remembering locations

Run the Customer Maintenance form again. Change the location of the form by clicking on the title bar and dragging the form to a new location. Now close the form by clicking on the form's Close button (X) in the top right corner of the screen.

Run the form again. You will notice that the form appears in the location where you last left it.

Change the size of the form. Notice that each of the form controls is proportionally resized as well. Close the form and run it again. The form appears in the same location and has the same dimensions as you last left it.

Experiment with running the form more than once, or changing the location of the toolbars. You will find that each form is offset slightly from the previously active form. You will also find that the toolbars remain visible until the last form is closed, and, if you have repositioned the toolbars, they reappear where you last positioned them.

Finally, exit the application and then restart it. This time, however, log in as a different user. You will find that the Customer Maintenance form reflects none of the changes from your previous session because all location and preference settings are user specific.

Design time and run time

All the features illustrated so far work identically whether you are running in the development environment or from a compiled APP or EXE. I prefer this behavior because it greatly reduces development time. For example, to test a code change, you can run the form immediately without first having to compile the application.

The only difference between the development and compile-time environments is that the MyFrame and DevTools menu pads do not appear in the compiled version.

One-to-many form (Customer Invoices)

Creating a one-to-many form for the first time can be somewhat of a challenge with any development tool. FoxPro is no exception. In this section, I'll review how to create a one-to-many form using the framework classes.

Step by step

Creating one-to-many forms involves many of the same steps required to develop the Customer Maintenance form in the previous section. Therefore, I will illustrate only the differences.

Create InvHdr, InvDet, and GlLedger tables

Three tables store billing information: InvHdr, InvDet, and GlLedger. To create the InvHdr table, run the New Table program by selecting DevTools | New Table from the system menu. Add three fields: Desc (character 30), CustomerID (integer), and StatusID (character 10).

Next, create the InvDet table and add the following fields: InvHdrID (integer), LineDesc (character 30), and Amount (currency). Create an index for InvHdrID to establish a relationship between the InvHdr and InvDet tables as shown in **Figure 17**.

Finally, create the GlLedger table, adding the following fields: Account (character 30) and Total (currency).

Create the billing form

To create the form, select DevTools | NewForm, and then save the form as "Billing" in the AppSource folder. In the property sheet, set the name of the form to "frmBilling" and set the caption to "Billing Entry." Add the following tables to the form's data environment and set the data environment's InitialSelectedAlias property to InvHdr.

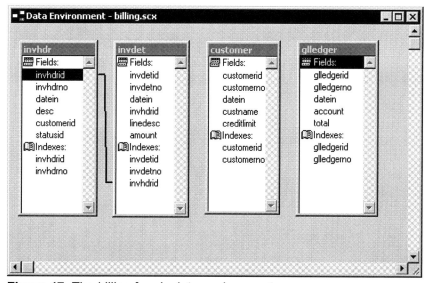

Figure 17. The billing form's data environment.

To add controls to the form, drag and drop the Fields icon from the InvHdr cursor onto the form. This should add text boxes and labels for each field in the InvHdr table. Unfortunately, text boxes are not acceptable for two of the fields, CustomerID and StatusID, so delete them from the form (txtCustomerID and txtStatusID). A more appropriate control for customer selection is a combo box (assuming, as is the case in this example, that the combo will not be displaying thousands of customers). To add a combo box to the form, select the Classes tab of the Billing project manager and locate the appBaseClasses class library. Drag the class smpaComboBox to the billing form and make changes in the property sheet as shown in **Figure 18**.

BoundColumn	2
ColumnWidths	150,0
Name	cboCustomerID
RowSource	customer.custname,customerid
RowSourceType	6 - Fields

Figure 18. Settings for the customer combo box.

The next control to add is smpmySysCodescbo, which can be found in the appComboBox class library. Drag it to the form, change its name to cboStatusID, and set its control source to invhdr.StatusID. In the next section, you'll set up status codes (Pending and Billed) by using the system codes utility.

Next, add a grid to the form to collect the invoice line items. To do this, open the form's data environment, select the InvDet title bar, and drag it to the form. The name of the grid should be grdInvDet. Run the FoxPro builder and make LineDesc and Amount the selected fields.

Unless you change the data mapping for multiple fields, the grid class you add to your form will most likely be the FoxPro base class. This will not be an issue for this example.

The next step is to add two command buttons to the form: one to add records to the InvDet table and one to delete them. To add the buttons to the form, locate the AppCommandButton class library by clicking on the Classes tab of the Billing project. Drag one AppMyNewCmd button and one AppMyDeleteCmd button from the class library to the form.

By default, the AppMyNewCmd and AppMyDeleteCmd buttons call the form's New() and Delete() methods, respectively. However, earlier in this section, I identified InvHdr as the InitialSelectedAlias of the data environment. The default behavior of these methods is to add records to or remove records from the selected table and to prompt the user if unsaved changes exist.

The New() and Delete() methods accept two parameters: tcAlias and tlOverrideChecks. To instruct the New() and Delete() methods to act on the InvDet table, you need to pass the name of the table, in this case InvDet, as the first parameter. To suppress the checks for unsaved changes, thereby allowing a user to add or delete multiple line items, you need to pass the value True as the second parameter.

A final change is that after a user has clicked the New or Delete buttons, the grid should get the focus. To do this, set the cSetFocusTo property of each button to Thisform.grdInvDet.

To easily make all these settings, right-click the AppMyNewCmd button and select Builder | FoxPro Builder from the context menu. Fill in the builder as shown in **Figure 19**. The builder settings for the Delete button are not shown, but the settings are similar to Figure 19 with the one exception that the value in the Method text box is "Delete."

Your form should appear similar to **Figure 20**.

Create the billing business object

Save your changes and run the form. To create the billing business object, "boBilling," select DevTools | Create Business Object. Notice that the resulting business object contains four cursors and one relation.

However, a couple of changes are needed to make this entry screen effective. First, the InvDet table has a foreign key that links it to a record in the InvHdr table. To ensure that each record contains the correct foreign key value, select the oInvDet cursor object and type the following into its OnSetForeignKeys() method:

```
REPLACE Invdet.InvHdrID WITH InvHdr.InvHdrID
```

Next, add a method, GetInvoiceTotal(), to the boBilling class. Place the following code in the GetInvoiceTotal() method to return the sum of all the lines of the currently selected invoice:

```
*--BoBilling.GetInvoiceTotal()
LOCAL lnSelect, lnRecNo, lnTotal

lnSelect = SELECT()
lnTotal= 0

THIS.oInvdet.SELECT()
lnRecNo = RECNO()

IF SEEK(InvHdr.InvHdrID,"InvDet","InvHdrID")
    SCAN WHILE InvDet.InvHdrID = InvHdr.InvHdrID
        lnTotal = lnTotal + InvDet.Amount
    ENDSCAN
ENDIF

IF lnRecNo > 0 AND lnRecNo < RECCOUNT("InvDet")
    GO lnRecNo
ENDIF
SELECT (lnSelect)

RETURN lnTotal
```

For now, those will be the only changes. You'll add one more change in the next section.

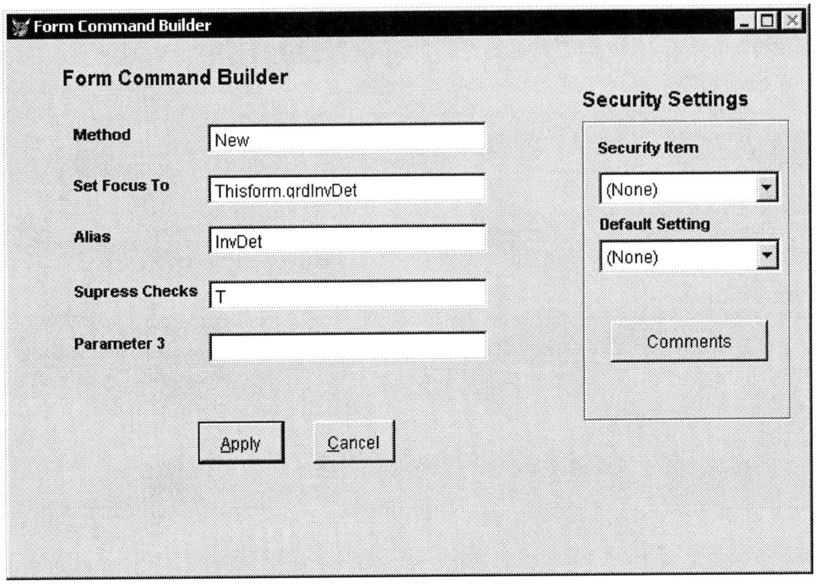

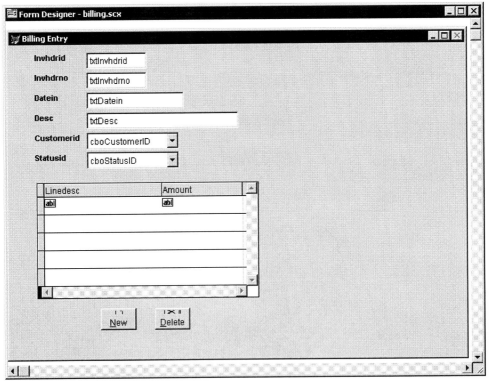

Figure 19. Builder settings for the New button.

Figure 20. The Billing Entry form.

Mixing system codes and business rules

One aspect of billing systems is that an invoice may be saved, but not added to the total billing of a company. For example, a user may be in the middle of billing a customer and realize he doesn't yet have all the information to complete the invoice. Rather than forcing the user to cancel the invoice and start over, you as a system designer decide that the status of the invoice is the trigger for writing information to the ledger table. To keep the example simple, our sample invoice will contain only two statuses: Pending and Billed. By default, each invoice will be Pending. When the user changes the status to Billed and saves the invoice, the line item amounts will be written to the ledger.

Creating system codes

Open the System Codes Management form by selecting MyFrame | System Codes from the system menu. Select InvCodes in the list box control on the left and you will see that InvCodes already contains two system codes: Pending and Billed, as shown in **Figure 21**. Not shown in Figure 21 is that the return value for Billed is 1, while Pending has a return value of 0. Notice that the return type for each code is integer ("I").

Modify Billing.scx. Right-click the cmbStatusID combo box you added earlier, and then select Builder | MyFrame Builder from the menu. Select the framework builder and select the settings as shown in **Figure 22**.

When the form is run, the combo box will be populated with the Pending and Billed statuses.

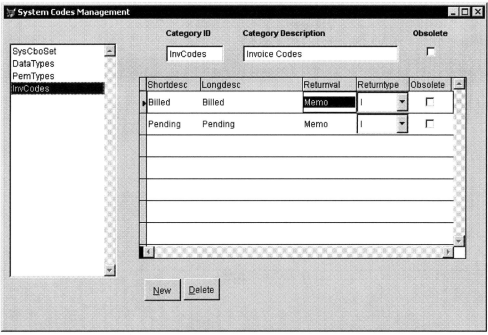

Figure 21. The System Codes Management form for invoice codes.

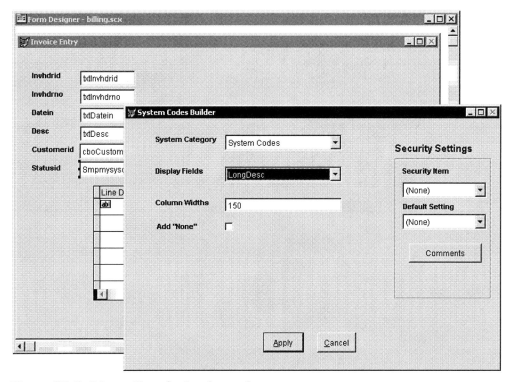

Figure 22. *Builder settings for invoice codes.*

The final business rule is to save the amount of an invoice when the user changes its status to Billed. The business rule could be stated as, "When an invoice is marked complete, write the value of the invoice to the ledger table. In no circumstances should the invoice be considered complete if the value of the invoice is not successfully recorded in the ledger table."

To determine whether the invoice is billed, the program checks the return value of the system code. For this example, a return value of 1 indicates that the invoice is billed, while a return value of 0 indicates that the invoice is pending. The following code, placed in the billing business object's OnAfterSave() method, obtains the value associated with the invoice code and writes the value of the invoice to the ledger.

```
*--boBilling.OnAfterSave()
LOCAL llOK, lnInvoiceBilled,loGLRecord
llOK = .T.

lnInvoiceBilled = _SCREEN.goSysCodes.GetReturnValue(InvHdr.StatusID)

IF ! ISNULL(lnInvoiceBilled ) AND ;
      lnInvoiceBilled = 1

   THIS.oGlLedger.New()
   loGLRecord = THIS.oGlLedger.GetCurrentRecord()
   loGLRecord.Account = "Billing"
   loGLRecord.Total = THIS.GetInvoiceTotal()
```

```
THIS.oGlLedger.SetCurrentRecord(loGLRecord)

THIS.oGlLedger.New()
loGLRecord = THIS.oGlLedger.GetCurrentRecord()
loGLRecord.Account = "AcctsReceivable"
loGLRecord.Total = THIS.GetInvoiceTotal()*-1
THIS.oGlLedger.SetCurrentRecord(loGLRecord)

llOK = THIS.oGlLedger.SAVE()
ENDIF

RETURN llOK
```

The business rule stated that if the ledger cannot be updated, the changes to the InvHdr and InvDet tables should not be saved either. The OnAfterSave() method fires after the changes to the invoice have been updated, but prior to committing the transaction. Notice that a logical value of llOK is returned from the OnAfterSave() method. The business object wraps all updates in a transaction. A value of False returned from the OnAfterSave() method results in a rollback of the transaction and thereby reverts all pending changes.

Design review

To this point, you've been able to build the one-to-many form with the help of some builders and a little code. However, the style presented illustrates a one-to-many entry form with child records edited in a grid.

Some developers prefer not to allow editing in a grid. Additionally, the InvDet table contained only a few records. Regardless of your grid preference, wide tables are extremely poor candidates for grid editing.

The solution is to create a separate form for editing the child records. In the example code accompanying this book, I've created a second invoice form named Billing_NoGrid. The name of the form to edit InvDet line items is InvDet.scx. The InvDet form has its WindowType property set to 1-Modal, has no tables in its data environment, and its DataSession property is set to 1, default. This results in the InvDet form using the data in the Billing_NoGrd environment.

I have also added an AppMyEditCmd command button from the AppCommandButton class library to the Billing_NoGrid form. The following code, placed in both the Add button and the Edit button, opens the InvDet form while the appropriate InvDet record is selected.

```
IF DODEFAULT()
    DO FORM InvDet.scx
ENDIF
```

Finally, the grdInvDet grid is set to read-only. This forces all data entry to occur in the InvDet form.

The sample application included in the source code accompanying this book contains two versions of the Billing form. The first is Billing and the second is Billing_NoGrid. An example of the Billing_NoGrid form is shown in **Figure 23**.

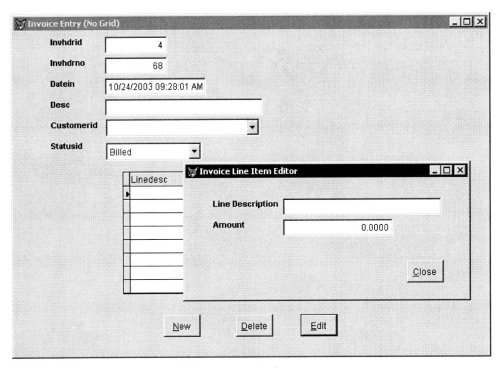

Figure 23. Editing child records in a separate form.

Adding security (menu options)

Earlier in the chapter, you added security to the Customer Maintenance form that restricted access to the txtCreditLimit field. You can use the same setup to restrict access to the billing system. Add a new menu pad to the AppMenu | Forms pad and name it Billing_Grid. Add a second menu pad and name it Billing_NoGrid. Place the following code in the SKIP FOR text box on the Billing_NoGrid menu pad.

```
_Screen.GoSecurity.IsAuthorized("BILLING")
```

Then add the following commands to Billing_Grid and Billing_NoGrid, respectively.

```
DO FORM Billing_Grid
DO FORM Billing_NoGrid
```

Save and generate the AppMenu menu code. Then, run the main program to reload the menus. You'll see that you still have access to both menus because in the development environment you are automatically signed in as Joe Developer. Compile the application as Billing.exe and log in as Connie Controller. You will see that the Billing_NoGrid menu pad is disabled.

Using remote data

Although the MyCursor and MyCursorAdapter classes were created to work with local and remote data in similar ways, there are still differences in how you create applications using local and remote data. The primary difference is that when accessing data through a data connection, you want to access only the records that you need at that time.

For example, earlier in the chapter you created an entry form to maintain customer information. That form used a business object, boCustomer, which in turn had one cursor, oCustomer. The Customer Maintenance form has the ability to navigate a list of customers as well as update individual records. When designing for remote data access, these functionalities should be separated.

In this example, you'll create a business object, boCustomer_Remote, which accesses the customer table using ODBC. The business object will contain two CursorAdapters: Customer_Nav and Customers. Customer_Nav will supply a list of customers, and Customers will contain the specific customer record to be viewed or edited. Then, you'll modify the Customer Maintenance form created earlier in the chapter to work with your newly created boCustomer_Remote business object.

Creating the business class

To create the class, you'll use the application classes smpMyDataEnvironment and smpMyCursorAdapter. These classes were created during the project creation step earlier in the chapter.

The first step is to create the boCustomer_Remote class. To do this, select the Classes tab of the Billing project and then select the appBusinessObjects class library (see **Figure 24**). Click the New button. Enter "boCustomer_Remote" for the name of the class and instruct it to inherit from ("Based On") smpMyDataEnvironment, which is located in the appData class library. Click the OK button.

Adding a "Customer" CursorAdapter

The boCustomer_Remote class will appear in the Class Designer. Right-click the class and select Builder from the context menu that appears, and then select the FoxPro builder.

In the FoxPro builder, select ODBC from the combo box, select the "Use connection string" option button, and enter a connection string as shown in **Figure 25**.

Assuming you have placed the examples that accompany this book in the C:\ directory, the following connection string will enable you to connect to the Billing database:

```
DSN=Visual FoxPro Tables;UID=;PWD=;
SourceDB=C:\Dev\Billing\AppData\Billing.dbc;
SourceType=DBC;
Exclusive=No;BackgroundFetch=Yes;Collate=Machine;Null=Yes;Deleted=Yes;
```

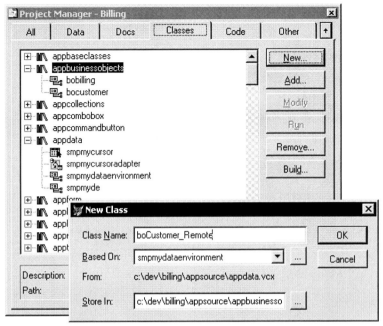

Figure 24. Creating the boCustomer_Remote business object.

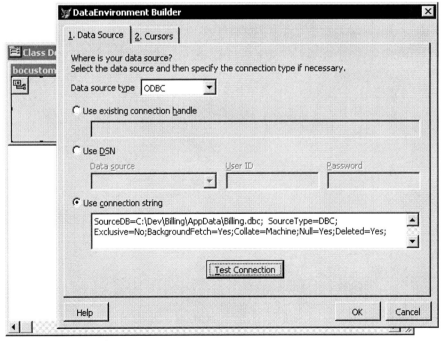

Figure 25. Identifying a data source.

Next, select the Cursors tab and click the Add button. When prompted to find a class, select the smpMyCursorAdapter class from the appData class library. Another builder will appear so that you can configure the CursorAdapter. Change the name of the cursor to oCustomer and the alias to Customer, and then select the "Use DataEnvironment data source" check box. The first page should appear similar to **Figure 26**.

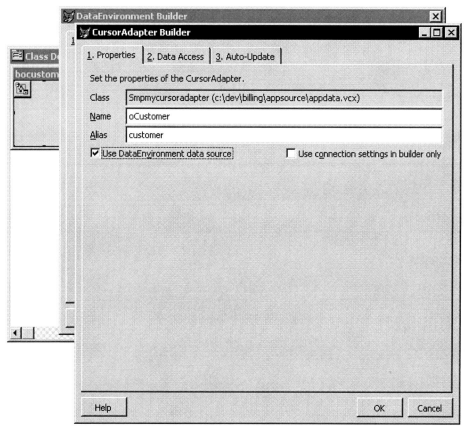

Figure 26. Naming the CursorAdapter.

Next, select the Data Access tab and click the Build button. When prompted to select a table from the Billing database, select the Customer table and then select "customer.*" to indicate that you want to update all fields in the Customer table. The completed selection box is shown in **Figure 27**.

After completing the Select Command Builder, the CursorAdapter Builder will appear as shown in **Figure 28**.

Next, select which fields should be updated. Select the Auto-Update tab and then select the "Send updates" and "Auto-update" check boxes. Select the individual fields as shown in **Figure 29**.

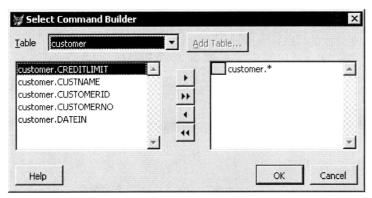

Figure 27. *Specifying a table to update.*

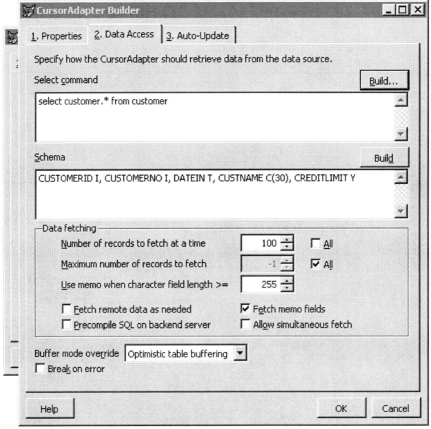

Figure 28. *The completed data access page.*

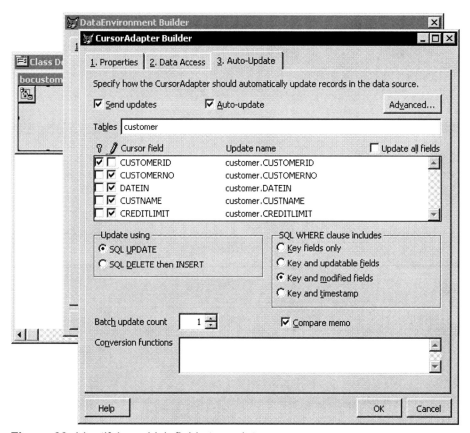

Figure 29. *Identifying which fields to update.*

Click the OK button to close the CursorAdapter and DataEnvironment builders.

The final step is to identify the data type of the primary key. To do this, open the property sheet for the CursorAdapter and change the cPKType property to N.

Be sure to check that the DataSourceType of the DataEnvironment class is set to "ODBC." It appears that on some occasions, the builder does not properly set this property.

Adding the navigation cursor

Repeat the steps outlined in the earlier section, "Adding a 'Customer' CursorAdapter," but make the following changes. Change the name of the CursorAdapter to oCustomer_Nav and the alias to Customer_Nav (refer back to Figure 26). Additionally, you do not have to complete the Auto-Update page (see Figure 29) because the navigation cursor will not receive updates.

Remove wizard code

In Chapter 10, "Business Objects," in the section titled "Connecting to remote data," I listed the reasons why I don't like the wizard-generated code that is placed in the BeforeOpenTables() method of the data environment. To summarize, the wizard code does not generate a DODEFAULT(), which prevents inherited code from running, and the connection string is hard coded, which is problematic if you have many forms and need to change the connection string.

The solution I chose for MyFrame is to remove the generated code entirely, and place the connection string in the cConnectionString property of the application class smpApplication. To do this, open the boCustomer_Remote class in the Class Designer (if it is not already open) and modify the BeforeOpenTables() method. Copy the connection string to the clipboard (highlight the connection string and press CTRL-C) and then delete all of the code. Save and close the class.

Next, modify Main.prg and locate the cConnectionString property of smpApplication. Paste the connection string between the quotation marks. If prompted to release the class from memory, choose yes. Your connection string should appear as shown here (assuming the framework source code is on your C:\ drive:

```
*--The connection string property in smpApplication
cConnectionString = "DSN=Visual FoxPro Tables;UID=;PWD=;
        SourceDB=C:\Dev\billing\AppData\billing.dbc;
        SourceType=DBC; Exclusive=No;BackgroundFetch=Yes;
        Collate=Machine;Null=Yes;Deleted=Yes;"
```

Creating the Customer_Remote Form

The final step in the remote example is to create an entry form that points to the boCustomer_Remote business object. For this example, you'll start with the Customer form created earlier in the chapter and make a few changes so that the Customer form works with the boCustomer_Remote class.

First, modify the Customer form and save it as Customer_Remote. Next, change the DEClass property from boCustomer to boCustomer_Remote. To do this, select the Customer Maintenance form and open the property sheet. Select the DEClass property and click the ellipsis button (…) located toward the upper right corner of the property sheet. Then select the boCustomer_Remote class from the appBusinessObjects class library as shown in **Figure 30**.

The final modifications are to specify source and target aliases for the list box navigation control, smpMyNavlst1. Select the control, and using the property sheet, change the cSourceAlias property to Customer_Nav and the cTargetAlias to Customer. Additionally, change the RecordSource property from "Customer.custname,customerid" to "Customer_Nav.custname,customerid." This instructs the list box to get its list of customers from the Customer_Nav cursor and to direct navigation requests to the Customer cursor. Save and run the form. You should see that it behaves just like the Customer Maintenance form created earlier in the chapter.

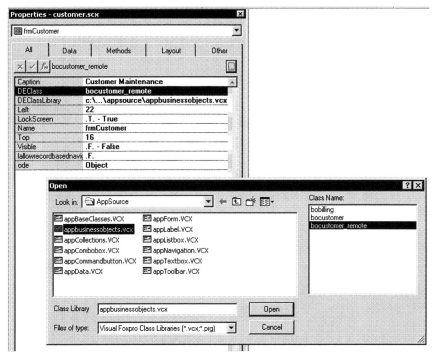

Figure 30. Selecting the boCustomer_Remote class.

Summary

In Chapter 1, I defined a framework as a reusable integration of components engineered to facilitate development of a particular type of application. I also explained that building a framework can be broken into four phases: planning, component development, integration, and productivity enhancement. Throughout the book, I explained the important aspects of each phase, and brought it all together in this chapter, showing how to create an application using the MyFrame framework.

The most challenging aspect of working with frameworks is the time it takes to understand them. However, once understood, a framework can be a tremendous productivity enhancer. For example, even with the significant time you invested in reading this book and completing the example, you (most likely) could not have reproduced this sample application, with all the features associated with this framework, in fewer hours.

This book has offered a solid methodology for developing your own framework, and I hope it has also given you ideas that you would like to include in your framework. The features you choose to include in your framework, and how you implement them, are all decisions you will have to make when creating your own framework. Having read this book, you should be in a better position to understand the effort required to produce a framework and be in a better position to successfully build your own framework.

Updates and corrections to this chapter can be found on Hentzenwerke's Web site, **www.hentzenwerke.com**. Click "Catalog" and navigate to the page for this book.

Index

Note that you can download the PDF file for this book from **www.hentzenwerke.com** (see the section "How to download files" at the beginning of this book). The PDF is completely searchable and will provide additional keyword lookup capabilities not practical in an index.